THE BANTAMS

SIDNEY ALLINSON

The Bantams

THE UNTOLD STORY OF WORLD WAR 1

HOWARD BAKER

LONDON

THE BANTAMS

by Sidney Allinson

© Copyright, Sidney Allinson, 1981

First published 1981

ISBN : 0 7030 0201 5

A HOWARD BAKER BOOK

Published by Howard Baker Press Ltd.,
27a Arterberry Road, Wimbledon, London SW20.
Typesetting by Triste Ltd., Croydon, Surrey.
Printed and Bound by
A. Wheaton and Company of Exeter.

In Memory of My Father
Pte. Thomas William Allinson
1898 – 1976
4th Battalion
The Green Howards Regiment

ba'ntam, n. Small kind of
domestic fowl, of which the
cockerel is very pugnacious;
small but spirited person.

— Oxford Dictionary

The British Bantams.

There is a bonnie brood of Bantams
　　As yet unknown to fame,
Who have joined the British Roosters
　　To earn a glorious name,
They are sturdy and they're willing
　　And sure to stand the test,
What price the German Eagle
　　When the Bantams leave their nest.

Each one a Pocket Hercules
　　Just five feet and a bit,
A kind of Bovril Essence
　　Of six feet British Grit,
He is out for Death or Glory Boys
　　In the Cockpits East and West,
Who'll back the German Vulture
　　When the Bantams leave their nest.

His heart a perfect reservoir
　　Of pluck that is known as grit,
You'll find no mouldy slackers
　　Where the British Bantams trot,
His beak a two edged bayonet
　　He flaunts a blood red crest,
Who says a slice of Turkey
　　When the Bantams leave their nest.

Each one is tipped with armour
　　For there is serious work ahead,
God help the Baby-killers
　　When the Bantams sees the dead,
And if he stops a bullet
　　He makes one last request,
Will some one feed the young uns
　　When the Bantams leave their nest.

Contents

List of Illustrations·

1. At 4ft. 9ins., New Yorker Henry Thridgould claimed to be the shortest Corporal in the British Army.

2. Lord Kitchener stands on the steps of St. George's Hall, Liverpool as Bantam battalions march past.

3. The marching song of the 216th Toronto Bantams was composed by Captain Stanley Bennett with whom in this picture is the youth who would later be celebrated as Sir Billy Butlin, MBE, developer of popular Butlin's Holiday Camps.

4. Members of the 17th Battalion, Royal Scots and the cause of many a cruel accident to small men on the march: the Long Lee-Enfield.

5. Poet Isaac Rosenberg returned from South Africa to serve in the King's Own. Killed in 1918, his work has steadily gained in popularity in recent years.

6. Far British Columbia raised a Bantam battalion despite poaching of volunteers by other regiments.

7. Welsh Bantams included many sturdy miners who were often employed between battles in carrying up supplies to the front line.

8. The war is over for this wounded Bantam and for the helpful German prisoner he is escorting back to the POW cage behind the British line on the Somme, Summer, 1916.

The illustrations appear following pages 192 and 208

THE BANTAMS

Introduction

The little men in khaki all seemed unbelievably small to be British soldiers. Barely over five feet in height, they swarmed over the decks of the Channel steamer *Caesarea,* moving briskly to shouted orders of sergeants, to sling rifles, packs, and kitbags, then file quickly down the ribbed gangplank to the Le Havre quay. Short legs bowed under their heavy loads of equipment, they tramped ashore — loudly and cheerfully baahing.

The tiny soldiers of the Cheshire Regiment amazed the French onlookers. After two years of war, the local civilians thought themselves blasé to the variety of types of soldiers the British Empire brought through the port. They had seen black Nigerians, giant Australians, bronzed New Zealanders and Maoris, colourful Rajputs and Sikhs, confident Canadians, splendid Grenadiers, and even blue-uniformed Chinese labourers, but never anything like these almost Lilliputian newcomers. Certainly, no unit ever arrived with such an irreverent display.

Boots polished to a black sheen, buttons and brasses glinting in the grey early morning, trousers pressed and puttees tight, soft peaked caps set square on heads, the men were like miniature Guardsmen in their smart military turn-out, but the noises they made were like nothing ever heard at Caterham Barracks. "Baaaah! Baaah! Baaah!"

T3 - 3

After being shunted across southern England in crowded trains for over twenty-four hours, packed into a wallowing tub of a ship through a night of miserable Channel weather, denied breakfast, and kept standing on deck in full marching order for two more weary hours, the sturdy little men saluted their orders to finally march ashore by giving tongue to a chorus of prolonged sheep-like noises.

"Baaaah! Baaaah! Baaaah!" They swung down the gangway onto the docks. Seeing these uniformly small soldiers loaded with the kit of war, struggling gamely under the weight, yet cheerfully voicing their opinion of all set in authority over them, convulsed many French onlookers. The laughter grew as furious N.C.O.'s and Provost Corpsmen barked orders for silence and chivvied the troops into more orderly groups. The mirth spread infectiously to the soldiers themselves, until the docks were a chaos of hilarity.

A red-faced Rail Transport Officer clattered up on a horse, to take a horrified look at the scene of hundreds of British soldiers laughing amidst civilians. Apparently singling out one particularly offensive individual, he was heard to roar, "Take that man's name!" The result was only to further convulse the crowd. The RTO rode up to an amused young lieutenant of the Cheshire Regiment, hauled back on his reins and shouted, "You! Take charge of this damned rabble!"

At this point, the mishandled horse shied, slipped on the wet cobblestones, and sent the officer into a frenzy of desperate horsemanship to retain his seat. When the RTO recovered himself, he was the centre of more laughter, and shrieked at the young officer, "Dammit, straighten out the little bastards!" He cantered away to find more respectful units.

The troops quickly settled down at a colour-sergeant's bellow of "Attention!" Further orders and a good deal of hissed threatening by corporals helped shake them out of their laughter and succumb again to accustomed discipline. "Riiii-ght dress!" brought short muscular forearms snapping out to punch the shoulder of each man next along the ranks.

Polished boots shuffled into straight lines. "Ey-ees front!" . . . "Le-heft tarn!" . . . "Qui-hick march!" The Cheshires moved off in column of fours, quick-timing through the streets of Le Havre towards Top-of-The-Hill Camp.

After this less-than-dignified arrival, the troops began to be taunted by French townspeople, who cried out, *"Hey, piccininy! Piccininy-soldat!"* The taunt began to be taken up more and more while the men marched along, drawing crowds as they moved into residential streets of the town itself.

More thoughtful observers on that cold January morning in 1916 must have wondered at the new arrivals for other reasons than their novelty. Here were perhaps living symbols of the extreme poverty of British manpower reserves, that such undersized men had now to be flung into battle against the Germans.

The small troops themselves took the name-calling with a resigned silence born of similar gibes in a succession of training camps from North Wales, to Yorkshire, to Salisbury Plain. They strode along the grimy streets, staring at the prosaic reality of surroundings which were disappointingly less exotic than what they had somehow expected to see in France. For they, like most of their generation, had never previously been abroad beyond the industrial towns or isolated farms of their childhood. The taunts of the French left them unmoved as being those of inferiors, foreigners, whom they casually despised, as befitted the outlook of Englishmen of that time.

There was less acceptance of the jeering after the Cheshires were halted at a railway crossing, for one of the inexplicable delays inflicted on all soldiers in transit. Standing in rows, with kitbags down, and rifles at "Stand easy" the objects of ridicule looked reassuringly small and were under strict military order again. The taunting reached an ugly pitch after some lounging young munitions workers came out of an *estaminet*.

These Frenchmen, all exempt from military service because of their employment, took exception to the flirtations which quickly began between the soldiers and some girls from a nearby shell factory, whose prettiness was not marred by the yellowish tinge lent to their skin as a result of handling explosives. The girls were giggling at the advances and roguish jokes of the Englishmen, delivered with twinkling good humour and obvious meaning that needed little translation. The overtures were made in such a comical manner, with much eye-rolling, twirling of waxed moustaches, and dances of eagerness by the miniature soldiers that the girls were soon crowding around, enjoying the entertainment of such gallant little suitors.

The young men from the factory were irritated, and began to chant "Pic-in-ni-ni" even harder, and to hoot their disdain of such apparently puny soldiery. Some accounts say the troops were physically jostled by the munitions workers, others say the troops were simply tired of standing fast under such gibes, especially with girls looking on.

One eye witness, Corporal Joseph Mainwaring of the Service Corps, recalls, "It was bad enough for them to put up with all that slanging, but when some of the civvies started pushing the little fellers about, that put the top hat on it!" Whatever the trigger, several of the soldiers suddenly erupted in rage and proceeded to attack their tormentors. Fists toughened by a lifetime at the coalface, in warehouses, or in farm fields, now began to thump satisfyingly into sneering civilian faces, to the accompaniment of strange Northern curses, the shrill of officers' whistles, and bellows of "Steady on, lads!" from harrassed sergeants.

The flurry was over in moments, halted mainly by the prompt flight of the opponents, and sealed by six or eight infantrymen being placed under arrest. Refreshed by their first scuffle in foreign parts, the little men swaggered off towards the war, bellowing a bawdy chorus of "Madam'me'sel from Armenteers, Parly-Voo!" The first of the Bantams had arrived – volunteers all – and keen to be getting their chance to fight at last. Less than half of them would live to see England again.

Twenty more battalions like theirs would follow, to fight, and many to die, and then be almost forgotten. Slaughtered, ignored, their survivors even dismissed as failures, the Bantams formed one of the most unusual and little-known chapters in the annals of the British Army.

The idea for this book began with a single photograph noticed in a yellowed newspaper of 1916. It showed a strapping Guardsman in shirtsleeves towering over a boyish soldier almost half his size. Each was in shirtsleeves, suspenders dangling, thrusting bayonetted rifles at each other with looks of mutual exasperation. The caption read, "Burly Guardsman trains one of Bantams how to skewer Hun!"

Bantams? Though a lifelong student of military history, I had never heard of such troops. Who were they? Were they ever used in combat? Over the next couple of years of reading, I idly kept an eye open for further references to them. Finding none, I made a few enquiries, which drew blank stares, except for a few almost embarrassed hints of a topic vaguely "infra dig".

Intrigued by this apparent mystery, I decided to solve it for my own interest. What I learned was that here was a neglected story which involved over fifty thousand British and Canadian soldiers who never quite made it into the war books. They had volunteered to serve when they could have stayed safely at home, had suffered physical hardship often beyond their capacities and sometimes endured with good humour the ridicule of less courageous men, all for the privilege of fighting for their country in some of the fiercest battles of the Great War. Their reward was now virtually total obscurity, or from the few who had heard of them, a condescending shrug, "Nice try, of course, but . . . "

The Bantams seemed to deserve more than that and I set out to put together their saga. It was to send me off on journeys that ranged over Britain and France, and from coast to coast in North America. Hundreds of letters from all over the world, and many personal interviews with survivors, relatives, and military men provided me with details which confirmed that the Bantams warrant a place beside all those other gallant men who served in the Great War. This is their story.

Chapter One

Blood of the Breed

Later, the world might wonder at it. Yet, at the time – August, 1914 – few people thought it strange that millions of men and boys were rushing to join the British army. Hordes of them converged on recruiting offices all over the country, to stand for hours in the heat or rain, struggling to push their way ahead of each other to the enlistment tables, there if necessary to lie about their ages, health, and family responsibilities in their frenzied desire to be accepted as volunteers. Within the first month, over five hundred thousand managed to enlist for the chance to throw themselves into the worst, the bloodiest war that mankind ever endured.

What was referred to as a "boom" in recruiting started in London when the Central Recruiting Office in Great Scotland Yard opened on August 5th. The building and courtyard was filled with so many men eagerly trying to sign up that a dozen extra doctors had to be brought from nearby hospitals to handle the medical examinations.

Hoarding blossomed with posters and newspaper advertisements which appeared overnight urging, "Your King & Country Need You! Single men between 19 and 30 in good health, height 5 ft. 3 ins., and upwards, chest 34 inches minimum, are urgently required now. Terms of service: for a period of 3 years or until the war is concluded. Join the Army!"

The provision for three years' service was a hint that Lord Kitchener, who led the recruiting drive, did not share the popular delusion that hostilities with Germany would last only a matter of weeks.

One volunteer that day — rejected as being too short — was Cyril Wright, who explained how most people then felt about the war, "You have to remember that nobody expected the war to last very long. We all thought it would be over by Christmas, or the Spring of 1915 at the latest; so every man Jack of us wanted to have a crack at the fighting before it was too late."

The advertising campaign was part of the Kitchener Plan to recruit a massive army of civilian volunteers to augment the Regulars — who were already on their fateful way to France. This appeal seems to have tapped some deep chord of response among British males of the day, if we can judge by the overwhelming number of applicants who besieged recruiting offices. Upbringing, schooling, the popular press, or a combination of all the factors which made up British national pride, created a driving compulsion to enlist.

A surviving officer of the Green Howards recalled the simple morality of the time, "People in England then were far more influenced by the traditional ideas of right, wrong, and duty. While few amongst the officers had a clear idea of the history and politics of the Balkans, which had brought on the war, every private knew that Belgium had been brutally attacked, and that unless Belgium was rescued, it might be Britain's turn. It was that point, and no other, that brought the crowds to the recruiting offices, and it was that point which maintained morale until 1918, in spite of colossal casualties."

This overwhelming urge to get into the army was an aftermath of the night of August 4th. By dusk, the whole of London was wound up tight like a giant clock, waiting to see what the stroke of eleven would signal. People began to pour into the centre of the metropolis, forming huge, strangely excited crowds in Trafalgar Square, Piccadilly, The Strand, and Whitehall — the traditional open spaces where Londoners gather in times of stress or of joy.

Thousands tried to press their way into Downing Street, peering through a cordon of police at the bustling visitors to Number 10, while awaiting first news of Germany's reply to the British ultimatum. Shortly after Big Ben struck eleven, confirmation that war was declared reached the street and the people burst into loud cheering which lasted for twenty minutes.

Crowds rippled and moved from Downing Street and Parliament Square, surging towards the War Office, and down the Mall to Buckingham Palace. There, they sang the National Anthem over and over again. Union Jacks were waving everywhere, as astute flag hawkers arrived to do lively trade. The pedestals of Nelson's Column, statues in Whitehall, and the windows of government offices became grandstands for the demonstrators.

The party atmosphere grew more intense as the night went on, with every main street jammed tight with cheering masses, among which scores of motor cars moved slowly carrying champagne-drinking groups of men and women in formal evening dress. The area in front of Buckingham Palace became the most congested, until "not an inch of ground was to be seen and the Albert Memorial was black with people".

For more than four hours, the crowd kept up its singing and cheering there, pausing only when King George and Queen Mary finally showed themselves on the balcony. This brought tumultuous applause and the mass singing of "For he's a jolly good fellow". Drunk with patriotism — and some no doubt with a good deal of brown ale — the people kept up their loud enthusiasm until the King and Queen returned to the balcony, this time with the popular young Prince of Wales.

When her loyal subjects began a laughing chant of "We'll

hang the bloody Kaiser!" the ex-Princess Mary of Teck must have been a little disconcerted, as must the King who was after all the German monarch's cousin.

Clyde Davis was among the twenty thousand American tourists caught in London at the outbreak of war. He remembers, "After the King went inside for the third time, the crowds fell quiet. Everybody moved off to go home, and it took me hours just to get to the Underground station. A lot of the women were close to tears and I guess it was dawning on them that war was not a picnic to be looked forward to. I overheard one very small man carrying a sleeping child say to his wife who held a baby, "Well, Mary, I'll have to join up in the morning." She stopped short, looking stricken and said, "If you go, what'll happen to the babby?"

Such fears did not hold back volunteers, for so many began to enlist next day that mounted police were needed to patrol Great Scotland Yard to keep the way clear for the streams of men anxious to serve their country. Even the heavy rain which fell during the afternoon of August 5th had no affect on the crowds which gathered to watch the early arrivals. Many onlookers ended up inside the recruiting office themselves, caught by the fever. When the doors were shut at 4.30 p.m., hundreds of men still waiting were told to come back next day.

Among the millions of men trying to join up, there was a particular group of repeatedly frustrated volunteers. These were men below the regulation minimum height of 5 ft. 3 ins. Strong or weak, no undersized recruit was accepted for even a medical examination. The authorities saw no need for reducing height standards for soldiers, however spirited or patriotic, while they could have the pick of Britain's finest manhood.

Even as a more realistic policy began to relax general standards of physique and the authorities began to take virtually any healthy recruit who stepped forward, there was no wavering from the rules of height requirements. With either kindness or ridicule, small men were turned away in their tens of thousands as the bugle call found a response in the hearts of tiny patriots who were themselves barely taller than a rifle.

From all accounts, there was then a fairly large number of under-height Britons — their lack of stature either a result of the hideous living conditions and poor nutrition of industrialized cities or, in Wales and in the North, merely the evolvement of populations employed as coal miners for many generations.

Central London recruiting station alluded "it is unfortunate that so many otherwise fit men must be turned down for lack of the regulation height". In late August, the Rugby town recruiting committee was mildly reprimanded for "attempting to pass very small men into the army", as zeal to create volume overtook the rules. But usually there were no exceptions made to accommodate the querulous bands of little men who pestered the staff at every recruiting office in the country.

At the headquarters of the London Scottish Regiment in Buckingham Gate, an officer told a reporter, "We needed only sixty men, and today we have completed our establishment". One of the men turned down there was James Robertson, a coal-heaver from North Lambeth. "They didn't even let me inside", he recalls. "They said, 'Get away home, Titch!' I told them 'I'm all Scottish', but they just laughed and said, 'To get in, there'd have to be two of you!'" Robertson was 5 ft. 2 ins., and he was to wait another two years before being allowed to wear the tartan of a Highland regiment.

Patriotism reached out in many ways. A police constable in Whitehall was approached by a young man who said "I am a deserter from the Marines. I cannot stand by now. I want to go back and do my share in the war". Charged at Bow Street, he was whisked back to his unit by a sympathetic magistrate. Another repentant young man, Able Seaman Tom Linns, gave himself up to police at the Guildhall. He was a stoker who had deserted from *H.M.S. Commonwealth.* His pleas to go back to his ship were also quickly answered. So many cases of surrendered deserters were reported that on August 8th a War Office telegram was sent to Marylebone Police Court asking that all deserters should be given a railway pass and sent off to their depots without bothering with prosecutions.

Within hours of the declaration of war, over four thousand applications arrived at the War Office from ex-service officers in all parts of the Empire. That same day, another four thousand five hundred ex-officers came forward in person to seek commissions in London, and hundreds more applied every hour. Their burning enthusiasm to serve can be perhaps measured in one personal tragedy briefly reported in *The Times* of August 9th, 1914:

"At an inquest on the body of Arthur Sydney Evelyn Annesley, aged 49, formerly a captain in the Rifle Brigade, who committed suicide by flinging himself under a heavy van at Pimlico, the Coroner stated that worry caused by the feeling that he was not going to be accepted for service led him to take his life."

If the rest of Britain reacted to news of war less demonstrably than London, it was not because of any lack of patriotism. Outside the capital, people were simply further removed from the immediacy of events and the provincial populations were inclined to be more restrained by temperament, particularly in the North.

Alice Turner says they still tell the tale of how the news arrived at the public house of a small village near Bradford, Yorkshire. "A very red-faced sporting gentleman dashed in, waving the newspaper and began shouting 'It's war, and every man must do his duty!' He raved on in this way for quite five minutes while the locals peered silently over their beer mugs. Then the publican responded solemnly, "Oh, aye?". The excited fox-hunter said angrily, "Every man must join up! Don't you understand?" "I do an' all", the publican said, " 'Appen you'll be leavin' us t'join oop in t'mornin', then?"

The populous cities of Manchester and Birmingham, Liverpool and Bradford, Leeds, Newcastle, Glasgow and Cardiff took the fact of war in their stride. For many people there, it may have been almost casual interest at first, another incidental to their more immediate concerns of earning a living or of finding their next meal.

Life was never easy in the industrial cities, mill towns, and colliery villages where many people still existed in Dickensian conditions that shared none of the splendours of Empire. Though conditions had improved greatly since the turn of the century, the threat of want and even starvation was still real to Britain's working class in 1914. Nowhere was it more bitterly obvious than in the Midlands, South Wales, Northern England, and in much of Lowland Scotland. There, the closing of a mill, a coal mine, or a shipbuilding yard could bring misery overnight to the endless rows of terraced houses undulating across a polluted landscape under smoke-filled and often rainy skies.

At first, war brought more problems to industrial Britain — the Manchester Ship Canal empty, mills closed in Salford and Nottingham, coal shipments halted. Only Birmingham prospered immediately as its giant weapons factories began to turn out the cannon and small arms hastily ordered in the nervous days of late July.

The grimy streets of Manchester were virtually deserted the morning after war was declared. Only the polished brass knockers and freshly yellow-stoned doorsteps, the housewives' morning ritual of defiance against poverty, showed any sign of people being abroad. "We little ones had to stay in that day," recalls Winnie Parker. "As soon as he heard about the Germans, my Dad said, 'This'll be bad on the docks. I'd best go and see.' We were kept in because my

Mam was worried about him losing the two days work a week he had, I suppose.

"He came back in a little while to tell us that the Canal was completely at a standstill and there'd be no more work for who-knows how long. My oldest brother Tom was seventeen, and he told Mam not to worry, as he'd join the army and give her his pay. 'I'll be a general in no time,' he said. The dear lad was always cheering us up. 'They'll never take you', my Dad said, 'You're not the height of two-penny-worth of coppers!' But he was big enough for the Bantams, and lay dead in France less than two years later".

With cotton mills closed and the Ship Canal halted, Lancashire could have been expected to raise an outcry. Yet as it happened no-one spoke against the war's effects on the local population, even though Lancashire held grim memories of war. The widespread deprivations suffered during the Napoleonic Wars were followed by the strike-breaking sabres of Dragoons at Peterloo. During the American Civil War, Lancashire folk stoutly supported the anti-slavery Union, even when cotton shortages brought an end to jobs in the mills.

There were no flags waving, no cheering mobs anywhere, as Northerners went about their business, stolidly prepared to shoulder the inevitable load of patriotic duties they would no doubt hear about in due time. For the young men, of course, there were the recruiting halls to be visited, with matter-of-fact readiness to fight 'yon Germans'.

The same urgency to get into the war swept across the world to distant cities of the British Empire. Crowds filled the streets of Sydney and Perth, Auckland and Wellington, Durban and Capetown, chanting their ardour to enlist and battle the suddenly hated Hun.

Nowhere was the enthusiasm to fight greater than in Toronto, Canada. Then a city of 470,000, it was ultra-patriotic, with most of its population either of direct British descent or recent immigrants from the United Kingdom.

Though the most Americanized of Empire cities – the open U.S. border being close by – Toronto showed where its heart lay in a surge of emotion towards the "Old Country" during the final days before the declaration of war.

Dependent for international news on the pages of the *Toronto Star,* the *Telegram,* the *Globe,* and *The Mail & Empire,* people had little forewarning of war until a week before it began. Though the shooting in Sarajevo had been reported in Canada, and the sabre-rattling speeches of the Kaiser were acknowledged, there was no hint in Toronto of a major European conflict until the last days of July.

Then, daily dispatches of armies on the march and threats from Berlin, Paris and London began to spread across the front pages of newspapers, until all other news was forced aside. "Blood of the Breed Quickens!" was a headline in the *Star,* echoing the belicose mood of Torontonians during those hot August days.

Civic holidays freed most people from their normal activities on August 3rd, allowing many to relax and escape the heat by boating at Centre Island, picnicking in High Park, or even by taking the train for a day up at Lake Simcoe. But thousands more did not take part in these usual summertime diversions. Instead, huge crowds began to flood into the downtown area during the afternoon, restless for the latest word on the ultimatum then running out. The crowds began to pack the humid city streets in the newspaper region – Richmond, Bay, King and Melinda Streets. Shouting with enthusiasm (called "slogans of Britishism" in contemporary accounts), the crowds circled the newspaper offices, snatching each papers' edition from the hands of newsboys before they had stepped out from the doors.

The next day, August 4, 1914, before it was known Britain had declared war, Toronto was in the grip of patriotic fever, with hundreds of volunteers lining the pavement outside every regimental depot in the area. There was a continual lineup of men moving into the Military Headquarters in

Simcoe Street, jostling each other in their keenness to be signed up for service. Uniforms were to be seen everywhere, as Reserve men in thick khaki serge or bell-bottomed blues marched proudly about, despite the punishing heat. The Queen's Own Rifles had to close its doors at noon because of the crush of volunteers, and the 48th Highlanders appealed for "a more orderly progression of applications."

"Schoolboys went running through the streets next day, waving his newspaper and shouting, 'Hurray, it's war!'" said Adelaide Kemmel, a schoolgirl herself at the time. "Everybody was so excited, laughing and talking of nothing else. All the boys I knew wanted to get into uniform of any description. As they were too young for the army, they started going to the Boy Scouts or joining the Young Soldiers' Clubs that sprang up everywhere."

The stark headline "WAR" was the headline that sold three extra editions of the *Toronto Star* that August 5th. Boldly displayed amongst the breathless prose on the front page, was mention of the British War Office advertisement that "King and Country Needs YOU!" A lead story explained to eager readers that the Empire was on the brink of the greatest war in history, and that there was an appeal out for all unmarried men between eighteen and thirty to volunteer immediately.

Relative to population, the response in Toronto was as overwhelming as it had been in the United Kingdom. On August 6th, over two hundred and fifty men signed up with the Queen's Own, and the same numbers were taken on strength by the 48th Highlanders and other regiments.

Thousands more got their names taken down as being ready to enlist. Confident of their attraction, the Royal Grenadiers opened recruit classes. At that stage, the regiment insisted that would-be soldiers were first groomed before being accepted.

A new spectator sport began, as people began to jam the public galleries of the Armories and stand five deep around army parade grounds, enjoying the sight of local men being put through the earnest movements of military footdrill. A great number of men were barred by the rigorous standards of medical fitness and, in some units, lack of the proven ability to shoot straight.

Soon, the volunteers were being signed up at the rate of seven hundred a day, and competition grew keen. "One boy I knew was a six-footer, though only seventeen, and a fine athlete as well," said Adelaide Kemmell. "He had three regiments after him, yet was rejected after all because of poor eyesight."

Military men became the lions of the moment, and were lavishly quoted in the press. "I have just come from the Armories," General F.L. Lessard told *The Globe*. "I counted twenty-five men in one group who came to volunteer; all fine, well set up, likely-looking fellows."

Not only were physical standards high in those early days, there was to be no nonsense with deportment, either, as Major General Davies made clear while addressing a training corps meeting. "Long hair may be all right for the knuts and dudes, but it has nothing to do with soldiers," he pronounced. "There is a great deal too much hair about. It gives soldiers the appearance of something between a civilian and a foreigner. It is unsoldierly and distinctly un-English!" Evidently, military men then were agonizing over some of the same issues as they do today.

Within days, large drafts of reservists were leaving from Union Station, bound for their regiments or ships to Britain. They were universally envied by the men still trying to get accepted for training, and seen off by such large and wildly enthusiastic crowds, that a special squad of police constables were detailed to manage the daily events.

"We used to go and see leavetaking every day," said Miss Kemmell. "It was quite the thing to see — men shouting, singing, quite a few of them pretty drunk, and roaring threats about what they would do to the Kaiser. The soldiers would

ГЗ - С

come down to the station, with a big banner at the front to say which regiment they belonged to. We children would each have a Union Jack to wave back at them. Toronto was a small place then, so there was usually somebody we knew personally among the men going away.

"I still remember that the wives would hold up their little ones so they could see over the crowd for a last sight of Daddy. The only women I recall to do any cheering were the flirty young girls who were caught up in the excitement. Even then, I used to feel sad when I'd notice how some of the married women would be crying loudly, while many more had tears swimming in their eyes as the trains pulled away with their men singing in them until you couldn't hear them anymore."

As the British reservists were cleared through the system, more organized methods were developed to gather the eager crop of volunteers being swept up in the desire to board the troop trains. One of the hopefuls to arrive at the University Avenue Armories in late August got no further than the front steps. Alexander Batchelor* was a nineteen-year-old ex-miner from Staffordshire who had become a familiar sight at recruiting offices all across the city during the past few days. Though sturdily built, he was only five feet high, and for that reason had already been turned down by the Mississauga Horse, the Signals, the Engineers and the Queen's Own Rifles.

Like many young men of his age, he was desperately keen to get into the army, well-prepared to give up a good job with the Street Railway for the privilege of going overseas. Now, as he elbowed his way through the queue, he was halted by the powerful voice of the Imperial recruiting sergeant. "You again! Don't bother going inside. There isn't a place for you here either."

Batchelor still remembers the sympathetic glances of the other volunteers pressing forward around him. Squaring up, the immigrant youth who had been in the country less than

---

* Name changed at request of widow.

a year said, "Come on, Sergeant, give us a break. I hear that they need men to be cooks. You don't have to be big for that, do you?"

Scoffed the sergeant, "Last I heard, you was a miner. Don't tell me you can cook, too!" "Been doing it all my life," said Batchelor, desperately.

Resplendent in red sash, compaign medals and a luxuriant moustache, the recruiting sergeant exulted in over six feet of muscular height as he pronounced sentence. "Just you hop it, lad. You're far too small to ever wear the King's uniform, so quit pestering us."

"But, I can march as well as any man, and I can shoot right well," said Batchelor. "Somebody must want to take me."

"Well, not on this side of the water, sonny," the sergeant turned away, then as an afterthought threw over his shoulder, "You might make it in the old Country though. I hear they're taking just about anyone in Kitchener's mob over there."

The new force in England — more respectfully known as Kitchener's Army — was planned to consist of five hundred battalions, organized in thirty divisions. Each new battalion raised was to be considered as an additional battalion of regiments of Infantry of the Line for absorption by their parent units.

Army Order 324, dated August 21, 1914, detailed how the new battalions were given numbers consecutive to the existing battalions of their regiments, and were to be identified by the word "Service" after the unit number. Groups of six service battalions were organized to form divisions of the four new armies: — the First Army, 9th to 14th Divisions; Second Army, 15th to 20th Divisions; Third Army, 21st to 26th Divisions; and Fourth Army, 30th to 35th Divisions. Soon after, the Fifth Army was raised, which included the 36th (Ulster) and the 38th (Welsh) Divisions recruited in Northern Ireland and Wales.

THE BANTAMS

Among these new formations were the 35th and 40th Divisions which would be further distinguished for a while by the word "(Bantam)" in their title. The uniqueness of their origin and their great popularity at the time makes their later demise all the more poignant.

Chapter Two

"B.B.B." Battalions

Today, no-one knows his name. The first Bantam was a short, wide-shouldered coalminer who had walked the entire one hundred and fifty miles from Durham to Birkenhead — crossing the Pennine Mountains and the Lancashire plain, visiting Preston, Manchester and Liverpool on the way, doggedly trying to enlist in the army. Each time he was turned down because of his lack of height, he set out again on foot to find a regiment that would accept him. His journey finally took him across the Mersey River to Cheshire, where he met the one man in England able to recognize a fresh new source of manpower.

Alfred Bigland was the Member of Parliament for Birkenhead, a large vigorous man who had thrown his powerful personality into recruiting local men to answer Lord Kitchener's call for volunteers. He headed the City Recruiting Committee, working tirelessly to stage public rallies.

He was particularly effective in cutting through the red tape which threatened to hamper every advance of his Committee. Stores, accommodation, and food were in desperate need as tens of thousands of men poured into Birkenhead, eager to enlist. Time and again, Bigland would slash through the delays and bureaucratic procedures set up by civil servants and officials which might otherwise have delayed the effectiveness of his recruiting drive. He was not only interested in signing up a satisfactory volume of bodies; his attention never wavered from the human side of war.

Bigland later wrote, "It was painful and discouraging to find how many cases of severe hardship existed owing to the men who had joined up having failed to fill in the forms correctly as to wives, children, parents, or others absolutely dependent on them. It was our first duty to get all the papers in working order.

"It was brought to the notice of my Committee that totally inadequate accommodation was furnished for the thousands of men being sent to Chester to create Kitchener's Army: a deputation of the Committee waited on the G.O.C. of the Western Command and insisted on an immediate improvement in the whole system of billeting the new recruits, which the authorities in Chester quickly adopted.

"The next matter this Committee decided was that as Army Regulations closed all Recruiting Offices at 6.30 p.m., we should open one at our own cost to carry on the work from 6.30 p.m. to 9.30 p.m., the very hours that the men were most about the streets. The Committee divided itself so that three members should be in attendance every evening to answer questions, give advice and attend to complaints."

How the Durham miner's arrival caused the Bantams idea to be born is best told in Mr. Alfred Bigland's own words: —

"One morning, Mr. Alfred Mansfield, who was an active member of the Committee, came to me and said that they had had a lively scene in the recruiting office the night before — a young man who presented himself for enlistment. The sergeant said: "Take off your hat and stand under that machine." He did so, and the sergeant said: "Nothing doing, you must get out" — the young fellow demanded an explanation, and the reply was — "Army regulation height is five feet three inches, you are only five feet two."

"Then ensued the scene — the aspirant for fighting the Boche turned round and offered to fight any man in the room — he scoffed at the idea that an inch in height precluded him from joining the Army. Though he raged and swore, the sergeant was obdurate and refused to give him the usual papers and with great difficulty, got him out of the office.

"Mansfield said: 'This is a serious matter: when we only wanted a small army a regulation height of five feet three inches might be good, but now every available man is wanted, and the subject should be reconsidered.'

"After discussion, it was decided that I should write direct to Lord Kitchener and inform him of our view that a very valuable contingent of his army could be raised of "Bantams"— five feet to five feet three inches, provided they were strong, sturdy fellows and suggesting that by stipulating for an extra inch in the chest measurement over the regulation 33 inches, sickly weedy men with insufficient stamina would be excluded. Although we could not raise a battalion of such men in Birkenhead alone, we expressed the opinion that if he saw his way to give us authority to enlist over the whole of the country, we could do it.

"I wrote accordingly, but did not get a reply direct from Lord Kitchener. However, in a few days there came an intimation that Sir Henry McKinnon, the G.O.C. of the Western Division, desired to see me. I waited on Sir Henry, and he informed me that the War Office was interested in the idea of Bantam battalions but were too much pressed to undertake the formation of a new type of regiment.

"However, he had authority to say that if the Birkenhead Recruiting Committee would undertake the whole service we should have every assistance from the War Office — that for specially raised battalions, regulations had already been drafted fixing a definite amount of so much for housing, a ration allowance, and payment for uniforms and equipment. The War Office would provide rifles, baggage wagons, etc., but all other matters must be undertaken by the parties raising the battalion.

"I summoned my Committee and put before them Sir Henry McKinnon's message. They suggested that the Town should become responsible, as it was quite possible the sums named might prove quite inadequate to house, feed and equip the men and someone must be responsible for such a deficit if it occurred.

"I saw the Mayor, but after consulting the Town City Clerk, he said it would be quite impossible, as the members of the Town Council would be personally charged if they voted to undertake the work and there was a deficit. No charge, even if voted by the Council, could be met by the ratepayers. My Committee, too, declined to take responsibility for an unknown liability and it looked as though the bright idea would fall through.

"So keen was I, however, to form a Bantam battalion, that I studied the financial risk very carefully and came to the conclusion that the appropriations in aid fixed by the War Office might, with good management, be made to fit the bill. I saw Sir Henry McKinnon again, told him I would take the risk myself, and so it was agreed."

Bigland estimated that he would likely be able to raise the whole battalion of one thousand men in a Bantam unit. He began reserving dining rooms, stables for officers' horses, drilling grounds and housing for the men. He looked around and found all these facilities under the roof of the local Agricultural Show Ground. He briskly set about taking over the buildings for his new project.

He somehow managed to pass along specifying information about the Bantams to every recruiting office in the United Kingdom within a matter of days. His announcement informed each local medical officer about the requirements for men with chest measurements of 34 inches, minimum height of 5 ft., and a maximum height of 5 ft. 3 inches. These men would be provided with railway warrants to Birkenhead where they could join the newly designated 15th (Service) Battalion 1st Birkenhead, The Cheshire Regiment.

"On the morning of November 30th, 1914, we had everything in readiness to receive one thousand one hundred men," wrote Bigland. "As each man coming from a distance would already have passed a medical board before he received his railway warrant, we provided half a dozen doctors to examine all recruits coming from our own neighbourhood. As I passed along these volunteers, I was depressed to find large numbers of them being turned down as ineligible. A very considerable number were satisfactory, but they could not expand their chest measurement to the required 34 inches and I began to fear for my promised thousand.

"But throughout the day telegrams were received from many distant towns stating the number of recruits who had passed their examination and were coming. The next morning more telegrams were received from Ireland, Scotland, South Wales, London, and so on, saying more and more men were coming. By noon that day, we added the total and found to our consternation that instead of the eleven hundred men we had provided for, two thousand had arrived or were on their way!

"I telephoned to Chester to wire the principal recruiting centres that the Bantam Battalion was full, and to stop enlistment. We were up against a real difficulty – only housing and sleeping accommodation for one thousand one hundred men, and what were we to do with the thousand more – all needing food and sleeping places to be found within a few hours! The Mayor opened the Town Hall to house them for the night, and fortunately I was able to get the promise of two thousand blankets which the Army Stores Department at Burscough said would be delivered in Liverpool by eight p.m. if I would have carts in attendance to bring them over the Mersey.

"We ransacked the town for bread, ham, and other comestibles, and as each party arrived we were able to feed them. To keep them cheerful and merry, we organized a concert and found that many of our Bantams were ready with songs to while away the time until the blankets arrived. To our dismay, nine and ten o'clock came and still no blankets.

However, just before eleven the welcome news came that the carts were at the door. By twelve-thirty we had them settled in for the night — sleeping on the floor of the concert hall, in the passages, and the committee room — two blankets for every man.

"It spoke well for the way they would face greater hardships at the front to see the cheerful adaptability of these good fellows in taking the situation with the merriment of boys out for a picnic. The next day, we commandeered the most modern school in the town, secured mattresses from shipping companies' stores, and had the second thousand comfortably settled in by nightfall. I came to know many of these men individually and their stories of self-sacrifice — their belief that they would be looked after — their keenness to learn and to serve touched me to the quick.

"Most of them brought a small bundle of spare clothes and a little money, but one attracted my attention and I asked him where his kit was. He naively replied he had it all on his back. Think of it, leaving home, with no money, no spare clothes, no food; trusting himself absolutely without a thought to the care of those who called for his service. These things became known; the townspeople soon made them welcome, arranging clothing centres and amusements of all kinds, and were never tired of planning pleasant surprises to meet the exigencies of the day."

A new wrinkle was added to speed up the process of attestation. Several trams were bedecked with the rooster symbol and posters exhorting short men to join the Bantams on the spot. These mobile recruiting stations were sent touring city streets in Birkenhead and Liverpool, enabling volunteers to step aboard and be signed into the battalion while en route to the depot. It was an innovation so successful that "recruiting trams" became a familiar sight on city streets all over Britain throughout the war years.

Arnold Weymouth was a schoolboy at the time. He recalls the impact of these recruits when they arrived in town.

"I and some of my pals walked by the main railway station every morning on our way to school. We were already used to seeing hundreds of men come crowding off the trains, clutching their brown paper parcels on their way to recruiting stations. However, on that particular morning, we were amazed to see what seemed like thousands of very small men, swarming off the trains, laughing, and singing and fairly skipping in their eagerness to get down to the town hall. They had a holiday air about them; chattering and shouting excitedly, and often formed into groups with arms linked to sing the popular songs of the day. Many of them were Welshmen, and I can still remember their beautiful voices raised in song, booming against the high glass roof of the railway station.

"Though a good many of the Bantam volunteers were obviously from poor homes, most of them were dressed up in their best Sunday blue suits, though many of them did not have collars and ties. I particularly remember a large group of Lancashire men dressed in their best clothes, yet wearing heavy clogs, doing an impromptu tap dance in a crowd, then making their way towards the station exit by the expedient of leap-frogging over each other in turn as a sign of their exuberance."

After a decade of peace, during which Parliament had refused to allocate funds for more than basic military needs, the War Department was unprepared in August, 1914, to equip a suddenly burgeoning army. Massive orders were placed for stores; injecting millions of pounds into the economy and creating hundreds of thousands of jobs in Britain's industrial towns — rifles from Birmingham; uniforms from Manchester and Leeds; machinery, food, transport, ammunition, boots, tents, from London, Glasgow and hundreds of other manufacturing centres.

Suddenly, businesses that had become stagnant had un-dreamed-of demands placed on them by their biggest customer ever. The remarkable genius and power which was the industrial base of post-Edwardian Britain was unleashed to produce stores in record time. But in the meanwhile, the army found itself unable to equip the hundreds of thousands of men who had already flocked to join up.

From the start, the Birkenhead Bantams enjoyed the support of local citizens who saw to it that the men did not lack what the government was yet unable to supply. It was a very personal solicitude that was later to show itself wherever else a Bantam unit was raised.

Uniforms would have been a problem for these "big men on short legs" at the best of times. With arms, thighs and chests thickened by hard work at the coalface and on the docks, yet being disproportionately short in the leg, Bantams were not easy to properly clothe from normal stocks. Those chaotic early days made it doubly impossible to hope for any kind of uniforms suitable for the Bantams. The organizing committees proceeded to make do.

This problem was partly solved by an energetic greengrocer called Fred Parsons who appointed himself as an unofficial quartermaster of the battalion. He proved to be a valuable man in finding and appropriating many supplies with a briskness that would have been the envy of even the most ruthless "scrounger" on the Western Front.

An early and valuable contribution of Parsons was the provision of four hundred Boer War tunics which he uncovered and somehow prized away from a reluctant Army depot in Manchester. What these garments lacked in style and fit was overlooked by their merit as being at least military in appearance. As there were no khaki trousers to match the tunics, most of the men were to be seen wearing an assortment ranging from labourers' corduroys to banker's striped pants. Another outré touch was added by those men who improvised puttees around their legs with strips of red baize torn from seats of the Bebington Grandstand.

Members of the recruiting committee dug down into their own pockets to see the men kitted out. Mr. Bigland,

Thomas McArthur and his son Theodore Hunter McArthur bought several hundred Post Office uniforms within ten days and issued them during a midnight parade.

Cyril Wright remembers how it felt as a new soldier to be dressed in this unexpected way. "I had rather shamefacedly been walking around in blue railway-men's overalls for a week or so, the best they could find for my platoon at the time. Now, I was dressed up as a postman.

"We were pretty disappointed at first, as we had been looking forward to khaki and brass buttons. But there we were, all done up in blue G.P.O. outfits with red piping around the edges. It wasn't long though before we began to see the funny side of it, and all manner of jokes started. We used to tell the girls that Bantams dressed like that because we soon were going to be 'posted' to France!"

Some of the more affluent recruits scorned the non-military clothes offered, and travelled to Liverpool to buy "Lewis suits." These were smartly-cut uniforms of officer-quality cloth, provided by a Mr. Lewis, a tailor who expressed his patriotism by supplying them at prices even some privates could afford.

Though the regulations specified the minimum height of Bantams to be five feet, there appears to have been a good deal of latitude applied by recruiters. It became common for men of well below this height to be accepted in the general rush to sign up two thousand men for the new battalions.

"I was exactly four foot ten inches when they accepted me," recalls Cyril Wright, a shipyard worker from Wirall, Cheshire. "I turned up at the Town Hall office with very little hope of getting in, but as I was a strong, healthy lad otherwise, they just said my heart was big enough to make up for height, and a soldier I became."

Other surviving Bantams proudly tell of being below five feet high — Jeff Pritchard, a miner, 4 ft., 11 ins., Graham Carr, a clerk, 4 ft., 10 ins., Nobby Streeter, a foundryman, 4 ft., 9½ ins. But for the most part, the two Cheshire battalions were recruited from men close to five feet three inches, with chest measurements often much greater than minimum requirements. However, as the war moved on and the Bantam movement spread to other parts of Britain, the original standards were to be often ignored with ultimately disastrous results.

Throughout the war, recruiters had a continual problem in watching for young boys, some no older than fourteen, slipping into the army. This was prevalent in every regiment, but was particularly difficult for the Bantams. Many mature men in these battalions were "boy-sized" and eighteen-year-olds often looked five or six years younger.

John Jones of Warrington recalls, "I may be one of the very few Bantams still around now because I joined up so young in the first place. I gave my age as nineteen years two months, although I was just sixteen at the time."

Harry Hurst recalls, "As for my being in France at the age of fourteen – my parents were dead and, of course, I falsified my age when enlisting. The A.B. 64 Paybook I still have shows my age on enlistment as nineteen. Being tall for my age, and the recruiting sergeant being presumably blind, I found myself on the Somme in July, 1916."

"I was very keen to get into the army," says Jeff Pritchard. "The only problem was my age – fourteen and a half. My mother was poorly in a county home and my father had six other mouths to feed. So one morning, I just walked away from my job as a cart-handler down the mine and went to the recruiting office. "How old are you, lad?" the doctor said. I looked him in the eye and said "Eighteen, sir." "Hmm," he said, "And what does your mother think of you going for a soldier?" I told him she was dying, and he just patted me on the shoulder and signed my acceptance without another word."

Most local recruiting secretaries saw the merit in Bigland's idea and campaigned aggressively to get small men to send to The Cheshires. Hundreds of Durham miners were inspired to follow their fellows who were the original Bantams.

"When the war broke out, I was seventeen and a half years old, working down the pit at Berwick Main," recalls George Embley. "I went to Newcastle barracks to join up but they told me I was under-age and too small (5 ft. 2 ins.). On my way home over the high level bridge, I saw a notice — "Join Bigland's Birkenhead Bantams!" Next day, I was in Birkenhead, at Rock Ferry school signing up with the 16th Battalion, and I still have the King's silver badge they gave me, engraved with "BBB" for Bigland's Birkenhead Bantams."

From the start of the Bantam movement, many Welshmen came forward to join it. Being the major recruiting centre closest to North Wales, Birkenhead was a natural lure for Welsh would-be soldiers. They came in by train and foot every day; from Anglesey and Cardigan, from the Rhondda Valley and distant Cardiff. They were coal miners and farmworkers, most of whom were in excellent health and who made ready recruits. Among the miners, scores were below the minimum height yet tremendously toughened by their jobs underground which often had begun at the age of nine.

"When some of my oppos and me set out for Birkenhead, we had never heard of the Bantam," confessed Albert Lewis. "We were miners in our late teens, and we set out to join the new Tunnelling Companies that were being formed. An agent had come to the pit and told us we could work as Army Moles, digging under the German lines, and be paid as much as five shillings a day. That was big wages in those days, so we set off to make our fortunes!"

Lewis and his friends arrived in Birkenhead and were about to take a train to London, when they were mistaken for Bantam recruits and directed to that unit's barracks. "We came across a lot of old friends there. When we heard they expected to be fighting Germans in a few weeks, we changed our minds and joined the Cheshires instead. We just laughed when we heard we'd be getting one shilling a day."

With such an embarrassment of rank and file, Bigland and

his committee were then faced with the urgent need to find officers and N.C.O.'s. Many trained officers and drill instructors had already gone away either to the front or to more fashionable units. Very few of the available remaining officers were keen to take on the new military venture of Bantams.

Bigland shrewdly decided to take advantage of the local flavour of the battalion. Given a free hand to find and appoint his own officers, the resourceful Member of Parliament set about getting them by looking among his own circle of acquaintances.

Members of the Corn Exchange, various ship building firms, and the sons of business executives he knew provided a ready core of officer candidates. He told each of the men he selected to be officers that they should buy their own kit, and after three months of training they would have to pass inspection. He warned them that if after their trial period they failed to pass, they would be dismissed and their uniforms would be charged to them. It says something for the astuteness of Alfred Bigland that not one of the officers he selected failed the training course, and many of them had distinguished careers with the Birkenhead battalion and some other regiments.

One of these officers was Theodore Hunter McArthur, earlier among the buyers of postal uniforms. He had been active since the beginning in helping to recruit the unit and was appointed as a Lieutenant. Tremendously popular with his men, McArthur played a key role in the training of the battalion, and in building the troops' morale as a disciplined fighting outfit. Two years later, as a twenty-year-old captain, he was to lead his beloved Bantams into battle on the Somme.

Not even the damp cold of early morning could subdue the two new battalions when they were paraded together for review on the Bebington Show Grounds. The still-eager recruits, dressed in their ill-fitting motley of post office blues,

Boer War tunics, or railway overalls must have struck a strange contrast with the group of tall staff officers in immaculate uniforms who came to review them.

Lord Derby himself, in his silk hat and cutaway coat, was there to look over the Bantams for the first time. Before he had managed to make more than five minutes of his prepared speech, the enthusiastic men gave him a drawn-out roar of applause, a gesture which that dignitary must have received with mixed emotions.

It was obvious that the Bantams did not need rousing speeches to get them into a fighting mood. The men already fairly throbbed with martial ardour, eager to go to France tomorrow if possible, and asked only to be equipped, trained, and shipped across the Channel without delay. They were in for a long wait.

TB - D

Chapter Three

Hard up for Troops

By early 1915, it was obvious that the war had become a nightmare of killing that could go on for years. The opposing armies lay shivering in an almost unbroken line of ditches which stretched from the Swiss border to the Belgian beaches. Static trench warfare, with its massed artillery and machine guns, had already slaughtered most of the professional troops and created a new demand for huge citizen armies to feed a conflict of attrition. To accommodate these, Lord Kitchener announced the formation of "Service" battalions and promised them the same status as regular units.

The authorities launched an even more intensive drive to boost recruiting. While volunteers still came forward, there was already a faint dulling of the original patriotic keenness, a hint of wary discernment among men of military age. A busy recruiting officer in Bristol rebuked a crowd with "I never thought I would see the day that young Britons would actually question the course of the war, and ask how long they would be serving!"

Newspapers in Britain began to do their editorial best to counter this trend by featuring front-line stories of high adventure: "Tommies Show Jerry What For!", "Boy Soldier Leads Gallant Raid!". Between these effusions — written second-hand by war correspondents forbidden by the

General Staff to visit the trenches — the papers sandwiched lengthy appeals for volunteers. Using alternates of praise for heroes and contempt for "slackers," reporters described the enlistment of men into units forged from shared interests or origins — The Legion of Frontiersmen, Sharpshooters, Tunnelling Companies, Soccer Rifles, Sportsmens' Battalions, Artists' Rifles, Golfers' & Cyclists' Company, and the many City Pals' Battalions.

It is the volunteerism, the eager self-sacrifice, that so impresses anyone today looking back on that era. Wherever in the world there were people of British stock, the opportunity to serve formed a magnetic pull back to the Old Country. Five hundred men banded together under the name of the 'Australians of Western America' entrained from California, and sailed from New York in a body. Five orphaned sons of English railwaymen arrived from Russia, and went straight from the boat-train to the Piccadilly recruiting station. Men came from the African veldt, from the far North of Canada, and from nameless islets of the Pacific, paying their own passage, giving up their livelihoods and offering their lives.

Despite this worldwide fervour, one could think of few more isolated or unlikely prospects for recruits than the wind-swept plains of Patagonia. There, in Chubut Province of Southern Argentina, several hundred Welsh farmers and sheepherders had settled over half a century before. Though scattered all along the Chubut Valley, they were mostly concentrated around the towns they had founded, Rawson, Trelew, and Puerto Madryn.

Content to work hard, live free under a big sky, and mind their own business, these Cymric-Argentines had scant obligation to fight for a distant land that had offered little to their forefathers. Yet even here, the war's progress was followed closely through the months'-old newspapers from Britain and the English language *Herald* of Buenos Aires. Among these hardy folk, who discussed the war as often in

Welsh and Spanish as in English, was a young ranch-hand named Jack Enrique Jones.

Argentine-born, twenty-year-old Jones had never seen the green hills of Wales described so often by his grandmother, and was on amiable terms with local settlers of German descent, yet he burned with the urge to join a Welsh regiment and fight in France. He was to set off on an Odyssey that brought him his wish within a few months, to survive the worst of the trenches, and spend the rest of his life in the United States, where he left a remarkable account of his career as a Bantam.

"What an exciting time that was to be a youngster!" Jones recalled. "The European War seemed to be on some distant planet, and to be fought by gods. Chubut was such a backwater to my mind then. I didn't have any parents left alive, my sister was married, and I was left to my own devices. I was strong for my size, and knew a lot about caring for sheep and cattle, so I never lacked for work. But all I could think of was how to get across the seas to Wales and sign up as a soldier.

"Some of the local old men had been in the British army many years ago, and the newspaper stories set their tongues wagging with memories of life in the ranks. Of course, there was more than a bit of embroidery of those stories, as I realized later on. However, at the time I was not to know that, and thought the army to be a fine life, especially the fighting part. Probably that's why there'll always be wars, as long as young men are excited by the idea of risking their lives and testing their courage against enemy bayonets.

"There was only one veteran who tried to warn me. He was very old, having actually been in the Crimean War, and I remember him saying, 'War is all murder, but trench war is the worst murder of them all.' I often thought about the truth of his words in the next few years."

Jones finally left his pampas homeland, running through a stormy night to catch a coastal vessel at Puerto Madryn.

He worked his passage to Buenos Aires, a city which in itself was thrillingly different from anything he had known before. The British Military Attaché was not impressed by the stunted, wild-looking youth who came back every day for a week before being allowed inside the Embassy. Though there were no funds provided for the many hundreds of Anglo-Argentine volunteers who had already set out for England, most of them had at least been given an audience and some kind of encouraging advice. When Jones finally gained entrance, he was allowed no further than the front hallway. There, an official voice brayed at the commissionaire, "Do get rid of the little fool. We're not *that* hard up for troops!"

At this point, it would have been understandable if Jones had gone home, after a heartfelt "To hell with them!" Instead, his determination to go to war for Wales was only redoubled, and he set about making his own way overseas.

His first need was to get a job, as what little money he had was spent and he had been without food for two days. After a difficult time – "I wouldn't steal, not even food" – he found work at the cattle pens near the docks. There he learned that men with a knowledge of livestock could sometimes work their passage to Britain aboard cattle ships. These berths were in great demand, and it took some weeks of persistence before a skipper looked beyond his small stature to give him a job.

"It's funny, but I wasn't at all surprised when the captain told me that his ship would end the voyage in Cardiff, Wales. It just seemed meant to be. I fairly sang the whole way while I shovelled cow manure in the hold, working sixteen hours a day tending cattle that weren't as seasick as me, and one of which repaid me by standing on my foot hard enough to break it." So it was in the spring of 1915 that Jack Enrique Jones of Patagonia limped ashore at Tiger Bay, in the land of his fathers at last.

Though Wales was less inclined than other regions to turn away small men from the army, his 5 ft. 1 in. height kept him under the absolute minimum for acceptance. After being turned down at several depots, he was told by one jovial doctor to "Put some manure in your boots to help you grow." "I just tried that, boyo," Jones shot back. "It don't work at all."

By the time he had arrived, there were already over a dozen units eager to accept men like Jones. Three famous Welsh regiments were among these, although it was to be some time before he learned of them.

The early hostility of some Army spokesmen towards Bantam troops fell hastily silent after the favourable comments made by Field Marshal Kitchener. The authorities were further swayed to a policy of widespread recruiting of men below minimum height by a paper presented by the Royal Sanitary Institute in February, 1915.

Discussion of the Topic "Tall men versus Short Men for the Army" was led by Dr. M.S. Pembrey, Lecturer on Physiology, Guy's Hospital.

"When I was asked by the Council to open a discussion upon the question whether tall or short men make the better soldiers, I agreed because it appeared to be a suitable time," he began. "During the opening stages of the war the standard for recruits was raised for a time, and this official action was interpreted by some as evidence that there were too many recruits, and by others that better material was required. The standard was soon restored, and later on was reduced when the so-called "Bantams" were enlisted. Can this lowering of the standard be defended, and if so, are there other arguments than those of necessity?

"The official view that height in a soldier is an advantage is a reflection of the general view of the layman. There is often some truth in an opinion which is held by the mass of the people; it is necessary, however, to consider the evidence, for popular views may be based on insufficient data or traditions handed down from times when fighting was very different from what it is now.

"There will be no difficulty in proving that there is no evidence to justify a dogmatic opinion. The civilian has no experience of active service; the military men who have served in the field during the minor wars in the past have an experience based upon a small but highly-trained regular army, which was recruited in times of peace from a limited portion of the population.

"In times of peace, the need of employment is frequently the stimulus to enlistment, and height is then a recognized standard for recruits, for most men will agree that a tall soldier is more imposing, docile and dignified than a short man. An unjustified bias may thus arise in favour of the tall man.

"A definition of terms is a necessary preliminary to an examination of the evidence. A man may be considered tall when his height is four or five inches greater than that of the average of his countrymen; on the other hand he is short when his height is a similar number of inches below the average.

"All comparisons must take into account racial differences. A typical Scot would be considered a tall Welshman. The average height of the men of Great Britain and Ireland is uncertain, for there is not sufficient data; there has been no anthropometric survey of the country.

"According to the figures collected by the Anthropometric Committee of the British Association for the Advancement of Science, the average for 8,585 men between the ages of 23 and 50 years are: Scottish, 68.71, Irish, 67.90, English, 67.36, and Welsh, 67.66 inches. The mean of these figures is 67—66 inches.

"An adult Englishman of typical proportions has in the opinion of this Committee a stature of 67.5 inches, a chest girth of 36.5 inches, and a weight of 10 st. 10lbs. Professor Parsons, from an examination of two or three hundred thigh-bones, concluded that in the 13th, 14th, and 15th centuries the Midland Englishman had an average stature of 65.75 inches. There is no evidence of any sudden change in stature, nor is there any proof of the somewhat prevalent view that the population of this country shows physical deterioration.

"The average height of the recruits for our Army during the period 1901–1910 was 66.1 inches. These anatomical data are of value, but are based upon too small a number of cases. Even if this objection were removed, it would be impossible to estimate a man's capacity by height. Physiological estimates must be expressed in physiological terms.

"It is now necessary to consider whether the greater stature of the tall man is distributed evenly throughout the body. It is not so distributed for the difference in height of men sitting down, but the individual differences become apparent directly they stand up. Thus a man 6 ft. 4½ in. in height was of course 10½ in. taller than a man 5 ft. 6 in., but compared in the sitting position he was only 3¼ in. taller. Height, therefore, is due chiefly to a greater growth of the lower limbs What are the causes of difference in growth?

"In the first place, there is the racial factor already mentioned; as instances may be given the tall Russian and the short Japanese. Growth depends upon the correlated activity of certain glands, which produce internal secretions.

"Something is known about the relationship of the thyroid, pituitary, thymus, and the generative glands to growth; qualitative and quantitative changes in the secretory activity of these glands may result in retarded or defective growth, in the production of dwarfs, or on the other hand in excessive growth, such as that of giants.

"These two extremes are pathological and would be rejected by a medical man. Puberty is generally accompanied by a marked accentuation of growth. Associated with the influence of the glands are the effects of nutrition, muscular work, and climate. A good supply of food, active exercise and exposure to the stimulating effects of a variable climate, such as our own, will produce a sturdy growth, but all these factors are subordinate to the racial influence.

"These considerations show that the selection of recruits requires as much intelligence and experience as the selection of horses or cattle. The tap-measure can never serve as an accurate guide. The "points" of a soldier are related to the functions which he has to perform.

"The duty of a soldier is to defend whole heartedly the interests of his country; the test of his efficiency is not his height nor his weight nor his girth, but his ability to bear the physical and mental stress of active service, to march, to shoot straight, and to subordinate his own interests to those of the race. If the question be reviewed in this light, it will be obvious that physiology and psychology, the sciences which deal with the working of the body and mind, are involved more than anatomy which is concerned with structure.

"At the present time the desire of the short men to fight is a psychological testimonial of their value; they are willing to give up good positions, to undergo hardships and to bear, what is often the hardest part of all, the slight regard or even contempt for the short soldier. The volunteer is better than the pressed man. Cromwell's army, on the "new model", showed the value of the phychological factor.

"The essential organs are in the head and trunk; these are often better developed in the short man than in the tall man. During the period, 1891–1902, the chief cause of the rejection of recruits for our Army was not defective stature; most men were rejected because they were under chest-measurement and under weight. The weight of the brain is relatively greater in the short man, but this anatomical fact is no evidence of quality. The reaction-time of the short man is not so long, and associated with this may be his greater alertness and pugnacity. The tall man, of full proportions, are generally heavy, docile, and slow.

"The physiological reasons for the greater agility and activity of the short man are well founded in the relation between the surface and the mass of the body. The small man possesses a relatively greater surface, and this, in many ways, is an advantage. His exchange of material is relatively greater, although absolutely less than that of the tall man. His small size is in favour of rapidity of action, strength and endurance. During muscular work in hot weather, he would be less liable to suffer from heat-stroke, for he has a relatively greater surface to expose to the cooling effect of the evaporation of sweat.

"There are mechanical advantages and disadvantages in height, but a consideration of these in relation to marching, digging, and exposure shows that the resultant is not against, but in favour of the short man under the conditions of modern warfare. The short man has a smaller weight of body to carry, and the weight of his clothing and equipment is less; he is lighter upon a horse; he does not require so deep a trench, and offers a smaller target to the enemy. He is more firmly placed upon his feet, for his centre of gravity is lower. It is true that in relation to his size he requires more food, drink and clothing, but his absolute needs are less, and thus there is a saving to the transport.

"The short man need not fear a comparison in relation to his capacity for work, endurance, and resistance to disease. Sir Charles Cameron, in his evidence before the Committee on Physical Deterioration, mentions that the big men of the Cameron Highlanders were always the first to fall out on the march. This is what would be expected upon physiological grounds, for the essential and resisting part of a man are in his head and trunk, not in his lower limbs.

"The evidence from the fighting capacity of tall and short races or of tall or short men of the same race is not against the short man. Numerous instances could be obtained from the military history of recent times. The following figures, which were kindly supplied by Mr. J.M. Bulloch from his forthcoming book on *Territorial Soldiering in the North-East of Scotland, 1759–1814*", are of interest, for they relate to the Gordon Highlanders whose fighting capacity no one will question. The prevalent idea that they were gigantic men is quite erroneous. The average height of nine hundred and fourteen of the first recruits to the Gordon Highlanders in 1794 was 5 ft. 5½ ins. Dr. J. F. Tocher, who examined the lists, found that the figures for stature were very similar to those he had obtained for Scottish populations of the present day.

"In conclusion, I wish to point out the danger of extremes; the man who comes up to the average of his countrymen is, other things being equal, the man to select, for it is probable that his development has proceeded along normal lines. There may be some abnormality, present or past, to account for the extremes in stature, but in the absence of such, there are strong physiological reasons in favour of the short man."

Dr. Leonard Hill agreed with the physiological tenets put forward by Dr. Pembrey, and held strongly that they should have bantam regiments. He found from a Japanese military friend that the Japanese ordinary standard was 5 ft. 3 in., but in a national emergency they went down to 5 ft., and it seemed to him in this country they could go down to that too. There was everything in favour of the 5-foot man in regard to his power of endurance and of his size for lessening the danger of being shot.

Then he required less clothing, his boots would require less leather; when he got into the trenches and was exposed to cold, he required less shelter and was more easily wrapped up and protected. A long lean man was more exposed to cold in the trenches, and the trench would have to be deeper to conceal him.

Surgeon-General Evatt of Camberley said, "As regards height, those who have served throughout the Empire knew that the Gurkha, who was a small-sized man, is a splendid fighter. The prejudice in favour of the tall man was a survival of the old days of shock tactics, but in these days great campaigns were not won by shock tactics, and the question of height could be largely neglected."

In the old days, in his own regiment, the tall men were put into the Grenadier Company on the right of the line; and there was an advantage in having big men to throw grenades, but now the grenadiers had been abolished. He attached very little importance to the question of height in the soldier, if otherwise he was of good physical type.

It was left to the Institute's chairman, Surgeon-General Sir Launcelot Gubbins, to put the conclusions of his colleagues in clinching military terms. He considered that the chief point they had to consider was, what was the typical height of the race? If they took officers and men, there was a difference of at least two inches. The average height of cadets at Woolwich and Sandhurst was about 5 ft. 9½ in. Two years ago he made an inspection at Woolwich, and was shown a junior class, one hundred and twenty strong, whose average height was 5 ft. 10 in. The soldier class was about 5 ft. 7 in. The only way in which he thought they could account for the difference was the better feeding and better sanitary surroundings.

For the officer class, he would look on the most useful type as 5 ft. 9 in., and his experience was that the medium man was the best on active service and generally. "With regard to the bantams," sir Launcelot concluded, "It is ridiculous to refuse a small man if he does not come up to the standard, provided his physical requirements are otherwise good."

Reassuring as these findings were, the Army had already issued instructions to regimental headquarters all over Britain to begin active recruiting of Bantam troops, "so long as rigorous standards regarding medical fitness are observed."

The intensive campaign which ensued in the next few months to enlist short men was followed with unusually close interest by a general public one would have thought already blasé towards any new efforts devised to sign up the nation's young manhood for war. As a result, the general public, the clergy, and military men began to debate the issue in the press. Because the need for more British soldiers was already acute, most debaters came down strongly on the "pro" side for the Bantams, drowning out their critics and urging full-speed recruitment.

Reverend John S. Vaughan, of St. Bede's College, Manchester, wrote: "From Caesar to Nelson, from Napoleon to our own Lord "Bobs" Roberts, some of the greatest soldiers have been some of the smallest men."

A military officer added his voice in a magazine article which foreshadowed the fall of Singapore and Saigon in future wars. Major Darnley Stuart-Stephens observed: "The restrictions as to height have shut out from the fighting line a large section of our manhood. There still remains in military circles in this country the old-time and surely absurd prejudice against the little men.

"When Russia embarked upon that stupendous campaign in the Far East, I heard long-legged officers of the Tsar's Imperial Guard speak with most absolute contempt of the cheek of the little Jap daring to throw down the glove to the long, stalwart soldiers of Russia.

"We have all known what these so-called under-sized Japanese soldiers have done, and their little sailors, despite their want of height, proved that under Togo they were admirably efficient in the handling of the newest forms of naval armament. The little man in that war established himself as quite as good a fighter as the longer "Ruski"."

The bantam-sized applicants themselves had few delusions. Some, like George Hughes, wrote with straightforward simplicity about their personal desire to serve:

"I am willing to join the Bantams. I have been rejected on three different occasions for Kitchener's Army because I am only 5 feet 2¼ ins. In chest measurement I am 39½, and I am thirty-seven years old. We don't kid ourselves we are likely to be as useful as the

Grenadier Guards, but give the little ones a chance to show their worth to King and Country!"

His letter published in the press resulted in his acceptance at London Bridge recruiting office one week later.

Even the stages of music halls began to echo the Bantam call. Entertainers had already found that any patriotic theme was popular with audiences, so when Stephen West wrote a new song, with music by Edward Watson, it was soon being sung in theatres all over Britain. To modern ears, it has a crudely obvious naiveté, but when considered in the atmosphere of early 1915, it was no doubt thought to be a cheerful ditty as well as being an effective singing commercial for recruitment.

"Have you ever seen a Bantam in a fight?
No other bird can 'stick it.'
Like a Bantam, or can 'lick it,'
And you never saw a Bantam taking fright!

So what does it matter what the height may be?
If it's five foot one or five foot ten?
If a Briton's heart beats right,
And he's longing for a fight,
And the Dear Old Country calls out now for Men?"

It could have been response to the rooster symbol that appeared everywhere on hoardings, posters, and omnibuses, or perhaps something about the very jauntiness of the miniature soldiers themselves who offered to fight alongside larger men — whatever the reason, the civilian population took the Bantams to their hearts. Bantam picture postcards, souvenir drinking-mugs, songs and poems, even embroidered cushion-covers blossomed in 1915 Britain to salute "the wee heroes."

This popular interest, so high at the time, makes today's scanty knowledge of the Bantams all the more puzzling.

The current Commanding Officer of a famed regiment, which once readily recruited an entire battalion of Bantams, recently dismissed a writer's enquiries with a frosty, "It is unlikely that we would have ever had such sub-standard men in our ranks."

A unit museum pronounced that, "Such battalions were never used for much more than as labour or reserve troops." Another regimental secretary announced that, "We found after all that we did indeed have Bantams. Not much more than a couple of lines in the records about them, though." A Ph. D. research specialist in a university military history department stated that, "It is hardly worthy of study, as the Bantams were complete failures."

The sacrifice, the spirit, and the contributions of the Bantams are now virtually unknown; yet they once proudly shared the exploits of some of the finest fighting regiments in the British army.

Chapter Four

The Devil Dwarfs

Precisely at eleven o'clock in the morning on each November 11th, the haunting melody of bagpipes playing *"The Flowers 'o the Forest"* would skirl across the hushed back streets around Lyons Road, Glasgow. Women and children huddled close in doorways and stern-faced men pulled off cloth caps while they watched the kilted pipe-major march slowly back and forth.

As the wailing tune died away, there would be a silence broken only by the sound of women's sobs and the fluttering of red, white and blue bunting strung overhead. All eyes would turn to look at the corner of Garscube Road. There stood a giant black cross adorned with a wreath of poppies, and beside it a Roll of Honour in a golden frame, brought out from Kieran's Bar for the day.

The scroll had on it the names of dozens of Lyons Road men who had left that one short street to die in the First World War — some said there were more killed from the little road than any other in all Scotland. Among the names were over a score of men who served as Bantams. They and their comrades were remembered by this unique ceremony which was repeated each Armistice Day for over twenty years.

At the end of two minutes silence, another soldier stepped forward, put a bugle to his lips and played *"The Last Post."* After the brassy salute died away, the two riflemen briskly marched back to Maryhill Barracks. The Highland Light Infantry had honoured its dead once more.

From Hong Kong to Halifax, wherever the British Army served, there were few warnings able to drain the ruddy cheeks of Sergeant-Majors or strike dread into Military Policemen as could the simple words, "The H.L.I. are coming!"

Recruited mainly in the streets of Glasgow and industrial towns along the Clyde, not many members of the Highland Light Infantry had so much as ever seen a heather-covered mountain. Yet if their regimental name belied their origin, it certainly described their ability. As infantry, the H.L.I. were arch-typical fighting soldiers. Zestfully as ready to punch-up a pubful of English soldiers as to storm a German trench, their quarrelsome reputation was legendary.

Though all the regiment had a special relationship with the civilians of Glasgow, there was a special affection for the "wee fellas" of the 18th Battalion. Over two hundred thousand men and women from the city were to serve in various armed forces during the Great War, yet few drew greater crowds than those which gathered to see the H.L.I. Bantams strutting along.

The onlookers would often call out jeers – "Look oot, laddies, there's a girt big cat loose!" and "Dinna trip o'er yon matchstick!" – among the cheers, but the fondness was there for these men who seemed to represent the spirit of Glasgow's anonymous "little man in the street," and his cocky resentment of anyone placed over him in temporary wartime authority.

The populace was also proud of the fact that the 18th was originally raised in direct defiance of the War Office. When an offer was made in early 1915 to recruit a Bantam Scottish battalion, the authorities in London curtly refused to sanction its formation. Not in the least cowed, the Rotary Club, the Lord Provost, and the City Fathers set up a recruiting organization anyway. Within hours, over one thousand two hundred men sent in their names to join.

T3 – E

Setting a target of a full battalion, a Bantam Recruiting Week was inaugurated on February 16th, 1915. City tram-cars were placarded with the slogan, "Bantams For The Front — 3,000 Wanted — Apply 46 Bath Street." Soon after the drive was completed, the promoters were able to approach the War Office again, with two thousand recruits already formed into a battalion. The authorities this time graciously accepted, and the unit went into training at Girvan, Ayrshire.

Long before they reached France, the cantankerous 18th battalion had earned their nickname, "The Devil Dwarfs." It was soon awarded for their record for brawling and general mischief which almost eclipsed even the awesome reputation of their sister battalions in the H.L.I.

Alec Findlay witnessed over forty men being paraded for disciplinary sentences after a particularly riotous night before. The Company Sergeant Major added his own contribution to the C.O.'s punishments, by royally tongue-lashing the unrepentant group in forceful and obscene terms.

Exhausting his lengthy vocabulary of abuse, the C.S.M. turned his scowling face away to hide a reluctant grin. "Ach, tak' the wee bastards away," he whispered. "There's no' a man o' them that I wouldna' be proud tae lead o'er the top!"

For all their recalcitrance, they had proved to be readily trained into smart soldiers on the barrack square and the assault course. They excelled at foot drill and seemed tireless on route marches. One incident which endeared the battalion to Glaswegians was when the 18th made a forced march from Girvan to Ballantrae.

They set out with a well-known police band in the lead, but when the march ended the police had all dropped out along the way. That the "Peelers" could not stand the pace set by the Bantams was a small triumph for the troops and for those of their fellow citizens whose relationship with the police was not always cordial.

While these fierce Scots began training, greater impetus

was put behind the campaign already underway to recruit several similar – if hopefully more docile – battalions in England. The authorities had been impressed by the success of independent civic enterprise in Birkenhead and Glasgow in raising Bantam units so quickly. Such enthusiastic response and the evident surplus of volunteers spurred the generals to instruct several regiments to recruit enough bantams to form an entire army division.

This was an ambitious enterprise, as a division was composed of slightly more than twenty thousand men. Each division had three infantry brigades, plus artillery, engineers, medical and transport services. Brigades usually had four infantry battalions, of about one thousand men each.

The physical toughness of miners being already well noted, efforts to build the 35th and 40th Bantam Divisions were particularly directed towards those regions of England and Scotland where pit-workers were numerous. As the Welsh National Executive Committee was at the time looking after its own recruiting, that area was treated as a separate case. (The sensitive political situation in Ireland precluded putting in a further unit recruiting campaign there, and it was rightly assumed that there would soon be no lack of Irish applicants, anyway). However, all counties were surveyed, whether they had collieries or not, to select the most likely regiments to host this particular type of Kitchener battalions.

Even in peacetime, crowded Lancashire had always been a ready source of recruits for the army. The region was the home of several famous county regiments, four of which were instructed in December, 1914, to raise Bantam battalions among the other new Service battalions being formed. A large reservoir of suitable men was already known to be available in the mining towns and cotton-working cities there.

The Bantam recruiting drive through the Palatinate made frequent reference to a comment by one Dr. E. H. T. Nash, "The Lancashire miner is much the same type as the Welsh.

They are sturdy and hard as nails, and better fighting and more quarrelsome men you could not find. The authorities could take 5 ft. 2 in. men from among this class and raise some of the finest battalions possible." It became a phrase repeated so often that one luckless recruiter mouthing it in Salford was hooted off his street-corner platform by a group of miners passing by on their way to enlist at the Town Hall.

The Lancashire Fusiliers began the war with eight battalions, a large component of Britain's peacetime army. Before the Great War ended, the regiment had expanded to thirty-three battalions.

There was then still a strong tradition of local involvement with regiments, making the raising of military units an intensely personal matter. So it was that again one man spearheaded Bantam recruitment, as was often to be the case.

Sir Ryland Adkin, M.P., obtained the consent of the War Office to raise a Bantam unit in the regimental area, and formed a committee of powerful no-nonsense Lancashiremen to get the project moving without delay. Funds, supplies, publicity and industrial and civic support was assured with the impressive line-up of talent Sir Ryland put to work – Sir F. Cawley M.P., Sir G. Toulman M.P., Mr. T. C. Taylor M.P., the Mayors of Bury, Rochdale, Middleton and Heywood, the chairmen of the District Councils of Radcliffe, Ramsbottom, Whitefield, and Wardle, the Rev. J. C. Hill, Rector of Bury, Colonels R. W. Deane, G. E. Wike, and C. L. Robinson, and Major B. Smythe.

The committee named Colonel Wike, former C.O. of the 5th Battalion, to be the official raiser. When he opened his recruiting campaign on January 2nd, 1915, the response was overwhelming. The 17th Battalion reached its full strength of one thousand three hundred and fifty within five days, and assembled them at their depot in Oldham, under the command of Lieut. Colonel W. J. McWhinnie.

By January 20th, the 18th Battalion was also up to full establishment in their depot at Garswood, commanded by

Lt. Col. R. A. Irvine. There was such a surplus of volunteers, that the Lancashire Fusiliers were able to form yet another Bantam battalion, the 20th raised by Mr. Montague Barlow, M.P. at Salford, with Lt. Colonel C. R. G. Mayne, D.S.O. in command. These units were grouped in the 35th Division's 104th Brigade, along with the 23rd Battalion, The Manchester Regiment.

The latter was raised by the Lord Mayor and placed under Lt. Col. Sir Henry Hill at a separate depot in Morecambe. A famed city regiment, The Manchesters had been active in wars since before the American Revolution, where they first took their nickname of "The Bloodsuckers." This derived from their fleur-de-lis cap-badge, jokingly said to resemble the fever mosquitos which had thinned the regiment's ranks in the swamps of New Jersey.

Their Bantam component, officially known as the 23rd (Service) Battalion (8th City), The Manchester Regiment, reached full establishment by the end of December, 1914, largely due to the organizing ability of Mr. D. E. Anderson of the National Service League.

The Manchester Bantams filled their ranks so quickly that it caught the imagination of another newspaperman:

"Many collier lads were forthcoming last evening. Some of them had gone straight to the Town Hall from the pits. As a class they were said to be 'a sturdy set of fellows, and men who will make capital fighters.' Among the acceptances last evening was a youth from Glossop, who was drenched to the skin, and who had the appearance of having walked the dozen miles in the rain. The attestation form of another of last night's recruits showed that he was the father of no fewer than eight children under fifteen years of age."

Though there was a large number of coal-miners from Wigan in its ranks, the 23rd also attracted many city office workers and prosperous businessmen. This mixture formed a highly disciplined unit, based more on friendship than on fear, a delicate balance which was typical of the "Pals" battalions being raised all over Britain.

The 105th Brigade was composed of the 15/16 Cheshires, the 14th Gloucesters, and the 15th Sherwood Foresters. The two pioneer Cheshire units were by now well established, under the respective leadership of Lieut. Colonels. F. H. M. Newell and R. Browne-Clayton. Proper military uniforms had been issued, some unfit men weeded out, and a programme of regular military training was underway. Living conditions had been greatly improved for the rankers, after being forced for a while to endure uncomfortable living quarters in bell-tents, relieved only by the kindness of local citizens.

Miss F. Musgrave tells how her father heard of the Bantams being camped at the nearby Bebington Show Ground in very primitive conditions, he converted part of his home into a meeting place for the young recruits. "He had a bath installed, complete with a huge boiler, so that the youngsters were able to come there for a warm bath. Afterwards, they could chat with their comrades in comparative comfort, play games, or read the many books and magazines the family provided in an adjoining room."

The men were moved into a number of schools in the area, one of which was Ionic Street School in Rock Ferry. They were amused to note that they entered their billets through a door marked "Infants Department." Dozens of neighbours there adopted the men.

"I lived with my family alongside the Ionic Street School and I can still remember the Bantams marching down Lees Avenue," said Mrs. Harriet Williams, "They were a fine lot of chaps and my dear old mother was very good to them. She used to wash their shirts and socks, and many a jug of cocoa was given to them at nights when they would come on over to our house for a few hours for relaxation.

"They would cause much laughter among our family of

twelve with their merry jokes and carefree disposition. They were stationed in the school for several months and I can still remember hearing the bugle playing reveille at five in the morning, and half an hour later the bugle calling the Bantams to the cook house."

"In 1914, I was a 15 year-old girl and employed at a confectioners' shop," recalls Mrs. Amy Swift. "One day we looked out of the window and saw a band of rather small soldiers marching by. We found out that these were the Bantams. They were stationed in a school very near to the shop. Most days or nights they would come in for a ham sandwich and a mug of tea. Sandwiches cost two pence and the tea a halfpenny.

"They were a grand little band of men; always cheerful and bright, and flirtatious without being rude, but they did not seem to have much money to spend. I served them with sandwiches and many a mug of tea, for which I did not charge them. They often joked about their own lack of inches, but they were the grandest bunch of men I ever knew.

"After a time, they moved on and we were outside the shop waving them goodbye. That was the last I saw of the Bantams. Later we heard what had happened to them and remembered them with pity."

When the two battalions left Birkenhead for training at Masham, Yorkshire, and his original idea was adopted on a national scale, Alfred Bigland went on to aid Britain's war effort elsewhere. His administrative ability was recognized by the government, which appointed him a Deputy Director of Munitions. He set to work organizing Merseyside factories in a massive programme to manufacture glycerine for high-explosives.

He was later sent to the United States as co-ordinator of food purchasing, a job he did so well as to be later credited with helping avoid what could have been severe food shortages in Britain. In any field, Bigland had a rare ability — he got things done.

This redoubtable Member of Parliament had his final moment of local glory on Sunday, March 21st, 1915. That day, Bigland stood with Lord Kitchener on the steps of St. George's Hall, Liverpool, to review a march-past of twelve New Army units, including the Cheshire Bantams.

In the next couple of days, the Commander-in-Chief reviewed troops throughout Lancashire, paying flying visits to Salford, Bury, and Manchester. Each time, there were Bantams marching by, and Kitchener picked them out in his speeches as symbols of the nation's fighting spirit.

One witness was Harry Stanton, then a lieutenant in The Manchester Regiment. "After the march-past in Albert Square, Lord Kitchener made a complimentary speech about the smartness of the Bantam troops. However, one aspect of the parade disquieted Kitchener. While the men had been recruited in the Wigan and Manchester regions, the officers had been selected by the War Office. By some quirk of administrative planning, officers posted to the 23rd Battalion were mostly men of six feet or taller.

"Lord Kitchener was devastatingly critical of this fact, pointing out that in action the officers would be immediately singled out as an easy target for snipers. It was therefore ordained that all the officers in the Brigade should be measured individually, and the thirty or so of the shortest (5 ft. 9 in. or so) should be drafted to the 23rd Battalion, and those of great height should be posted to other battalions of the Brigade."

About this time, the vagaries of army routine had also brought the 16th Cheshires an incongruous new recruit in the lanky 6 ft. 5 in. shape of Benjamin Pierson. After being rejected by several regiments because of his great height, he was finally accepted by the Cheshires, who assigned him to the Bantams, of all units. His disconcerted superiors responded promptly making him a sergeant.

Fortunately, he proved to be popular with the men, who

accepted without resentment the tall rookie being promoted so quickly. The incongruity of Sgt. Pierson towering over his charges became one of the entertainments of the parade-ground. As he was still somewhat vague about military matters, his platoon would good-naturedly chorus their own drill orders, then march and counter-march, slope and present arms, over and over until the privates had taught the sergeant. This turnabout method was so effective that "Lofty" Pierson eventually gained the skills of a first-class drill instructor.

There is a fine line dividing well-trained troops from over-trained troops. This comes when men are held under iron discipline month after month – marched, paraded, put through foot drill, rifle drill, bayonet work, and bombing practice, polished, spruced, and generally trained to respond immediately to any order. The intent behind such relentless drilling is ideally to make the men able to save their own lives in an emergency by responding to orders instantly, without conscious thought.

However, if the process is drawn out too long, the men become over-trained, and discipline tends to deteriorate the moment this feeling sets in. Some Cheshires had been moved again, and spent many months at Kinmel Park Camp. There, they began to feel the strain of training and the daily un-certainty of not knowing when they would be shipped to France.

Some of the instructors brought to the battalion late in the training programme had not settled in to share the feeling of *esprit de corps* with the Bantams. One such Sergeant was a particularly vile-tempered disciplinarian. He began to pick on one soldier in particular, a young man by the name of Jenner. The Sergeant took every opportunity to badger Jenner on the most petty details of discipline, from continual orders to get his hair cut to assigning him to the more dirty fatigue duties around camp. The charges laid by the Sergeant against Jenner were more and more serious in their penalties, until Jenner was put into seven days detention.

On the last day of Jenner's sentence, the Camp was electrified by the news that a large draft of men was due to go to France. The men began to crowd around the headquarters notice board, scanning it for their names. The bullying sergeant, towering above the rest of the troops, had just walked up to the board when a rifle shot rang out. The bullet narrowly missed the Sergeant, went through a soldier's body, ricocheted off a tree trunk and slammed into another soldier's chest. The men took full advantage of their training and scattered from the scene.

N.C.O.'s carried away one dead soldier and one seriously injured man. Company Sergeant Major James Swarburgh and Sergeant Brian unlocked the door of the nearby guard-room, and found Jenner lying on the floor moaning, "I didn't mean to hit them." He had pulled a ventilator brick out of the bottom of the hut wall and fired through there.

Before the court martial for murder, C.Q.M.S. Swarburgh was called to see the Colonel, who said to him, "I'm sorry for you Swarburgh. You're a good man, but you realize it is your career on the line as well, as it was you who issued a weapon to the prisoner." The Supplies Sergeant went back to his office and spent the entire night studying the King's Regulations, and eventually found the Regulation he had followed, stating that a prisoner may have his full equipment available for cleaning purposes when preparing to go overseas. As Jenner was on the overseas draft, Swarburgh had been in his rights to issue the man his unloaded rifle. How he obtained a live round was a mystery.

However, the C.Q.M.S. was a principal witness at the trial, which was soon held before Chief Justice Bray. The prosecuting counsel said in his speech, "The rifle was pointed in the direction of the murdered man." Jenner shouted from the dock, "Sir, the rifle was *pointing!*"

The "Prisoner's Friend" — an officer appointed as defence counsel, took up this point. The court chose to agree that there was sufficient ambiguity between the two words to cast doubt on any intent to murder and Jenner's life was saved. He was declared guilty on the reduced charge of manslaughter, and received a sentence of eighteen years in prison.

The bullying N.C.O. who was unofficially known to have been the real target of the shot, was quietly transferred to another regiment immediately after the trial. Months later in France, when the Bantams were stationed near the other regiment, Jenner's comrades could still be seen fingering their rifles as they wistfully enquired about the whereabouts of a certain sergeant.

In May, attention was turned to the West Country and along the Bristol Channel, from where men of The Gloucester Regiment had left to gain battle honours in a dozen past wars. One adventure gained the regiment the exclusive right to wear its Sphinx badge at both the front and back of the hat, to commemorate their fighting back-to-back at the battle of Alexandria in 1801.*

Their marching song, "The Slashers," is said to echo the time in the American Revoluntionary War when some troops removed the ears of a judge they considered to have illtreated a woman.

The work was taken up with practiced skill by the Bristol Citizens' Recruiting Committee, which had already formed seven new "K-Force" units for the "Glorious Glosters" as the county regiment was fondly known. Enjoying a glamourous local fame, the unit was able to quickly draw more than enough recruits to fill the ranks of the 14th (Service) Battalion, (West of England Bantams).

To bring in rural applicants, posters were displayed outside village pubs, put up near village greens, and even on trees at crossroads through the Forest of Dean, where many miners lived. The wording proved to be effective:

BANTAMS

Lord Kitchener has heard that there are plenty of

---

* A later distinction, added in 1951, was the blue ribbon of a U.S. Presidential Unit Citation awarded in Korea.

little and good men in Gloucester. The War Office has therefore instructed the Bristol Recruiting Committee to proceed at once with raising a West of England

BANTAM BATTALION

Height 5 ft. 3 in. Chest expansion 34 inches
Enlist at the nearest recruiting office!

The response was particularly good in the city of Birmingham where there were then a large number of undersized workers. Officers were mostly Bristol men as was the original commanding officer, Major John Carr, previously the Chief Recruiting Officer for the city. A Birmingham teenager named George Palmer joined the battalion, "to see what I was made of." He was to change from a sheltered youth to a battle-hardened soldier within little more than a year.

About this time the regiment also took on strength an unusually tenacious recruit. James J. Blake was a mere 4 ft. 10 in height and could not be taken seriously by any of the eighteen regiments he approached. For his nineteenth attempt, Blake wrote directly to the King, asking for Royal intervention. A few weeks later, he received a letter from Buckingham Palace which he took along to Bristol. The august introduction had the desired effect and, virtually in minutes, he joined the 14th Battalion as Private No. 27026. Suitably enough, Blake later became Champion Bantamweight Boxer of the B.E.F. in France.

After a few months of strenuous training at Ashton Gate, deliberately hard so as to shake out weaker men, the battalion was pronounced to be "a remarkably intelligent and smart body of men." They were dubbed "Bristol's Fighting-Cocks" by the local citizenry who gave them a hearty reception when they marched through the streets. The 14th Gloucesters left the city in August, 1915, went off to

Chisledon, Wiltshire to become part of the 35th Division. Training was increased in tempo, with unusually practical emphasis on trench warfare, and they were to find themselves in France just nine months after their formation.

"Robin Hood's Own," the jocular name for The Sherwood Foresters (Notts & Derby Regiment), recruited its 15th Battalion within ten days of April 10, 1915, when Nottingham city council authorized a thousand pounds to fund a Bantam unit. The regiment kept alive its association with that romantic outlaw by wearing a green diamond "flash" on the back of their uniforms' collar. However, there was little memory of verdant woods for the nine hundred and fifty stunted men who left pit-villages and lace-factories in the two counties to enlist in the 15th Battalion at Normanton Depot, Derby. They were also joined by recruits from elsewhere in Britain, one of whom was a 19-year-old Oldham cotton-worker named John Taylor.

"We were sent to Nottingham Barracks, where we drew equipment at the near-by Lace Market. Each morning, all four companies had to fall in at the Guildhall, then march into the famous Forest. There we would do the usual square-bashing all morning. In the afternoon we were taken to the embankment alongside the River Trent and given more training.

"We were billeted in private homes; mine being on Huntingdon Street, with three other chaps. Our good landlady, Mrs. Hill, fed us well, and gave us a special treat each Saturday dinner. The two older men got a bottle of beer each, while we teenagers received a bottle of lemonade. When asked why we couldn't have beer, too, Mrs. Hill replied that we were too young for strong drink. Ten months later in France, we needed both strong drink and strong stomachs!"

The 106th Brigade was composed of Northerners – the 17th Royal Scots, 17th West Yorkshires, and the 19th Durham Light Infantry, each a battalion in regiments famed for rock-like reliability.

The Royal Scots were the senior regiment of British infantry-of-the-line, of such early origin that they proudly called themselves "Pontius Pilate's Bodyguard." The raising of a Bantam battalion in Edinburgh was the personal project of Lord Rosebery. That modest aristocrat had made several unpopular speeches appealing for a peaceful settlement with Germany before war was declared, but when hostilities began, he gave his total support to the patriotic effort.

A tireless public speaker, he made a series of speeches at rallies throughout Scotland to urge that "The war must be fought to the bitter end, with no patched-up truce!" He daily addressed huge crowds in Edinburgh. At one of these gatherings, on New Year's Eve, he pleaded earnestly for more Bantam battalions to be raised.

As his opening theme, Lord Rosebery quoted exerpts from a Dublin pamphlet published as long ago as 1733, entitled "The Humble Remonstrance of the Five-Foot Highians Against the Unchristian Practice of Using A Height Standard In Enlisting Soldiers." In part, this read "We believe that it will not be very easy to show that an inch of a man's height is any substantial proof of his capacity to serve the government, or that a man will make one bit the better soldier for being as tall as a church steeple . . .

"Is not courage the principal qualification in a soldier? Is courage to be measured by the yard? And, since the invention of firearms, have not the five-footians a manifest advantage over your long-legged gentry? Cannot they draw a trigger as well as the tallest Guardsman in the Prussian service?"

There were eight pages in this vein, echoing some forgotten plea by British bantams of two hundred years before, and Lord Rosebery's practised tones read out every word to support his argument. He made the same speech several times, with the result that the 17th Royal Scots soon had more applicants than could be accepted and the unit was dubbed "Rosebery's Own."

At first, there was neither uniforms nor billets for the men, so each was sent away after being signed up, with a primrose badge in his lapel and instructions to return when called. The unit could just as aptly have been called "Rotary's Own," as that organization's past-president, Mr. I. P. Dobbie had first proposed a "Short Stature" battalion on December 4, 1914.

The Edinburgh Rotary Club appointed a "Lord Rosebery Royal Scots Recruiting Committee," headed by Mr. Dobbie and W. L. Sleigh. The executive committee mobilized one thousand men, paid for their housing in St. Leonard's School, arranged for old soldiers to drill them in King's Park, and tried to obtain suitable uniforms. Lacking an official supply, Rotarian Alex Wilkie cleared out his factory, brought in sewing machines and produced virtually tailor-made uniforms in a matter of days.

Yet another Bantam battalion had been quickly formed by individual enterprise, and on January 20, 1915, the smartly dressed 17th Royal Scots went on parade to be inspected by Lord Rosebery and their new commander Lt. Colonel R.D. Cheales.

Within three months of the outbreak of war, seventeen new Service battalions had been formed by The Prince of Wales' Own (West Yorkshire Regiment). The largest county in England, Yorkshire spawns tough, stolid folk who have manned a half dozen famous regiments for centuries. Like them, the West Yorkshires have always fought in a way that reflects their flat, direct manner; calmly warning enemies, "Tha'd best get out't road, or 'appen tha'll get a bloody nose."

The regiment was raised in the West Riding, an area of open rolling moors and large wool-working cities. It proved a ready source of recruits who formed what was to be one of the most highly-decorated Bantam battalion of the war. The 17th West Yorks was raised in December, 1915, by J. E. Bedford, Lord Mayor of Leeds. Shepherds and miners came in from tiny villages to join up with hundreds of woolworkers from Bradford and Leeds, particularly from the Holbeck area.

In Yorkshire, it's not what you say that counts, it's what you do. That Yorkshire people have an unfounded reputation for being tight-fisted was again proven by their generous donation of money and hospitality towards maintenance of the 17th West Yorks. For many months, the 17th battalion was a civic unit, even wearing the Leeds City coat of arms as its cap-badge. Not until August, 1915, did the War Department take over the battalion, when it began to wear the Hanover Horse badge of The West Yorkshire Regiment.

In the meantime, the Leeds Bantams drilled busily away on Holbeck Moor, under the stentorian orders of Regimental Sergeant Major Archer, an imposing figure with bristling red hair and waxed moustaches. By May, he had them smart enough to even his exacting standards when the city turned out to cheer them on parade for Lieut. Colonel F. N. Atkinson and be marched off to Masham Camp.

The little men strutted jauntily away to the rousing music of *"Ca Ira."* The West Yorkshire's regimental march. A newspaperman commented that, "There surely has not been a more sprightly tread of boot-heels since the West Yorks stole the tune from the French they defeated in 1793!"

Ringing in their ears was a speech by Lord Mayor Bedford predicting that the Leeds Bantams would one day be likened to Gurkas when their turn came for fighting. This prediction was proven true time and again over the next two and a half bitter years, winning the battalion one Victoria Cross, a D.S.O., three M.C.'s, and two dozen M.M.'s and D.C.M.'s.

The cost of the stubborn courage of these tiny Yorkshiremen later sent entire villages and towns into mourning for the eleven officers and two hundred and seventy soldiers who were killed — a fatal casualty rate of over twenty-five percent.

Half a century later, on December 12, 1968, people stood in the streets of old Durham City weeping for the passing away of an entire regiment. On that day, the Colours of the

Durham Light Infantry were laid to rest in the Cathedral for the last time. The ceremony marked the end of the two hundred and ten year saga of one of the finest fighting regiments in the British Army — a victim of financial constraints and bureaucracy which merged it with three other disbanded regiments into The Light Infantry.

Soldiering has long been a tradition in County Durham, back to when it was the buffer-zone south of Hadrian's Roman Wall built to hold back the Scottish tribes. Viking raids and Danish settlements there instilled enough warlike qualities that William the Conqueror's alien garrison at Durham City was wiped out. Norman reprisals were so severe that every town was laid waste and the population was decimated so that much of the region remains sparsely populated to this day.

It was a mainly local private army which defeated the invading Scots at Neville's Cross, as the post of Bishop of Durham was for centuries more a military than religious function. The Palatinate was virtually autonomous for centuries, and Tynesiders played such a key role in the successful cause of King George I against the Scots that they are to this day known as "Geordies."

Politically and geographically isolated for generations, and enduring a hard struggle for sustenance, it is not surprising that Durham folk developed their own distinct characteristics, even their own language. Though markedly blunt in speech, which discourages conceit in others, their conversation is warmly sprinkled with the endearments "pet" and "hinny." However, to the uninitiated visitor it is often difficult to understand exactly what a Geordie is saying in his rapid, sing-song accent.

The Scandinavian influence is still strong in speech cadence, and many Geordie words are not heard anywhere else — "plodgin" for wading, "clarty" for muddy, "haem" for home. They are also much inclined to assure one with "Why, aye, man!" rather than a mere "yes." Overlaying dozens of

T3 - F

these quaint words, is yet another language.

"Pitmatic" is an almost secret dialect * developed among Durham coalminers who form a large part of the country's inhabitants. It was a jargon which drove some Southern recruiting officers wild, when the Durham Light Infantry began its phenomenal expansion in the Great War.

"The Faithful Durhams" had done well in the Crimean War and in the recent Boer War, when six battalions was considered a large body of troops. Always up to strength in peacetime, the D.L.I. had no problem in recruiting ten "K-Force" units in the last three months of 1914. By war's end, the Durham Light Infantry was to raise thirty-seven battalions, a nigh incredible number from a small county which then had only about half a million males of all ages in the population.

A government health survey at the turn of the century commented on the short stature of people in Durham mining villages. "The typical miner is inclined to smallness, with short legs and the chest protruding." With a tradition of underground work from long before the industrial revolution, the Durham miner was shaped by heredity and generations of troglodyte employment.

Poorly fed, worked hard from childhood on twelve-hour shifts amidst dirt and danger, the Durham miners would emerge filthy from the pit, with hawk-like eyes and little to look forward to each day beyond the ritual scrubbing. Now society was about to lure them out of the dripping coalmines and march them away from their long rows of one-up-one-down company housing to fight a bloody war. It might have seemed to be an attractive alternative, as the 19th (Bantam) Battalion, D.L.I. was fully mustered shortly after its announcement by the Durham Parliamentary Recruiting Committee.

Men streamed in from collieries at Percy Main and Esh Winning; from Shillbottle where men worked stripped naked because of the heat underground; from Washington, where

---

* Used in the Second World War by D.L.I. front-line radio operators, "Pitmatic" proved to be an unbreakable code which baffled Germans trying to listen-in.

had originated the ancestors of America's first President; and from pits at Morpeth, Cowpen, and Blaydon Main, and a dozen other coal-workings. Doctors were horrified at the condition of a batch of volunteers from Monkwearmouth Colliery whose bodies were covered with carbuncles and huge open sores caused by years of working in hot salt water seeping down from the North Sea far above the mine tunnels.

Bantams also stepped forward from the shipyards of Sunderland and Gateshead, and walked down out of the Pennines to converge on the battalion's depot at the Co-operative Building in West Hartlepool. There, the unit's first commanding officer, Lt. Colonel W. Thomlinson spread his energies between drilling his men and directing a colourful recruiting campaign.

The heady lure of enlistment fever prevalent then is described by Edwin Lofthouse, who joined the 18th D.L.I. at eighteen. "Just imagine a military band marching down the streets, all in bright uniforms and playing stirring tunes. One's eyes took in the regular pattern of the uniforms and the precise steps of the soldiers, and then the ear took special notice of the quick rhythm of the tunes, and one's heart started beating to the music. So much so, that one's feet were marching along with the soldiers.

"In this atmosphere, the crowd was drawn to some central place, where a recruiting address was given, and on the platform were some beautiful ladies who as their part in the war effort were prepared to give every man who joined a kiss. This then was the path which eventually led me straight into Hell itself."

Private Billy Watson of the 18th Durham Light Infantry was late in leaving his home in the mountains near Wearhead to return from embarkation leave. "When I started walking back down the road towards Durham, the sky turned dark and before very long I was struggling with my full pack, kitbag, and rifle through a heavy blizzard. The snow got thicker and thicker, it became dark, and there was not a soul on the road. I kept hoping that someone with a horse and trap (cart) would come by," he recalls. "But there was nobody at all on the high road, nor a light to be seen anywhere.

"Just when I began to think that I was going to freeze to death, a woman's voice called out, "Come haem with me, hinny," she said. "You look perished." We walked a long way across the fields and moorland, then over a couple of short hills, until we came to a cosy-looking farmhouse. We were greeted at the door by the canniest (prettiest) lass I had ever seen. She had red hair and lots of freckles, you know-ah. She greeted me shyly and I went inside where there was an old man sitting with his dog at his side, alongside a roaring coal fire.

"He greeted me, and handed me some tobacco which was a great luxury at that time, and told me to keep the tin for myself. The two women prepared a meal of boiled potatoes mashed with milk, and cups of strong black tea. There was a strange smell in the room and a strange look to the old man that I did not recognize at the time. Later when I had seen much active service, I knew the look and smell to be that of a man who was about to die soon."

"Although none of us spoke much I remember that night as one of the happiest I ever spent in my life," said Mr. Watson. "The girl and I got on well together, and I can say now that I fell fond of her on the spot and felt that she was feeling the same way about me. I remember now her mother, the old woman, although she can't have been really that old, seemed to spot what was going on and I would catch her smiling to herself as she looked at the pair of us. Even the dog took to me and he would spend a lot of time with his paw on my knee as I rubbed his ear and stroked his neck.

"I took notice of the handmade collar on the dog. It had bronze studs in an old strip of leather. I slept there by the fire in a chair that night, as they had not a spare bed for me. I awoke next morning to find the lass making me breakfast of porridge. I said goodbye to the old man and was walked to the front gate by the mother and the girl. The old woman said her goodbyes first and walked back to the house leaving me with the girl. We didn't say much but I touched her hand and said, 'I reckon I'll be back.' She smiled, sort of shy, you know, and said, 'I do hope you will.'

"I walked away laden down with my army kit, plodgin through the deep snow which was still falling but not as much as the night before. I turned back once and she was still there, a little figure waving to me. I went over the hill the way they had pointed, and after a long time found the road again and marched off to war."

Private Watson fought in the trenches for over two years with only one leave in all that time. He managed to get home in the summer of 1918 for seven days. He spent all of that time walking across the hills in the area he guessed the farmhouse would be, vainly searching for the family that had been so kind to him during the blizzard.

"You see, I know it sounds strange now," said Watson, "But I never thought to ask their last name and they never asked for mine. So I didn't know even their name to ask neighbours whereabouts the farm might be. I thought about that lass every night and every day while I was in the trenches. As soon as I was released from the army in 1919, I came home to Weardale and started to look about for her. I looked for many a week and every weekend, for I was back at my job of mining, one of the lucky ones. But no matter how much I roamed thereabouts, I couldn't find anything that looked like their farm.

"After a while, I gave up looking properly, but of a Sunday, I would still find myself taking a walk up and down the high road. A few years later, maybe 1922 or so, I was sitting on a bank having a smoke, thinking about that girl as a matter of fact, when I looked down and there was her dog. Sure as I stand here, it was her dog. The same black and white old dog with the same copper-studded leather collar.

I was so startled I could hardly speak for fear the dog was a ghost.

"Then I began to talk to him and he wagged his tail, and put his paw on my knee as he had done five or six years before. All that afternoon, I tried to get the dog to walk away so that I could follow him, but as much as I shouted to him, the more he wanted to stay. In the end I walked away back home and he followed me for a while, then I looked around and he'd gone into the dark.

"So I never did find that canny lass again and all my life I've felt sad about losing her and wondered how it might have been if we had met up again."

By mid-1915, the three infantry brigades were ready for grouping as a division, and in June they began assembling at Masham Camp, Yorkshire. The 35th (Bantam) Division was officially formed on July 5th, 1915, under the command of Major General R. J. Pinney.

The decision to place General Pinney in charge of the unconventional new force was a remarkably good one. Among the general staff officers at that time, there were few others who could have better utilized the Bantams or even seen their potential. Pinney was a man who looked on war with a clearer eye than many of his Blimpish colleagues. While serving with the 23rd Infantry Brigade at Neuve Chappelle some weeks earlier, Pinney had saved his men from total annihilation by the simple method – then rare for a Brigadier – of personally going into the front line to see what was the trouble.

There, he found men of the Scottish Rifles, the Devons, the Middlesex, and West Yorkshires piling up their dead and dying on the uncut German wire. Their orders, comfortably despatched from headquarters far to the rear, had sent the men of the 23rd in repeated charges to certain death. General Pinney struggled through shellfire, smashed trenches, and a carpet of dead and wounded until he was crouching with his men in enfiladed positions.

He called off the troops, ordering them into more sheltered positions, and telephoned the divisional gunners. He demanded heavier and more accurate shellfire on the wide sheet of barbed wire entanglements, now fringed with the tatters of khaki corpses. The directed barrage quickly blasted a path through the obstacle and gave the 23rd a better fighting chance when ordered forward again.

This open-minded and experienced soldier settled into his new job of moulding his new Bantam force into a fighting unit, despite the derision and negative expectations of visiting medical officers. "It is quite impossible to expect undersized men to be useful as soldiers in the British line in Flanders," one reported. "It is well-known that such little men cannot bear the physical and moral load of modern warfare. One has just to see their unsoldierly appearance on the parade-ground to realize the total unsuitability of Bantams."

Lieutenant Colonel MacQuarie's views were not untypical of the time, when staff officers were still ordering men to go over the top in parade-ground marching order to attack barbed wire and concrete machine gun emplacements. Pinney preferred a more optimistic approach, putting his faith in a programme of hard training.

The practicality of all training was reviewed by the 106th's new Brigade Major, a previously wounded member of the Royal Warwickshire Regiment, named Captain B. L. Montgomery. He was later to be better known as Field Marshal Lord Montgomery of Alamein.

Trench-digging, musketry, and artillery co-operation exercises began to show the men what tactics to expect on the Western Front. Though nothing but experience itself could demonstrate the grisliness the troops would also find out there, some veteran N.C.O. instructors did their best. After complaints by the camp laundry and supplies officers, orders were given that instructors must desist from splashing warm bullock's blood onto troops to simulate battle conditions.

Thus trained and honed, the 35th moved south in late August to Pereham Down on Salisbury Plain, Hampshire. There they stayed in mouldy bell-tents and leaking temporary huts, being endlessly trained and watching hundreds of thousands of troops crowding the huge Plain and then leaving in draft for France. As the months rolled on and the chilly sky poured ceaseless rain, the Bantams began to feel they would never get to war.

Donald Gray of Hemet, California, was then a young private in the 17th Royal Scots. "By the time we waited on Salisbury Plain, we had been in uniform for eight months and more. We had lived sheltered lives far removed from the dangers of trench warfare and were nothing more than second-class soldiers. We might as well have enlisted in the Boy Scouts for all the good we were doing for our country."

On a miserably cold morning in December, the Division was cheered to be notified it was about to sail off to sunny Mesopotamia. Full tropical kit was issued, including voluminous "shorts" which were so large that the men clowned by walking about with two of them in each garment. Even more hilarity was provoked by the solar topee helmets which made the Bantams look like giant mushrooms.

Within a month, orders were changed again. In late January, 1916, the tropical gear was changed for long woollen underwear. That made it official. The Bantams were destined for the Western Front after all.

Chapter Five

Extracts from an Officer's Diary

The Cheshire Bantams, first of such units to be raised, had waited fifteen months before being given their chance to fight. In the meantime, they had been endlessly drilled and trained, their ranks combed repeatedly to remove all but the very fittest physical specimens amongst them. When the 15th Cheshires finally reached France in early 1916, they were sent to the front almost immediately.

We are able to study first-hand the battalion's fortunes through the memoirs of Lt. Col. Harrison Johnston, D.S.O., a compassionate, clear-eyed soldier who later privately published them as *"Extracts From An Officer's Diary."* It reveals the day-to-day experiences of his men, written down while they happened and told with modest, straightforward simplicity. Among his matter-of-fact descriptions of trench warfare, mud, and death, Lt. Col. Johnston also brought out how the troops faced such horrors with a patient good humour which gained his warm affection.

"31st January, 1916. The C.O. marched the Battalion through Le Havre and about three miles outside, all the way uphill, to a rest camp! A pretty name given to a number of tents in rows in a wet, muddy field on the crest of a high, bleak hill. We told the men off to tents; the camp very dirty – twelve men to a tent. One tent to each Company Officer.

"The people seemed very interested in our men – they are

splendid – so cheery and bright under all circumstances, and I know they will show the world that the little men were not given their chance in vain. You'll see the money spent on their training has not been wasted.

"Thursday, 10th February, 1916. (Molingham) This place is very damp – canals, ditches, waterways, stagnant water – smells everywhere. I have had chloride of lime put down all over the place, and it smells yet. Should not care to live here.

"As I finished this, I heard horses' hoofs – looked up, and there was a full-blown General, with some of his staff coming down the lane, followed by a Lancer complete with flag. I went out. The guard on the next billet did not turn out. The sentry presented arms – I saluted as they passed, and the General wished me good afternoon.

"As soon as they had passed, I rushed up and asked why the guard had not turned out? A man called McLellan was the sentry, and he said "I asked him if I should turn out the guard and he said 'No'." My goodness – to think that a sentry in my Company should ask a General if he would like a salute!

"McLellan was a waiter in the Sergeants' Mess and has not been on parade much until we left England. They seem to have got all the real dead-beats on guard today. It is enough to make one weep.

"Monday, 21st February, 1916. We had first parade 10 a.m. – one hour's physical drill and one hour's bayonet fighting. The latter had to be done under cover in barns, so that aeroplanes could not see the men. Airmen were busy this morning. Our fellows brought down a Taube about two miles from here. He had ventured too far over our line. Some of our officers and men saw the fight and saw the German fall.

"This morning we have drawn fur coats (jackets) for all officers and men. We will look like a lot of Teddy Bears! The coats are nice and warm, and if the weather keeps like this we will need them. It froze all night, and has been snowing until now (11 a.m.). We've been at physical drill and bayonet fighting and now we are off for a route march — just a short one.

"Weather very severe — everything frozen stiff — ice so strong that I saw a man stand on a deep ditch this morning. It was a beautiful day — sun out for five or six hours. All officers had to visit Brigade concentration point today. They went separately with one Sergeant as orderly. These Sergeants will take out patrols of eight men each; first leaves at 6 p.m., last at 7.15. Each patrol should be back here in two hours. An officer has to be at the point to take times of arrival and check any noise or chattering.

"Kynaston volunteered for this duty and has just gone off, he will have a cold wait in a bleak spot, so have made him wrap up well — fur coat over overcoat on top. He has taken a N.C.O. for company.

"6.20 p.m. Cold is not the word for it. This is the worst drop of weather I have ever tasted. It is snowing hard and I have been out talking to the poor little fellows whom I am sending out on patrols. They have five or six miles to march, and I feel mean coming back to this warm room after chasing them out, but it has to be done. Partington is out at some lonely crossroads taking the times they arrive. He offered to go. I don't ever need to order my boys out on these unpleasant stunts, they always offer to go. I am truly thankful I was so lucky with my Company officers. They are a grand lot of fellows.

"The C.O. and Major Shaw paid a visit to the trenches today with two snipers out of my Company. They returned safely, but did not think much of the trenches we have to occupy. We started for the trenches at Givenchy with an officer to take us the first bit.

"Thursday, 2nd March. I found we had to provide three more fatigue parties, each of forty men and one officer, to go up near the line and repair trenches. I sent Robert, Kinny and Partington on these.

"I have just heard that we are sending out a big bombing party tonight to strafe the enemy. I wish I could be up to see it – that's the proper thing to do. I hear we are also sending out bags of rations – as samples of our grub – each containing a German letter describing the nice comfortable rest camps in England for German prisoners. This is to tempt the Hun to come and surrender!

"Friday, 3rd March, 5.15 p.m. I met "Sambo" (The C.O.'s servant) this morning standing outside the estaminet so I asked him where he was off to. "Up to the trenches with the Colonel, Sir." I said "Sambo, if anything happens to the C.O. you're for it. I'll have you put against the first tree and shot." He said "Quite right, sir, and serve me right, nothing can happen to him whilst I'm with him – I'm his sniper." Sambo is a good lad, he's always smiling, and a chap who's always merry and bright is the man for my money every time.

"Saturday, 4th March, 1916, 11 p.m. This morning when we wakened up, it was snowing hard and had been most of the night. Everywhere is white. It continued to snow until 3 p.m. and as we had to be knocking about all morning we got very "fed up" and wet.

"The relief was completed by 8 p.m., after being held up on the way whilst people in front drew gum boots. We got none, but some had been left in a keep here for us. Unfortunately, most of the men were wet through before we reached the boots! In places the water comes well above the knees, and some of my boys have been up to the thighs in it. There are some decent dug-outs, however, which is a blessing. We have no rum but have sent for some.

"Sunday, 5th March, 2.40 a.m. We "stood to" just after 5 a.m. and I went round the Company's line. Returned at 6.15 for the tea which had been promised, but none was forthcoming, so I lay down for a snooze on one of the two wire frames on the floor which form beds. The bally brazier had gone out long ago, and it was very cold.

"Immediately after breakfast, I started my morning tour.

I found all my men cheery and had a word with each. Their feet were cold and wet, but there was no grousing — each had a smile and a cheery word in reply to our bits of chaff. Lads who'll stand last night will stand anything. Up to their knees in snow water, most had been nearly up to their middles coming in. It froze during the night.

"I gave the necessary orders for our withdrawal. It turned out that we were the only Company of the 15th leaving the trenches that night. Remainder had to wait until 4 a.m. yesterday morning, the reason being that a great stunt was to take place in front of the bit of line we occupied. A big mine was to be "popped off" at midnight, which necessitated all the front and support trenches being cleared of troops.

"The mine was in three parts. It should not have been fired until the end of the week, but owing to the saps having collapsed, through bad weather, the R.E. decided to poop it right away. The show was elaborately arranged and Major Campbell came up to our dug-out to explain the operation orders to the officers concerned. Of course, the mine was the star turn, but there were a good many other side-shows.

"At 10 p.m. a bombing party were to go out and throw bombs where we cut the Germans' wire the day before. A pretty thin job as the Huns are sure to have machine guns trained on these breaches in their wire. Later an officer and eight men were to light smoke bombs (like big candles) and throw them over the parapet. This was to make the Huns think we were treating them to a gas attack, and get them out of their dug-outs with helmets on.

"Of course, all our saps and front line trenches had to be evacuated whilst the show was on, and reoccupied later. Coloured rockets had to be fired from the keep. Artillery were to commence a big strafe at midnight exactly.

"It was near midnight when I got on to the bed in my billet. I heard the mine go up and then the artillery got on the job. Until 12.30 there was a terrible row — then all quiet and I tried to sleep. It was very cold and the rats were noisy and running about over my legs. I don't mind rats, but they kept pulling papers off the table and making quite a noise. I could not sleep well – I suppose I was too tired. However, I slept some, and shivered a lot.

"Wednesday, March 15th. We went to Brigade H.Q. where a motor bus picked us up, and after a long drive we arrived at our destination. Here we witnessed a great display. Lines of infantry attacked lines of trenches and set up different kinds of smoke as they captured different lines (with no enemy). We enjoyed the spectacle as it is the first time we've watched others do the work.

"When this was over we had a firework display – all kinds of signal rockets and flares, even some mortars fired bombs which burst very high releasing balloons shaped as fish, men, tigers, and dogs, (these are known as 'Rockets, Japanese, liberating animals'); flare lights descended slowly on parachutes, stars of all kinds were thrown – but in daylight it seemed a waste and not very instructive.

"Monday, 20th March. We left our billets at Cornet Malo yesterday morning at 9.00 a.m. and marched seven miles to Epinette. The roads were very bad – one particularly, which is marked a first-class road on the map, was about a foot deep in mud and full of jolly holes. Glad I had my horse. All the men were carrying full packs, plus fur coats, oil-sheets and mackintosh capes. This, with rifles and one hundred and twenty rounds of ammunition per man, is a heavy load for little men.

"I only had one man fall out. He was ill and has been taken off in the ambulance this morning with high fever. Influenza, I think. He is a Scottish laddie (O'Neil) and I am sorry to lose him.

"I had quite a number of (disciplinary) cases for office hours today. Nearly all for dirty rifles. Nobody got less than the limit of my powers – seven days punishment. We have now to be extremely particular about the rifles being always absolutely perfect. The least bit of carelessness on the part of a man might cause a jam at a critical time.

"We are to have a concert tonight and are inviting the officers and men of the Gloucesters to come. We go into the trenches with this regiment, so the C.O. wants us to get to know each other — very wise.

"Monday, 27th March, 1.15 a.m. Each man carries two sandbags up to the trenches, also rations for next day, but now we have only to carry one hundred rounds of ammunition per man.

"We started our march as a Battalion and got into different formations at different points as we approached the front. Companies left after the long halt at ten minute intervals; then platoons at two hundred yards' intervals; then formed two-deep and kept to the side of the road; then single file into communications trench. Roads quite close up are in good condition — rough concrete. Our men marched in and relieved a regular regiment of the line like real old soldiers.

"I reported relief complete (by telephone) at 8.26 p.m. I had then to send a few messages and make various arrangements.

"Captain Earle, Brigade Bombing Officer, came up this morning. I told him our grenades would not quite reach, so he offered to bring up a few that would reach there. He came up with them and a lot of men, rifles (for grenades), etc., this afternoon, also a cake in a box and invited himself for tea. We were glad to see the lad. Earle's strafe came off all right, and he fired nineteen Newton grenades, nine of which landed plumb in Fritz's trench — not bad, eh?

"Saturday, 1st April, 3 p.m. Relief commenced to arrive about 8.45 — relief of my Company complete 9.30, but we had to wait for "W." They completed 10.15 and moved off — we followed.

"We had to leave by different communication trenches after passing along "W's" sub-sector — men all loaded up, dark night, strange country, mostly overloaded, in single file along very bad tracks, through wire, mud and water. Our men were silent and discipline good – but frequent halts necessary owing to losing touch.

We were not shelled at all coming down, but many stray bullets continually about. They seemed almost to follow us as if they could see us. Ricochets hum and whiz overhead. I think going up and coming back from front line is the most nervy part of our business, but I've never seen anybody of ours show funk yet. Arrived Battalion H.Q. 12.30 a.m. and when I went in to report the C.O. wanted to know why we were so late – nuf sed!

"Sunday, 2nd April. A beautiful hot day – such a treat. I sent out two patrols at night, or rather at 1 a.m. One, under Lance-Sergt. Slavitz, had to go towards a certain spot in the Hun line, report on the condition of the ground between (ditches, cover, &c., &c.). This information specially required, and each Company has to make a separate report this trip.

"4.15 p.m. We had two patrols and one wiring party out last night from 11 p.m. until 12.15 a.m. One, under Sergt. Brittain, brought useful information about condition of "No Man's Land." They lay by the Hun wire for a quarter of an hour and heard a working party busy on a new fort the enemy are building. When it is finished the artillery will blow it out. A Hun surrendered to the Battalion on our right last night. He was a young Jaeger about eighteen years old.

"Saturday, 8th April, 2.45 a.m. I have had a reward of £20 cash – an offer throughout this trip – for a live German brought to my H.Q., and a number of the boys were very sick that I had restricted their movements and would not let them raid the enemy trench to get one. Such action would defeat the scheme for a rather bigger stunt, to take place shortly, of which they know not.

"Here's Kynaston with his Lewis Gun, to which is attached a hyperscope. This excellent arrangement enables the gun to be fired over the parapet without any of the crew exposing themselves. It is a wooden frame attached below the gun and fitted with a periscope.

"Sunday, 9th April. The strafe was a great success, but it is very evident that we will have to get a stronger rifle, or some better arrangement for firing these new grenades. First shot, the stock of the rifle broke. This is the last we have left, as two broke yesterday. However, the boys tied it up with string and we were able to use it, although it had to be refastened at each shot.

"We were firing it with a long lanyard, and everybody had to take cover when each shot was fired for fear of accidents. It was a great success. We fired thirty five grenades out of which twenty three landed either right in, or just behind the enemy's trenches. Two landed plumb on top of a dug-out.

"Meantime Wilson, with his Lewis Gun, was making a nasty mess of some snipers' loopholes, which we had marked. We all quite enjoyed the fun. Old Fritz took it very quietly and did not retaliate. No doubt he will prepare some little treat to give us back.

"The Bantams' Comforts Fund are sending us out a splendid lot of stuff, and their parcels are continually arriving. We all feel very grateful to the ladies who are working so hard for us. The men know where their new socks, pipes, mufflers, &c., &c., are coming from and they are very thankful.

"Sunday, 29th April. We used Lewis guns with hyper-scopes to good effect during the afternoon. It is a grand arrangement for upsetting old Fritz. Our snipers have rigged up a splendid telescope in a loophole running through the parapet and it is fixed on a gap in the Hun line. A fat Hun worked there for a while, but we could only see his helmet; he was too careful!

"Last night there was a terrible strafe on our right a few miles away. The Hun used gas two or three times, and I hear that although he reached our trenches he was turned out in less than a quarter of an hour with heavy losses. We had no casualties from the gas, which speaks volumes for the efficiency of our gas helmets.

TB - G

"Sunday, 30th, 2.30 a.m. It's jolly cold in this new dug-out, very draughty. I had three wiring parties out between 11.30 p.m. and 1.30 a.m. I find that our wire is not so good as I thought. I was over the top twice tonight and had a good look round. The wire on right is fairly good, but left flank is very bad for thirty or forty yards and will need immediate attention.

"It is now 3.20 a.m. We will "stand to." It's getting quite light and the larks are singing.

"Wednesday, 3rd May. At "stand to" on Monday evening, the Boche sent three shells simultaneously over the Strand. I was at the extreme right flank of my Company frontage, when a message came to say that ten of my boys were hit. I was talking to Capt. Morgan, who is holding a bit of the reserve on my right flank.

"I asked him to send his stretcher bearers along. As I was returning I met Billy, so sent him off to Strand. I then telephoned the Dressing Station to warn the M.O. that I had cases coming along, and doubled down the communication trench to see what I could do. I went along and had a word with the lads and felt proud of them. One boy was dead and five were wounded. Everybody was cool and stretcher bearers worked quickly and well.

"On the Saturday evening I was very surprised to meet the C.O. coming round. He had been in London at 11 a.m. and was here at 5.30 p.m. Pretty quick, eh! Of course, he had been driven here straight from the boat on a good motor-car. It shows what can be done. He took three days to get home!

"Orders came announcing an inspection for next morning, by the new Brigadier. He has really arrived and is not the officer we expected. He is Col. A. H. Marindin, late Black Watch, now temporary Brigadier-General.

"Near Chappelle, Sunday, May 14th: My first impression of the line is a good one. The breastwork is quite good — parados good — but no administration trench. Dug-outs not very good. There are a few danger spots, where the Boche sniper may bag a few of us – but on the whole the line seems comfortable and cushy. The communication trenches are not good.

" The battered fragments of a few houses stand between us and the front line; behind this H.Q. are built or dug. The mess is a French steel dug-out of the usual type. The usual small offices and sleeping places all round. Signallers, orderly room, kitchen, sleeping quarters for the C.O., myself and Graham-Barnet has a bed in the orderly room. The R.S.M., officers' servants, orderlies, runners, orderly room staff, pioneers, &c., &c., are accommodated near by.

"It has been a delightful hot day. The evening is beautiful – a cloudless sky and no wind. Partridges are calling, blackbirds singing. A yellowhammer quite near is singing his chirpy little song. An occasional shot is fired and a ricochet sings over occasionally.

"About 8 p.m. last night one of our planes flew along the front, passing over the Hun line at a height that was too low for the Archies*, which can't fire below a certain height. All the Huns "stood to" and fired at the 'plane with machine guns and rifles – a perfect fusilade. The pilot was priceless and we all turned out to watch the display and thoroughly enjoyed it. He would fly over the Hun line, just where his friends fell this morning. He would turn round and fly away over our line, then back again, and each time he swooped down quite low and fired his machine gun at the trenches of the Hun.

"About 7.30 p.m. I went down to "B" lines with the C.O. He has had a rifle battery rigged up there. We tested the rifle battery and it was going later in earnest all night, and every night it sends its jolly messengers along a road behind the Hun lines – one he uses – and we can shoot straight up it from here.

"I found that in addition to the wiring parties, Billy had a patrol of five out. There was some confusion while this party was out. They met six Germans. Bombs were

---

* Anti-aircraft guns.

thrown from sap held by W. Company and two of our own men wounded. One, especially (Tunstall), behaved splendidly – searching for the men who had been hit. His name has been forwarded to Brigade. They are all in now.

"I got up in good time and went off to the dressing station to see these men in the morning about 7 o'clock. I got a lot of good information about the construction of the Hun obstacles, his sentries, the position of the M.G. and the strength of his garrison in the front line. They all insisted that the enemy trenches are quite as strongly held as ours. This is rather useful, as we had an idea that they were very thinly held. The wire was very strong and deep – consisting of double apron fence and then twenty feet of low wire about 3 ft. high fixed on wooden frames, like our concertina wire in formation, but held on the frames firmly and well picketed down.

"A new draft arrived from depot and also a small draft (67 to the Battalion) of cyclists. These are big men and I feel it is a pity for them to have sent the chaps to us, as it rather spoils the "Bantams" business. However, we frequently have to send men away, and we may be able to pass them on.

"We have got a gun back here, which gets Fritz ripe every day. She is called "Silent Sue." The explosion of the gun is not loud, but she throws a big shell. She is a "six inch" and fires continually. The Germans frequently shell where they think she is, but most of their stuff is going into a nice big field and doing no harm.

"Captain Gibbs was up today and he showed me some of the Huns' latest shrapnel. He had just dug it up – three pieces in one hole, two round lead bullets and one marble. You know what kiddies call "olleys" or "stoneys" – they are the cheapest kind of marble one can buy. Gibbs told me that his men had repeatedly reported that the Hun was using a mixture of stone marbles and leaden bullets, but he doubted it until he saw it. Fritz must be getting short of even the baser metals.

"Friday, 9th June. At "stand to" Willie was going round his Platoon when he heard sharp words of command coming from one of the bays. He halted and listened to the following amusing performance: Shields, who was my servant when I was attached to the artillery, was bossing the show. He had four men on the parapet. "Battery action" — pause — "No. 3 gun stand fast. Salvo fire" — pause — voices from the top, "No. 1 gun ready, sir; No. 2 gun ready, sir; No. 4 gun ready, sir." Shields (commanding battery of 18-pounders by the way); "Two minutes right." Reply: "No. 1 gun ready, sir; No. 2 gun ready, sir." Shields: "Battery salvo fire." The four rifles popped off at once — pause — "No. 1 gun ready, sir, &c." Battery Commander: "Repeat fire," off again altogether — pause — "Three-quarters of an hour left, add 50, repeat fire." Again, they fire. "Cease fire!" They worked as though they were really on a serious job, and when Willie walked along the bay; there was nothing unusual — all at their posts and never a smile.

"Don't you love these little men who can play amidst the serious business? There's not a dry shirt in the Company, and we are here until Saturday. We're very cold, and Captain Johnston is grousing about the condition of the equipment! How can a chap be expected to keep his equipment clean when he has to, &c. &c. — but we're in the Army and we've got to.

"Major Shaw called 4 a.m. He is getting as regular as the Hun. The latter gentleman started firing A.T.'s (aerial torpedoes) yesterday, and he fired every quarter of an hour to the minute for two and a quarter hours, then finished.

"A Patrol sent out by Z Company got bombed. They went up an old trench, intending to sit and listen at a certain spot, but Fritz was sitting there first, heard them coming and bombed them. Lieutenant Alexander and three men were hit, but all got back.

"I'll tell you a story that is true to finish off this little lot before I post it. A certain Brigadier in our Division is very keen on gas helmets and severely strafes anybody he finds without one. One day he was going round the front line, and suddenly discovered that he had forgotten his own. He asked Tommy to give him his helmet, but the Tommy refused and said that his Captain had told him that he must not part with it on any account. The Company Officer stepped forward and told the man to give the General his helmet at once, and he'd see it was replaced. The General marched off with the helmet slung on. As he came out of the communication trench he met a subaltern without a helmet and gave him "gyp," saying that he would not have officers and men going about without gas helmets. He finished up with, "Here, take mine," and gave him the one he had borrowed. As the subaltern turned away the Brigadier said, "Now you have one, do you know how to put it on?" "Yes, sir." "Well do so." The youth opened the satchel and revealed a dirty pair of socks! The poor Tommy responsible was crimed.

"Friday, 23rd June. Up at nine, but no parade until 11.15 for the march to the place we were to be inspected at. We passed Battalion starting point 11 a.m. and Brigade S.P. 11.30. The men felt the heat a good deal as we were in "marching orders."

"The 19th Northumberland Fusiliers, a Brigade of Artillery (which now consists of three batteries of 18-pounders and one battery of Hows), one field company R.E. divisional cyclists, 106th field ambulance, and the four battalions of our brigade were all massed on the large field. A long wait before our inspection, but perhaps not quite so long as usual. At last orders came down. General Pinnie "The parade will come to attention and slope arms," repeated along the line, the "General salute," "Present arms" Bugles played "General salute," and all infantry presented arms. "The parade will slope arms and order arms," repeated, then "The parade will stand at ease," &c. General Sir C. C. Munroe commanding the First Army is a short, rather stout man.

"He looked rather severe and had a black shade over one eye. He went round the artillery "like a cooper round a barrel," as Fred would say. He then came round us (on his horse). General Pinnie mentioned Col. Newell's name as he reached him and explained that he commanded the 15th Cheshires, and I heard him say to the C.O. "Your men look very well," and so he passed on.

"When the General had finished he went to a small table in front of which stood a group of heroes. He presented medals. Four or five officers received Military Crosses and a number of N.C.O.'s and men received D.C.M.'s and Military Medals.

"Then the General took his stand, and the march past commenced. Artillery led and they looked splendid. We followed and the boys were on their toes.

"As we passed, the General remarked that "These men are wonderfully steady." Such praise from an Army Commander was very gratifying. I believe General Pinnie was pleased.

"I met a funny character for the first time on the Brigade march on Tuesday. He is a 2nd Lieutenant and commanding a battery. He was in the main guard with me. He's a Lancashire lad and a very capable officer. Talks broad Lancashire and does not care a – for anybody. He's the sort of chap one could absolutely depend upon in a tight corner. Funny tales are told of him so I'll give you one or two. An official notice came round on one occasion "Please state by retreat tonight exactly how many trench boards have been broken up, and used by your battery as firewood." He just wrote across it "Scores!"

"I understand that he was put under arrest once and his Sam Browne belt taken away. He promptly wrote to the Brigadier complaining that he could not strop his razor as they had taken his belt away. His belt was returned to him.

"Monday, 3rd July. Morning, 8.30 a.m., and here I am in a smelly, bumpy third-class French railway carriage. Already we have left the flat country and are passing through un-dulating country pretty and, as usual, every available bit is cultivated. The crops are growing rapidly and look very well indeed. Let's hope the crops of the Central Powers are not so good. The people are all waving and shouting to us from the houses and fields. They wave handkerchiefs and the children throw kisses. Nearly all the children salute smartly in the English way. Our Tommies teach them wherever they are billeted.

"We arrived at the station, Bouquet Maison, to find a five-mile march to Sur St. Leger in front of us -- a hot day -- roads dusty. Nobody knew our destination until the C.O. got his instructions at the station. The march to billets was rather trying and told on the men, who were carrying packs and greatcoats again. We arrived about 2.30 p.m. We were all tired and went to sleep once we were fixed up and the men settled. The people are nice -- real French, not Flemish.

"Two new drafts arrived for us, one of one hundred and three men from the 11th Cheshires and another of sixty one from the 10th Battalion. These men are Bantams, and had been sent to the other battalions during the last two months. Now they are returned to our Bantam Battalions and they put us miles over strength."

Chapter Six

Into the Line

At night in February, 1916, you could stand on the cliffs at Folkestone on England's south coast and sometimes be able to hear the war going on. If the sky was clear and the wind was right, the eastern horizon would ripple with pale light, the glow alternating with the faint sound of gunfire. When the troopships reached Le Havre, the "wump-wump-wump" was a steady drumming in the air, a close reminder of what lay ahead. By the time the 35th Division went into camp in the Foret de Nieppe, near Merville, the noise of bombardment 12 kilometres away was so loud that some of the men were at first convinced that they had actually reached the firing line.

But before a group of fresh brigades could plunge into battle, there was a whole ritual of settling in to perform. Like some huge dog turning round and round in new grass, the Division had to be reformed, billeted, and marched here and there, while medical and signals units, gun parks, and supply-trains were organized.

The artillery, engineers, pioneers, and signallers of the 35th Division were standard-sized troops, not bantams, who had been assigned from other formations. They brought with them brand new guns and other support equipment which was readied for use by the 157th, 158th, and 159th Brigades of Artillery, 163rd Brigade of Howitzers, three

Royal Engineers companies, a Signals company, and the 19th (Pioneer) Battalion, Northumberland Fusiliers.

One of the 17th Battalion was Frank Heath, an eighteen year old Yorkshireman. He looks back on his early days in France with clarity, "We were first billeted in a paper mill, and our boudoir was a large warehouse filled with paper bales ready for pulping, on which we slept. As it was warm there, we were able to undress. When the women came to work at 6.30 a.m., and caught us nearly naked, they loved to wrestle with us and touch us up a bit. One lad named Felton was much younger than any of us and had a baby face with rosy cheeks. He was a particular favourite with all the women and they called him "Piccanini" and paid him very special attention every morning, loving to embarrass him in a certain way."

To ease them into the war, the Bantams were first allotted to XI Corps, which contained the 38th (Welsh) Division and the Guards' Brigade. Each battalion was marched towards their encampment in stages, and encouraged to mingle with the seasoned troops of the local parent units in the hope that some individual experience would rub off on the newcomers. As is often the case, a strong liking immediately grew between the very tall and very short soldiers, when Bantams and Guards met.

"There was a lot of chaffing going on today," wrote Guardsman Alec Thames to his brother at the time. "After we finished telling the Bants they had duck's disease, we had to take a lot of very funny insults in turn. Very sharp tongues they have, and we've taken to the little chaps right away."

The newcomers soon learned that in volunteering to fight they were accepted as equals in a purgatory which was a great leveller, and where survival was the only real priority. On his first day at the front, Private Harry Tillotson's unit was marching up a sunken road to relieve some Grenadier Guardsmen.

"As we were going up the line, they were coming down

the line," he recalls. "The big fellas looked at us with grins all over their faces. At first we thought it was because they were so tall and we were so small; but it wasn't, they were smiling just because they were coming out of the line and we were going in."

On the 11th of March, Lt. General Sir R. Haking awaited Lord Kitchener on the reviewing stand at Wardrecques, where the entire division was to be inspected once more by the Commander-in-Chief. "I shall never forget it," says Jack Paget, at the time a seventeen-and-a-half year old 2nd Lieutenant with the 18th Lancashire Fusiliers. "It rained in sheets all day and the whole Division just stood there, drenched, waiting for Lord Kitchener to turn up. When he did, he was hours late."

Just before dusk, Kitchener arrived to watch the parade of each battalion through the downpour, then made another congratulatory speech about the turn-out and appearance of the men he had been interested in since their origin. Still wet, the battalions went back that evening to hauling ammunition and supplies through freezing rain and snow, as the division pressed to ready itself for front line service.

While logistics were being put in place, cadres of officers and N.C.O.'s were selected to gain some first-hand experience of trench warfare. They were attached to fighting units, given a taste of the real thing for a few days at a time, then sent back to convey their scant knowledge as best they could. It was the method used by military machines throughout history, but the individual results were not always of practical use.

"Some of our officers didn't seem able to put into words what they'd seen," believes Nobby Streeter, by then a lance-corporal. "We had three or four days of it with the Welsh Division, and came back to set up a training course. Thank God, we had a few old sweats with us.

"Two of our officers had been sergeants in the South African do, and were able to get across the facts to the rest of the battalion. But by and large, our officers thought it wasn't "good form" or something to talk about what they'd seen. They stood there fingering their swagger-sticks and mumbling about how things were a bit sticky up there, old boy. They were good fellers, mind you, but they'd been brought up to keep a stiff upper lip, and not to seem to show off ever.

"One young two-pipper (1st Lt.) stumbled along this way for a bit in the middle of a training exercise until a South African veteran who had been made up to a captain stepped in front of the company and said dryly, "What he means, lads, is don't bunch together, keep your rifle clean and your arse down at all times!"

Members of the cadres were more often the subject of interest for the personal stories they brought back. On February 14th, Lt. Colonel Harrison Johnston of the Cheshires wrote in his diary, "Here's Billy Brown come back. He is full of terrible tales of the wicked Huns, but he's glad to get back to the fold. The experience has been invaluable. It has given him renewed confidence in our men, and he says "Well, Johnnie, I know our boys will do well." I've been telling him and others the same thing for many moons, but he knows now. The best little men in the world, you will see. If not, then I don't want to come home.

"Billy brought some pretty stories back with him. One being that a Sgt. Major of the company he was with captured a Hun in the last show they had, and was found carefully strangling the chap with a pull-through shortly afterwards. I don't quite see the point of choosing that special mode of disposing of the gentleman, but we all have our different forms of amusement."

The green units began to learn methods of how to save more lives, often at the cost of the few for the many. Fusilier Frank Harris describes how it worked. "Troops in the line were strung out; just a Lewis gun post about every hundred yards. Should the Germans come, the outposts were sacrificed, but gave alarm for most troops held further back. During the day, nothing moved, but after dusk you could hear the hoofs of mules and jingle of harness, cursing drivers, and see shadows of men moving up and down the duckboard tracks. Men had to be relieved every forty eight hours, or they would have died of exposure."

Some shivering Lancastrians in one such outpost on the night of February 23rd heard a large group of Germans approaching. They determined to wait in ambush, calmly laying out a row of grenades in front of each man, and being careful to quietly hold bolt-tension while the Lewis gun was cocked to avoid that tell-tale clatter. The enemy advanced in open order, beginning to eagerly run forward when it seemed they would be able to invade the British trenches unseen. The listening-post crew opened up a close range, killed or wounded several intruders and drove off the rest.

A few days later, the 17th Battalion received a note from the area commander, Brigadier-General, L. A. Price Davies, V.C. – "Please convey to the battalion my appreciation of the spirit they showed in the recent encounter with the enemy. The readiness of the listening patrol allowing the enemy to approach and then dealing with them is also an excellent sign."

An hour and a half after going into the Welsh trenches, the division had its first battle casualty on February 18th, when Private Caxton of the 17th West Yorkshires was shot in the head at Neuve Chapelle. More observers from the West Yorks and the 17/18 Lancashire Fusiliers were wounded in the next couple of weeks, three of whom later died. Around this time, the Cheshires began to take casualties during their first sampling of trench warfare.

Colonel Johnston led his men into the sector where they were to learn their trade. He wrote in his diary, "On entering the communication trench we stepped into a foot of water – "the duck walks" (under the water) were narrow and up the centre of the trenches only. The consequence was that at the corners (and often at other times when one's foot slipped off the boards) a leg would miss the duck walk and sink three feet (no exaggeration, I assure you) into the water which filled the trenches. The duck walks are on piles which are driven into the bottom of the trench, but in places they had become loose, one would step on one end, the other end would tip up and in one went! The sides of the trenches were wet and slimy, and people frequently fell.

"Absolute silence was observed. No cursing or exclamations, just the splashes. Any noise would have drawn fire on us at once. As it was I had one lad hit before we left by a stray bullet. When we arrived at the trenches we found them in very poor condition — narrow, badly kept — very wet owing to the snow-water and almost without dug-outs.

"The dug-out occupied by the officers — otherwise Company H.Q. — was a smelly hole in the earth, which had to be entered by crawling on all fours through a tunnel with a floor of sticky mud.

"During the strafe, a 60 lb. trench mortar shell fell just outside the door. This completely wrecked the Officers servants' quarters and kitchen, which was a light dug-out next door where food was prepared. The three servants were buried but got out all right and unwounded, although badly shaken. A large water-filled crater formed in the space between the trench and the dug-out — it was raining heavily. "C" Company on our left lost eight men, four killed and four wounded, by a rifle grenade. One man at "D" also got hit on the head this morning by a splinter from a whiz-bang, but it was only a light scalp wound."

Frank Heath was sent for his first taste of war: "We were moved along the La Bassee canal bank at night to the trenches at Givenchy. The Welsh Fusiliers were to give us instruction as this was our first time in the line for us. As we entered the communication trench, we were challenged "Who goes there?" followed by cries of "Make way for the dead and wounded!""

"When it was dawn, we moved into the front line, which was merely composed of shell holes. It was pretty quiet, except for a few bullets and an occasional shell whining its way to a target well behind. I was detailed to go to a trench a few holes away to bring breakfast for six men — a rasher of bacon and a hunk of bread. When I got out of the hole, a bullet whizzed just past my leg. It put the wind up me and I ducked with my head buried in the snow.

"After two days of this, we Lancashire Fusiliers were withdrawn as it was assumed we had learned enough to be able to hold the line on our own. We marched three miles to a barn for a rest and a sleep. You could hear the guns thundering away and see the Very lights. Whichever direction you looked, those coloured lights seemed to encircle you. After we had been asleep for all of two hours with our boots off, we were awakened by Sergeant Nightingale shouting, "Come on lads, we are going on a working party." The job was to carry barbed wire and duckboards for the Royal Engineers in the front line which we had just left."

Raised on accounts of mass slaughter on the Somme where 60,000 casualties were suffered in a single day, and on tales of whole battalions wiped out at Passchendaele, Lens, Vimy, and Belleau Wood, we now tend to think that was how it was that so many died in the Great War. Yet really, men died for the most part in a steady trickle — here, a green young lieutenant sniped near the latrines; there, a wiring party caught by a Spandau; a squad wiped out by a sudden trench mortar bomb; or perhaps the morning sun brewing up dormant phosgene gas from the bottom of a trench to send an exhausted platoon lying there into the deepest sleep of all.

Trench raids, sniping, salvos from the routine morning "hate," each killed thousands of men every day by the multiple handful rather than by the hundred. You could waver off the duckboard and quietly drown in liquid mud without anyone being the wiser, or die from one of a hundred other mishaps. At Suzanne, three Bantams fell asleep at the side of a deserted road and their remains were found at dawn, pulped under the heedless wheels of a passing ammunition wagon.

Accidental wounds and deaths were common where millions of loaded small arms lay casually everywhere. One such incident was seen by Fusilier Frank Heath. "A chap by the name of Willet was on the firestep, cleaning his rifle. He asked Jack Darraque to grab the end of his pull-through cord, which Jack did. Willet then closed the bolt and pressed the trigger. Darraque was shot right through the heart. Willet was court martialled, not only for killing Darraque but also for cleaning his rifle without first removing the bolt and magazine as laid down in regulations."

The same training cadre had another tragedy the next day, just after they came out of the line into reserve. A popular officer, Captain Tyas, was putting a detonator into a Mills bomb which exploded in his hands. His men sadly buried him the same day in the village cemetery at Savigny and were marched back to the line that night as a rations-carrying party.

Even training courses well behind the lines took a small but steady toll of men. Their next-of-kin wept no less bitterly over the fruits of a badly-aimed practice salvo or of a shortfall during mortar-bomb instruction. From a variety of such causes, over thirty officers and men were killed in two months in France, before the 35th Division officially went into action.

After two months of preparation, in which detachments from each battalion were given a taste of trench conditions, the Division was considered to have been "blooded." On March 10th, the entire 35th was sent in to occupy portions of the front line east of Festubert and bordering Neuve Chapelle.

The sector chosen for the Division to hold lay between Festubert and Laventie, in the lowest-lying part of the wet

Flanders Plain. There, trenches tended to peter out every few hundred yards into quagmires impossible to dig, so that breastworks of sandbags and brick rubble were as common as conventional ditches. Lacking firm lines, both sides tended to raid back and forth more frequently than elsewhere, tempted by the flimsy battlements of each other. By deliberately withdrawing from low ground, the Germans did have the advantage of better drainage, as was their more intelligent strategic habit throughout the war.

So much water on the surface or just below ground made Flanders and Northern France the very worst places on the face of Europe for trench warfare. The neat picture shown on military maps of an orderly line of trenches was not possible in reality. Streams and marshes constantly interrupted the lines all along the battlefield, making any form of dug-out impossible. Even on apparently firmer ground, the desperate shovels of infantrymen soon encountered permanent saturation close below the surface, which kept most trenches in a constant state of wetness. On higher ground, the problem was that rainfall could not drain off through the clay. As a result, men were often forced to spend their time in the line standing up to their ankles or knees in cold water and liquid mud. For the smaller Bantams, this problem was that much more severe.

"We were issued with two empty sandbags each before we went into the front line, the idea being to fill them so we could keep out of the mud and reach over the firestep more easily. The only trouble was, the wet soil and muck available for filler soon collapsed flat as a pancake. I've seen us up to the waist in slush and wet muck," recalled Cyril Wright. "We tried all kinds of tricks like cutting shelves in the trench wall high up to get us out of the water. This wasn't too good an idea, as it made it too easy for snipers and also reduced protection against shellfire. But the misery of standing in deep mud would become so bad, we would risk a bullet or a Jack Johnson just for a bit of respite and dry feet."

During the first week of March, 1916, the three brigades began to take over their sector. The 104th Brigade relieved the 58th Brigade from holding the sector around Plum Street, while the 106th Brigade relieved the 57th Brigade next door. The 105th Brigade had been in reserve under instruction in the trenches of the 38th Welsh, and it was decided to now let them take over in full.

A signaller with the 38th Division, Edgar Pursell, was repairing telephone lines in an observation post that night. "It was a fairly quiet part of the front," he says. "We had been there several weeks, and scarcely heard from the Germans. All was dark and quiet as the Bantams filtered in from the road, along the communications trenches, heading for the front line. Suddenly, all hell let loose.

"Until the Somme battles later, it was the heaviest bombardment I had experienced. Shells poured into the sector, blasting the new troops at the very moment they started to man their position. Within minutes of arrival, dozens of dead and wounded Bantams were being carried back along the C.T.'s.

"It was uncanny. Their baptism of fire was particularly savage and devastating. How? Why? On a well-known *quiet* front? As was common practice, the rookies had been given that inactive front to gain experience. It was everyone's opinion there that the Germans knew full well that the Bantams would be going in to man that sector that night. And they obviously knew the time to the very second."

This devastating welcome was the Division's first experience of the apparent German omnipotence in matters of military information. Next morning, survivors swear that they had another demonstration that the enemy knew the Bantams had moved into the sector. "A very scary thing happened the first morning we were getting ourselves sorted out at stand-to," was described by Graham Carr. "Listen to that!" said one of our sergeants. Clear as could be, we could hear the Gerries crowing — "arroo-arroo-arroo!" then laughing fit to bust. We didn't think anything of it beyond promising each other we'd soon make Gerry laugh out the other side of his face, but our sergeant made quite a fuss of it and kept saying, "How do the buggers know already?"

There is a persistent story that every time the Bantams occupied sections of the front line, the Germans opposite would begin to make derisive rooster calls to show they knew which troops had moved in. The same type of thing is mentioned by Scottish and Irish regiments who were greeted by Teutonic shouts of, "Hellow, Jock!" and "Top 'o' the mornin,' Paddy!"

Though the British troops may have developed an exaggerated awe of German military intelligence, there is no question that the enemy did frequently seem to know an uncomfortably detailed amount about local British troop dispositions. This may have been due to their being able to form a well-developed espionage net amongst the French population, a few of whom were apparently subverted by a combination of bribe money and old feelings of hostility towards Britain.

A few weeks after their arrival, the Division was able to solve one such problem, as Colonel Johnston described while writing home in April. "Did I tell you the story of the spy who gave our artillery away? When I was attached to the Battery the other day, an officer called my attention to a civilian ploughing in a large field. He was using two horses — a black one and a white one. It seems that some days he would plough for perhaps an hour without an alteration of the position of his horses. He would then change the horses over at the end of each furrow.

"It was noticed at last and he was watched. The gunners became convinced that he was giving information to Hun aeroplanes who were observing for their artillery. We had three or four Batteries close together, which were frequently moved slightly, but the Boche always got the range and chased them out of their new positions.

"The man was watched, and two nights after I left he was found in a hedge with a rifle watching the road. A number of troops had been shot on this road at night by a sniper. The man is dead now."

The first Bantam unit to experience the full weight of the enemy was the 18th H.L.I. They were occupying trenches which straddled the Duck's Bill, a salient bulging forward about 500 yards north of Neuve Chapelle. Some of the men were miners, and had reported hearing sounds of underground work there the night before. However, they were still in position at dawn on March 13th when the Germans fired a mine under the salient. It is believed that the explosion also touched off the British counter-mine doubling the blast effect and sending up an entire section of the forward trench. When the smoke and dust cleared, there was a long mound of foul-smelling clay where the men had been crouched on the firing step, caught at stand-to as the enemy had planned. Though several survivors were quickly dug out, it was found that thirty Scotsmen had been killed, and another thirty had been wounded.

Deafened and groggy from the eruption, the troops on each side of the crump stood firm at their posts, loosing off such a volume of fire that the enemy follow-up raid melted away.

The officers and N.C.O.'s showed remarkable coolness in the fire fight, running along behind the trenches in full sight of the enemy to rally the men. Among them, 2nd Lt. St. George Yorke was awarded the Military Cross for his leadership.

A few days later, the Corps Commander sent a message to be read to all ranks: "I am very pleased with the action taken by all ranks to deal with the situation at the Duck's Bill on the morning of March 14th (sic). I am also glad to hear that there was no sign of giving way amongst the men of the 18/Highland Light Infantry, who were exposed to the full effect of the mine. This shows that although these men have only recently arrived in this country, they are to be trusted to maintain their positions even in the most dangerous and difficult circumstances."

The 17th Lancashire Fusiliers were given a swampy section of line outside Richebourg to hold. As no trenches could be dug, the principal strong points were three sandbag forts named Boars Head, Post Number One, and Post Number Two. "We had our first casualties here," recalls Frank Heath. "Lieutenant Nuttal was hit with a bullet, then Dick Cannavan was killed running 200 yards from Boars Head to Post Number One over open ground while trying to get a stretcher. When we got him in that night, we found a bullet hole straight through the middle of his forehead."

In mid-March, it was decided to give the 17th Lancashire Fusiliers some experience in a large trench raid. They were withdrawn from the line and sent to Richebourg St. Vaast, and rehearsed for the raid against replica trenches. Selected to go over in the attack were three officers and fifty other ranks under the command of Captain E. T. Cowan.

An artillery barrage was started the day before, intended to cut wire along the enemy front. The men bunched up in a forward trench for several hours, delayed by a German searchlight, that was only put out after a prolonged fusilade. Finally, they went forward at 9.30 p.m., in a raging blizzard which blinded them while crossing No Man's Land, bridging ditches with a ladder they carried, and managed to get through the shell-torn wire.

The Germans were understandably on the alert after so much attention and when the snowstorm halted to clearly reveal the Fusiliers, the attackers were forced back by a shower of grenades at the very lip of the trenches. Machine-gun fire killed two Lancashiremen, and wounded ten more, before they had to withdraw. A limited allowance of 30 rounds prevented artillery from giving much support, and the raid was judged a failure.

Trench raiding was a way of life for British and Common-wealth troops throughout the Great War. Though every bit as warlike, the French and Germans did not raid as frequently, considering it to be an expensive and bothersome activity. The British High Command constantly badgered front line regimental officers to "present an aggressive stance at all times to maintain the men's fighting spirit."

Raids were ostensibly made to capture prisoners to be interrogated for intelligence gathering purposes, but their high cost in casualties — which often provided the enemy with exactly the same kinds of information — in reality negated their stated aim. Many officers who had to lead men on such dangerous sallies believed they were more for the purpose of justifying Staff Officers' existence at the cost of other men's lives.

Yet the average Tommy thought little of such subtleties, and did his job without much question. The pugnacious Bantams seem to have been very ready participants in raids within a short time of their arrival at the front, and there was never a lack of volunteers when a "stunt" was announced.

"We were continually sent out on trench raids, wiring repair parties, and listening patrols in No Man's Land," recalls Patrick Cassidy of the 18th H.L.I. "On trench raids, we had our faces blackened, put scarves on our heads, and then were each given a tablespoon of rum before setting out. I always found those raids to be a bit hectic. We would creep right into the German lines to take a prisoner or throw a few grenades, then got back as soon as possible to our own side.

"One night on a raid, we were caught by a Very light. As we took cover a Spandau started to fire at us. We'd been spotted and bullets hummed close all round us. I felt a blow and a sudden wet feeling on my back and legs. I thought I'd been hit for sure, but made it back to our lines. There, I found that a tin of condensed milk in my haversack had been hit and I was unharmed."

"Dutch Courage" was an important ritual before starting out on a raid — rough brandy for the Germans, *gnole* spirits for the French, and Services Rum, diluted for the British. As Private Cassidy mentioned, men were hardly given enough to warm their stomachs, let alone send them roaring drunk into combat, but this tiny drink was always carefully doled out before a raid.

Because of the dash and initiative needed by men taking part, a raiding party usually was composed of volunteers. However, some units would detail men to also take part if it appeared that they weren't generally pulling their weight in the trenches. Between twenty five and fifty men would go over, with their positions and functions well defined in advance. A small section armed with Lewis guns and grenades would bed down just outside the British wire to wait as a covering party. The rest would go on in small teams of bombers, bayonet-men, and rear bodyguards. Cold steel was emphasized, bayonets and daggers, as was a variety of clubs, iron bars, and knobkerries for purposes of stealth. The main weapon of raids, though, was the Mills grenade, that 1½ pound egg-shaped bomb with a sectioned cast iron case which is still in service with the British Army to this day.

George Palmer of the Glosters tells how, "If we met a Jerry patrol in No Man's Land, it was bayonets and entrenching tools and pick-handles — quite a useful cosh they made. Of course, there were casualties on both sides and we would take back whoever we could. There was no time to waste, as when Jerry got wind of us he would try to make sure we never got back if he could help it. Safe home again, it was time for a good supper of bully-beef, dog biscuits, and a sip of water out of a petrol can which was never washed out — the dirty buggers. So to bed until stand-to just before dawn."

The Battalion Diary of the 17/West Yorkshires tells how they spent that month of March. "No attacks. No raids. Heavy manual work, keeping trenches dug, pumping water, revetting trench-walls, carrying Engineer supplies. Bitterly cold which reduces the mud, then warm weather which miserably thaws the ground, then cold sleet and blizzards. Fewer casualties from enemy snipers, as men learn survival skills and counter-sniping. Constant bombardment by enemy guns and trench mortars."

They were relieved at month's end by the 19th Durhams. The Geordies were still recovering from a mine and gas attack which caused seventeen casualties on March 14th while they had been in trenches with the 59th Brigade. "We were under bombardment all the time after we relieved the Yorkies," says Billy Watson. "You couldn't just spend all day hiding down on your hunkers, so we would stand on the firestep by the hour watching Jerry's parapet for a chance to hit back. I didn't get a chance until I reckoned how to get him cross. I fired off five rounds rapid, then moved quickly aside about ten feet and watched near where I'd fired at. Sure enough, a bare head popped up behind a rifle, and I shot him while he was firing at where I'd been a minute before."

Several battalion commanders had offered cash bounties of up to fifty pounds sterling for the first prisoner to be brought in. The Sherwood Foresters captured the division's first German on April 6th, when a fed-up deserter from the 17th Bavarian Regiment wandered through their wire. This voluntary p.o.w. did not pay a prize, and though a few more daring individuals strained for the chance to claim a bounty, most were content to forgo trench raids for the moment. There were dangers enough as it was.

Some men of the 15th Cheshires at the bombing school narrowly escaped death on April 9th, when a student dropped a Mills grenade after pulling the pin. Sergeant-Major Shooter scooped it up and threw it clear a moment before it exploded. He was wounded in the thigh, the only one hurt among the nearby group of officers and men whom he saved.

The entire division now received orders to move slightly south to the Ferme du Bois sector, and several changes in command were arranged en route. At this time, the 104th Brigade received a new commander, Brigadier-General J. W. Sandilands, who stayed with them from then on right until the Lancashire unit disbanded in March, 1919.

The Bantams had been instructing the 1st Australian Division in trench warfare. Now they turned over the sector to their students and marched off to the quiet trenches in front of Richebourg l'Avoué. Immediately, the Germans greeted their arrival with a heavy bombardment of high explosive, gas shells and smoke canisters. Five members of the 15th Sherwood Foresters were killed, including the popular Major H. T. Thirlwell.

The accuracy of German intelligence was again demonstrated when they shelled the British reserve battalions out of their rest camp at Croix Barbée. The shellfire swept on by plan the next day, smothering a trench salient called The Neb and causing a dozen Cheshire casualties.

The division struck back with a series of night raids, sending men against the German listening-posts, with orders to "kill or demoralize the enemy." A fifty-man patrol of the 23rd Manchesters went over on May 1st to silence a machine-gun post at Les Brulot. They destroyed the guns, inflicted some casualties, and returned with only two men wounded.

Enemy bombardment continued unabated for the next month, despite the spirited counter-fire of divisional artillery. The Manchesters attempted to repeat their success and set out on another raid. This time, they were caught in Very lights at the enemy wire and had to withdraw, carrying their casualties back. Four men covered the retreat and evacuation of wounded so well that the Military Medal was later awarded to Sergeant Hare, Corporal O'Connor, and Privates Townley and Lee. German retaliation gunfire was very heavy, catching the raiders and their comrades in the forward trenches. In a half hour, eight Mancunians were dead and 15 were wounded, including the fatally injured

Major Bannatyne.

The Germans preferred to make more massive attacks in larger numbers, and on the night of May 30th, they came close to breaking the 35th's line. Recently, the weather had grown warm, raising the men's spirits and increasing the tempo of combat. Several British units decided to send out fighting patrols under cover of a rain squall, unaware that the enemy was planning to launch a major assault.

The German attack was partially foiled by one of the raids setting out from the 15th Cheshire's position, as later described by their war diarist: — "The Colonel thoughtfully sent up a feed for the men who were to go over the top — tinned tongue, cakes, etc. They fed at 10.00 p.m. Officers supervising dealing out of bombs and wire cutters, and at 11.45 p.m. all go over the parapet from a bay in W. Company's line.

"At 11.50 to the tick, the lid of hell was suddenly lifted, and Old Nick seemed to vomit an inferno of fire and noise. As I stood on the fire step I felt the whole breastwork heave. Trench mortars were all around and the air was full of shells — spurts of flame seemed to come from between my legs, from each side and behind me — 18-pounders screeched overhead. Machine guns and rifles cracked out, but seemed very insignificant. Heavy rods from our T.M. bombs whizzed back over our heads. Time passed very slowly. The little drain pipes from which T.M. bombs are fired seemed like pipes from the nether regions spitting fire. At last the artillery lifted and the T.M.'s stopped.

"A strong impulse seized me to go out to those lads — but I had to stop behind. I felt a worthless thing, but we can't all go, can we? I knew our lads were advancing then and I prayed for them as I stared out into "No Man's Land." Time never passed so slowly, minutes seemed like hours, straining my eyes to see what was going on, but nothing to be seen. Our shells passed in one hissing procession over our heads.

"Then Schofield's voice, "Is that Capt. Johnston? Can you see anything?" Next, Barnett with a message from the C.O. that I must immediately send a runner to him at W. Company's H.Q. directly I saw the O.K. flashes from Partington — which would mean that the raiding party had passed through the covering party on their way back.

"Time dragged on. Artillery stopped firing. My brain was busy with names of men I must take out with my search party. I gave an order for stretcher-bearers to be brought up to the bay in readiness without taking my eyes from the front. A flash from the darkness — only a Hun rifle, then another — a few dull explosions — one's lips formed the word bombs — a few rifle shots — a few flare lights but nothing more.

"It was just after one o'clock.

"More rifles crackled out from the Hun parapet — a few more dull explosions somewhere out there among the wheat and long grass. Companies on right and left are giving covering fire. W. Company's rapid fire is good.

"No sight of a flashlight. The rain pours down and the smoke hangs about everywhere. Barnett's voice asks if I'm keeping a sharp lookout for the signal. I say "Yes" — I must be civil. The boy doesn't understand that my lads are out there. Suddenly a scuffle at the end of the bay and a voice "Tell Capt. Johnston they're coming in."

"I sprang over two men, who were crouching down on the duckboards, and with a loud "Make way!" hurried to the end of the next bay. Here I found congestion, largely men who had pals out, and a few curious sentries from the next bay. They melted at my first remark. The two parties came over the top as a drill movement, in their sections, just in the order in which they had left, except that all the officers came last. I checked the party and bustled them back to our lines as fast as I could, after sending word to the C.O.

"Taking advantage of the dark, wet night, old man Boche had a big working party out, with a strong covering party in front of it. Our barrage on his parapet prevented their return. They had taken shelter in deep ditches. The first our chaps knew of this was a rustle in a ditch and the explosion of four bombs right in the middle of the party.

"The chaps scattered but were reorganized at once by the officers, who led them to the ditch. Willie threw the first bomb and the Huns retired as the others pasted the ditch, which runs diagonally into another big one near the German wire.

"As our party reached the second ditch, they again met opposition and had to bomb the blighters out of that as well. One Hun fell in the ditch and was seen by several of our men. There seems no doubt that others were also scuppered, but as our artillery had "ceased fire" altogether, and the Germans were lining their parapet and firing rifles, the party returned.

"Whilst the strafe was on I distinctly heard the horn (for stretcher-bearers) blown several times in the German trenches, and I have no doubt that we accounted for a few. We were very lucky and the few wounds were trivial."

The brunt of this German attack fell further along the line where the 18th Lancashire Fusiliers had found themselves crouching in their trenches under heavy bombardment at the very hour they were expecting to be relieved by the 17th Battalion.

Telephone lines were cut and there was no means of knowing what was happening on each side of their position or if this was part of a major attack. Corporal H. Bloor and Private Dunn set out through the shellfire to learn the true situation on the left of the Lancashires. Though Bloor was wounded, the pair managed to return with information that the neighbouring 15/Sherwood Foresters had been forced to vacate about 200 yards of front line. A Lewis gun section of the 17th Battalion already in the line under command of 2nd Lt. R. J. Tyhurst had moved to cover the gap.

The Lewis gunners received support from a company commanded by Lieutenant J. W. Strong, who organized the defences there just in time to repel a storming-party sent across by the viligant Germans. A bomb fight ensued, followed by hand-to-hand combat in the trenches before the enemy was repulsed.

The struggle for the thinly-held trench gap went on until 4.00 a.m. next morning, when reinforcements arrived from the 14th Gloucester Regiment. Congratulations and thanks for holding the line arrived from Lieut. General L. E. Kiggel, Chief of General Staff, along with awards of the Military Cross to Lieutenants Gardiner and Tyhurst and a Distinguished Conduct Medal to Corporal Bloor.

Next day, word spread through the Division that it had been a near thing. The Germans had intended this major raid as a counter-offensive to delay British preparations being made for the Somme Offensive. They took back with them one officer and thirty-seven men of the Sherwoods, many of whom were already dead, wounded, or shell-shocked from the massive bombardment which obliterated their trenches. Some idea of German intentions was gained from the large stocks of abandoned picks, shovels, and bags of hand-grenades. One other interesting find was also described — "When the Hun got into our trenches the other night, he left behind many things, including a cat-o-nine-tails. This showed signs of much use. It is evidently a form of encouragement used upon infantry who are not over-anxious to get upon our bayonets."

Night after night, the Bantams continued to harass the enemy; raiding across the festering real-estate, to kill Germans and to die themselves on the wire or in the inevitable counter-bombardments they provoked. One raid in particular, on June 8th, 1916, was to enter the folklore of the Division and provide colourful material for the busy war-boosters in Britain.

The 14th Gloucesters sent a 60-man raiding party against the trenches south-west of Les Brulots. A box-barrage isolated their target at 9.00 p.m., and they set out a few steps ahead of the German artillery counter-fire. The raiders split into three groups and advanced despite machine gun fire. They blasted their way into the trenches where the courageous Germans still held on after enduring the softening-up from artillery. The fight became a hand-to-hand brawl with every man for himself — a confusion of bursting grenades, shooting, stabbing, and clubbing, while men screamed the vile murderous voices of close combat. At the end of it, thirty Germans and eight Bantams lay dead, and the enemy fled into the box-barrage where many more were killed. The raiders scampered back to their own side, dragging a heavy Maxim machine-gun with them.

Lt. Meldrum later told the story of the capture in his own words: "We halted halfway until the barrage was lifted from the front line up to the support trenches, then the raiding party went into the enemy trenches. When I got in, I made my way along with my party to the right, bombing dug-outs as I passed them, and found the gun between an open emplacement on the parapet."

. "The crew of six were round trying to fire, but it had evidently jammed. My first bayonet man charged the crew and accounted for two and my bomber accounted for the rest with four or five grenades. One man who was scrambling over the parados, I shot in the back. I then tried to dismount the gun, so as to carry it back more easily, but could not, so with the help of two men, I lifted the whole thing and rolled it over the parapet.. After doing some more damage, I and my party made our way back to our trenches.

"Captain Butt, who was in charge of the raiding party, was wounded in the enemy trenches. While making his way back to our lines, he was unfortunately killed by a shell. Lt. Brown, who also led a party over, was unfortunately wounded just as he reached the enemy trenches, but before he went back he emptied his revolver into a crowd of Germans and also threw all his bombs. As I learned afterwards, Col. Roberts was hit by almost the first shell when the enemy retaliated, and died almost instantly."

For personal reasons, Major-General Pinney decided to present the gun to the city of Bristol, as he was a grandson of the Mr. Pinney who was Mayor there in 1831. As the battalion had been raised in Bristol, it was felt that the trophy was a useful method of publicizing the unit's adventures, and might help to stimulate more recruiting in the area. Ten days after the raid, crowds of Bristol people turned out to see the Maxim on display at the City Art Gallery in Queens Road, which justified the effort made to gain a propaganda coup with local flavour.

As part of the ceremonials, Lt. Meldrum was introduced to the Bristol City Council by the Lord Mayor. The dignitaries were surprised when they entered the council chambers to see the Maxim gun on a table in front of the mayoral chair. Mayor Baron read aloud a personal letter from Major-General Pinney: "To the Lord Mayor of Bristol, June 19th, 1916. The 14th Battalion Gloucestershire Regiment wish to present a German machine gun recently captured by them to their raisers, the Mayor and Corporation of Bristol. Lt. Meldrum who led the party is bringing you the gun. May I be allowed to express my personal thanks to your Lordship and Corporation for the good battalion you have given my division."

After reading aloud General Pinney's letter, the Lord Mayor asked the sword-bearer to bring Lt. Meldrum into the chamber, where he saluted the Council and took a vacant aldermanic seat. The doubtless embarrassed young officer sat through a good deal of the fulsome praise, though he probably thought that a small price to pay for a few days of blessed leave from the trenches.

After what must have seemed like an endless spate of oratory, his Lordship said that he thought the Council would desire that they all should send back their lively sense of gratitude to the men for the magnificent heroism they had displayed. He asked Lt. Meldrum — who was leaving for the trenches again in a couple of days — to take with him the city's sense of gratitude and every good wish for the battalion and that they would surely keep up the reputation of the old city.

"Some day," said the Mayor, "we will have the pleasure and honour of receiving these men back in our midst. In the meantime, the gun will be a cherished possession of the Corporation."

When Meldrum returned from his brief well-earned home leave, he found the Division humming with rumours of a Big Push being prepared, and read the personal letters posted on all notice boards conveying the congratulations of Army commanders for the successful repulse in early June:

"Corps Routine Orders by Lieut. General Sir R.C.B. Haking, K.C.B., Headquarters, 9/6/16. 360. The Corps Commander has much pleasure in publishing the following letter received this morning by First Army: 'The Commander-in-Chief is of the opinion that the behaviour of the troops of the 35th Division was most creditable. Signed, L. E. Kiggell, Lieut. General, Chief of General Staff.

To 11th Corps. The G.O.C. First Army has great pleasure in forwarding the above letter for your information, and in adding compliments for the gallant manner in which troops of the 104th and 105th Infantry Brigades withstood intense bombardment and delivered an immediate counterstroke to drive the enemy back. Signed, S. H. Wilson, Lieut. Col. G. S., First Army."

Evidently this valiant behaviour of the Bantam Division had done much to enhance their reputation and to silence their few remaining critics. All through their first five months of active service, they had staunchly done as well as other troops in routine front-line duties. Now that they had beaten off a major strategic attack, they were conclusively proven to be reliable fighting material, so long as their sturdy quality could be maintained by reinforcements.

Steadily, the 35th was being drained of its original Bantams by death, wounds, and illness, and already grave concern was being expressed by Divisional medical officers at the declining physical standards of new men coming out from Britain. These worrying comments were voiced just as the 35th Division received orders to move to a new front — the Somme.

Chapter Seven

The Gamecocks

When the 40th (Bantam) Division was first constituted in September, 1915, it was feared that most of the suitable human material had already been siphoned into the 35th Division. Recruiting for the latter had just received a boost when the National Registration Act was passed in July; then it became evident that their battalions were already filled and could take no more applicants until combat thinned their ranks. The proponents of the 40th Division went ahead with renewed confidence, which further increased with news of the Derby Scheme.

Under this system introduced by Lord Derby — "The King of Lancashire," newly appointed Director-General of Recruiting — all men of military age were enlisted for one day then immediately passed into the reserve with liability to be called up when required. Half of these 2,000,000 Derby registrants were married men, and the hint was clear that compulsory service was in the offing.

Conscription eventually did receive Royal Assent in January, 1916, but in the meantime there was definite social pressure on men to volunteer before being forced to go.

Helpful as this climate was for recruitment of new formations, the particular physical requirements of the 40th Division still presented problems. The authorities had learned from the experience of the 35th, and were leery of opening the doors to substandard men not up to the sturdy levels of the original Bantams. Medical boards were strictly warned against this when a number of British army regiments were given their guidelines for Bantam battalions.

The 40th Division was headquartered at Aldershot, with the administrative arrangements set up in a more orderly way than the ad-hoc origins of earlier units. It was placed under the command of Major-General H. G. Ruggles-Brise and planned to be a deliberate blend of English, Welsh, and Scottish troops. The new 119th Brigade under Brigadier C. Cuncliffe Owen would consist entirely of Welsh battalions — 19th Royal Welch Fusiliers, 12th South Wales Borderers, and the 17/18th Welch Regiment. The Anglo-Scots 120th Brigade under the formidably-named Brigadier-General Hon. C. S. Heathcote-Drummond-Willoughby was intended to receive the 11th King's Own, 13th Btn. The Cameronians, and the 14th Highland Light Infantry. Originally, the all-British 121st Brigade led by Brigadier J. Campbell was to get the 12th Suffolks, 13th Yorkshires, 12th South Lancashire Regiment, 18th Sherwood Foresters and the 22nd Middlesex Regiment.

The Welsh units of the 119th Brigade were expected to provide the most promising quality of bantam recruits, because of the very large proportion of hardy miners available and the local capability for enlistment. The bureaucratic machinery had been in place there for some time, so that the formation of Bantam units in the Principality was a swift and smooth operation. A meeting of the Welsh National Executive Committee in September, 1914, had set itself the task of raising a Welsh Army Corps, and had reached that goal within a few months. Ever since their ancestors stopped the Romans cold, and later used their longbows to win Crecy and Agincourt for England, Welshmen had been renowned as soldiers. They were keen to get into this latest war — which promised to be a good one, look-you — and filled every new battalion in days.

By origin and employment, the average Welshman was then inclined to be slightly shorter than a Scot or Englishman, and the coalmines of the Rhondda Valley and other colliery regions bred hardy men who were born to strenuous activity. Elsewhere in Wales, from the sheep farms of the mountains to the crowded homes of Cardiff and Newport, and among the coalpits and ironworks of Monmouthshire and Gwent, men stepped forward by the thousand.

The South Wales Borderers had a fighting record which went back to the 17th Century. After service in many campaigns, the Borderers acquitted themselves so well against Napoleon that they were awarded a Sphinx badge and the word "Egypt" in their cap-badge. They are probably best known for their tragic stand at Isandhlwana in 1879 when the 1st Battalion was annihilated, and the immortal defence of Rorke's Drift a few day's later. In that fight, one company of South Wales Borderers held out against thirty times their number of Zulu warriors and were awarded eight Victoria Crosses. It was a regiment which expected nothing but the best of its recruits and at first faced the prospect of "bloody dwarfs" with something less than enthusiam.

The Borderers braced themselves at Newport Depot when news arrived that they were to expect drafts for the 12th Battalion, (3rd Gwent). "I'll have no Tom-tiddlers in my regiment!" roared one giant Company Sergeant Major, and even refused to retract his remark after catching the eye of a somewhat diminutive Captain who was also the unit Medical Officer.

On parade that day in May, 1915, was Albert Lewis, the miner who had given up the chance to be a well-paid Tunneller by joining the Birkenhead Bantams instead. He and a company of his fellow Welshmen were transferred to the 12th S.W.B. to infuse a group of trained soldiers into the unit's recruit instructional programme. "They promised us we'd all be sergeant-instructors by month's end," said Lewis

"Fat bloody chance, boy! Every one of us left alive was still a shilling-a-day private at war's end."

Though the nucleus of ex-Cheshires was available, the battalion temporarily borrowed a number of drill-instructors from the local police to provide some modicum of barrack-square knowledge. Military training was slow until July, when veteran officers and N.C.O.'s were transferred to the 12th and the unit was moved to Prees Heath Camp in Shropshire.

It was here that the fiery Jack Enrique Jones arrived for training, a Welsh soldier at last. "I don't know how many regiments had turned me down before I got into the Borderers," Jones said, adding as disgusted evidence of his desperation, "I even tried to join some bloody English regiments, but they wouldn't have me either!

"There was a bit of let-down at the recruiting office though. The officer looked at the form I'd filled in and gave a sneer. 'What sort of dago are you? This isn't the flamin' Foreign Legion, you know!' I told him I was as Welsh as he was and I'd come all that way to fight and I'd just as soon start with him. He quietened down a bit at that and signed me up without any more of his lip. But from then on I kept quiet about Argentina, and dropped the Enrique part altogether after being called 'dago' a few more times.

"I'd just got a steady job in Cardiff when I found I could get into the Borderers, so I drew my week's pay and blew it all on beer. I wasn't a drinking man then, so I felt pretty bad the morning after when I arrived at Prees Heath."

Jones' bleary eyes saw entire trainloads of Welshmen arriving with uniformed companies from Newport and drafts of civilians from Ebbw Vale, Pontnewydd, and Tredegar. As well, there was a train filled with Welshmen recruited overnight in London and with a batch of twenty caught on the rebound after being turned down by the Royal Navy at Chatham. These men from different backgrounds were united by their Welsh origins and proved to be readily trained into a smartly disciplined unit with high morale.

Their pride was further heightened when orders were posted later in July by Lt. Col. E. A. Pope, their new C.O. He announced that the battalion was struck off the rolls of its original 115th Brigade and was now officially part of the 119th Welsh Bantam Brigade.

The second regiment to raise Bantams for the 119th Brigade was The Royal Welch Fusiliers, which carried one of the army's best-known dress distinctions. This is a fold of black ribbons on the back of the coat collar, a hold-over from the days when soldiers' hair was tied in a queue. So traditional a regiment selected St. David's Day, March 1st, 1915, as the appropriate date for announcement of formation of their 19th (Service) Battalion.

The centuries-old Royal Welch Fusiliers observes a number of colourful ceremonies on that day of their national saint, including "Eating the Leek." This ritual has the commanding officer visit the enlisted men's dining hall, accompanied by a drummer, the Goat Major, and the regimental mascot, a white goat. The animal is traditionally supplied to the regiment from the Royal herd, and is prominent at all ceremonies of the unit. On this particular day, the mascot is dressed in his splendidly decorated apron and has his horns painted gold for his duty of supervising the youngest officer who must stand on a chair and consume the Welsh national vegetable non-stop before the drum stops rolling.

According to David Jenkins, this was the spectacle which the first 19th Battalion recruits saw when they arrived at the barracks near Deganwy. All the uniformed troops wore green leeks in their caps and paraded around behind the pampered goat, which doubtless eyed the newcomers with contempt. Ceremonies ended with the civilians awkwardly clumped along the edge of the barracks square to witness the garrison lustily singing, with leek-laden aspirates, the stirring "Men of Harlech."

As the last pungent chorus died away, a drill-instructor

turned to the wide-eyed recruits and bellowed, " 'Ow am I ever goin' to make real soldiers like them out of 'orrible little men like you?" An ex-miner called back, "Easy, Corporal. Start feedin' us all on onions like that bloody goat, an' we'll be able to *gas* the Jerries to death!"

Though this irreverent newcomer spent his first night in the army at cleaning latrines, he may have been gratified that his wisecrack was later often repeated by comrades to draw a laugh even under shellfire.

Their county of origin is recorded in the sub-titles of two Bantam battalions recruited for The Welch Regiment — 17th (1st Glamorgan) and 18th (2nd Glamorgan). They had been quickly raised in the Rhondda Valley in January, 1915, and sent respectively to Rhyl and Porthcawl, first attached to the 43rd Division. There the recruits were trained by old soldiers of the regiment brought back as instructors. Under such grizzled leaders, the Glamorgan men learned how to become adept at rifle-drill and the weapon's more important use on the firing range.

Like most Kitchener battalions in training, the Welch Bantams were issued with the old-fashioned Long Lee Enfield, Mark II, which weighed 9 lb. 4 oz. and was 49.5 inches long. As these rifles were not much shorter than the men themselves, they caused some difficulty in attempts to master arms-drill. When marching at slope-arms with 18-inch bayonets fixed, the exercise was downright dangerous for all but men in the first rank, and there were a number of nasty head wounds inflicted until troops learned how to hold the rifle at a rigid angle.

Firing the Long rifle was also difficult for any short-armed man, because of the butt length. The .303 Lee Enfield fired a 174-grain bullet with a muzzle velocity of 2,440 feet per second, with a proportionately vicious recoil. Even trained soldiers can experience a bruised shoulder after rapid fire with the "Lee En;" this punishment must have been much more severe for any Bantams who were unable to hold the butt properly, hard against the shoulder.

This was an important consideration at a time when the entire British Army training was based on fielding soldiers able to fire at least ten aimed rounds a minute. (Trained soldiers of the Regular Army could fire over 20 aimed rounds a minute. So devastating was rapid fire from the Lee Enfield that, during the retreat from Mons in 1914, the Germans believed it was machine-gun fire). This problem was recognized early and musketry training overcame it for Bantams through special instruction and practice.

When they embarked for France, their aged weapons were exchanged for the Short Magazine Lee Enfield, then the standard active service rifle. The S.M.L.E. was 5 inches shorter and more than a pound lighter, thus a more comfortable weapon for all troops, but particularly so for Bantams. The Royal Small Arms Factory, when told of this problem for smaller troops, introduced a rifle modification with a half-inch shorter butt. These were identified by the letter "S" stamped into the brass heel-plate. Further modification which reduced the butt by one inch, marked "B" for Bantam stock, was not officially introduced until September 1st, 1918, long after most Bantams were dead or gone.

In the summer of 1915, the 17/18 Welch Regiment arrived at Aldershot — each now also equipped with the obligatory Welsh mascot goat — and managed to cause a good deal of comment among the civilians of that Army-dominated town. The Welch settled down alongside their fellow-countrymen in the 119th and weighed up the other battalions in the 40th Division. "I don' know which is worse," Jack Jones announced, "both bunches of them talk sort of funny, look-you."

The units he maligned were English and Scots, who were having enough trouble without the prospect of fighting a three-way brawl every pay night. The 120th and 121st Brigades were undergoing a series of drastic weeding out of sub-standard men which was to continue until early 1916 and for a while threaten the existence of the whole division.

Not everyone found the Bantams to be an admirable body of men. One disappointed observer was the poet Isaac Rosenberg, himself a new recruit to the 12th Suffolk Battalion. Though not in the least warlike, Rosenberg had returned from South Africa to join the army, just as his writings were gaining him a small but growing reputation. Originally turned down by the Royal Army Medical Corps, he commented in a letter, "I could not get the work I might, so I have joined this Bantam Battalion (as I was too short for any other), which seems to be the most rascally affair in the world."

He scathingly referred to his fellow volunteers, mostly Cockneys from London, as "A horrible rabble. Falstaff's scarecrows were nothing on these. Three out of four have been scavengers; the fourth is a ticket-of-leave." The sense of fellowship seems to have caught him later however, when he wrote that joke that "The King inspected us Thursday. He must have waited for us to stand up a good while. At a distance we look like soldiers sitting down, you know, legs so short."

Rosenberg left Bury St. Edmunds with a draft of Suffolks which went to help make up yet another Bantam unit being formed in Lancashire.

There had been a large number of under-sized volunteers still on the rolls of the Warrington recruiting committee in September, 1915. Lacking only a battalion able to accept them, the authorities created the 12th (Service) Battalion, South Lancashire Regiment. Lt. Col. W. B. Ritchie, DSO, was appointed as commanding officer, and he initiated a vigorous training programme when the battalion went to Blackdown Camp, Aldershot. It formed part of the 120th Brigade, 40th Division, and "showed fine spirit in the traditions of the South Lancs."

However, the new battalion was no sooner trained than it was disbanded in April, 1916. Most of its fit officers and men were transferred to the 11th Battalion, King's Own Royal Lancaster Regiment, and Lt. Col. Ritchie was given the command.

So it was that cadres of Londoners, East Anglians and Lancashire miners found themselves melded into a regiment mainly formed of tough moorland men. When The King's Own Royal Lancaster Regiment announced the "urgent formation" of the 11th Battalion, it made no mention of the word Bantam. The height standards were given as between 5 ft. and 5 ft. 2 ins., chest expansion 33 ins., and age between nineteen to forty. The posters did promise that "You and your friends will be kept together and trained at Lancaster as far as is possible."

The recruiting base for this new battalion was the same as for the previous units raised by the King's Own, a semi-circle of towns from the Lancashire coastal resorts of Blackpool and Morecambe to Barrow, Ulverston, and Garstang, and the mountain villages of Cumbria. It was evidently a region which had not been previously combed for bantam-sized men, for the response was overwhelming in numbers, considering that by then the first flush of enthusiasm for war had ebbed across Britain.

The regiment made an extra aggressive drive to fill the unit by touring the countryside in motor coaches. The missionary party consisted of a brass band, an adjutant, quartermaster, medical officers, recruiting sergeants, and parliamentary speech-makers.

The resulting flock of recruits were looked after by a local retired officer, Major F. V. Churchill until the arrival of a permanent C.O., Lt. Colonel G. W. Priestley. Together they did their best to make the men as comfortable as possible in a collection of tents and hutments in Coulston Road field behind the Depot.

One of the first to walk between the granite pillars of Bowerham Barracks, past the regimental dogs' burial plot, and into the arrivals office, was the late Harry Stansfield.

"The place was bedlam," he recalled. * "Groups of soldiers and civilians mixed together were being drilled on every patch of open space inside and out. They were so mixed up, I was given two medicals and two sets of uniforms. Strangely enough, they both fitted me well, so I guess the army had the Bantams' clothing problem licked by then.

"We were well received by the regulars at the depot who worked hard enough on our training that we won the regimental prize cup for general smartness at our passing-out parade eight weeks later. Our drill sergeant was a Liverpool Irishman, an amusing character who said we would never be sent abroad as we wouldn't be able to see over the parapet. How wrong he was."

The Highland Light Infantry had by now recruited a second Bantam unit, the 14th Battalion, but was also experiencing difficulty in maintaining physical standards. "We had a lot of wee lads who never should have been accepted," says George Cunningham. "Short and wide was the style we needed, and here were boys and old men. I was fair disgusted at the medics for taking them in at all. We youngsters with a bit more heft to us could see there wasn't much chance for a fighting battalion until they got rid of the runts."

The same concern was expressed for the 12th Battalion, Royal Suffolk Regiment, whose officers now regretted passing along fit men to the King's Own. Among them had been "well-knit men from Suffolk, Cambridgeshire, The Isle of Ely, and Essex." The promising start of the 12th Battalion was set back not only by the drafting away of some fit men, and medical discharges but by the further loss of one hundred and thirty three "men" who were sent home after a careful check proved they were well under minimum age.

The Suffolk Regiment** was founded in 1685, and always took pride in retaining its regional character as much as possible. However, when faced with the need of additional

---

* Gallantly recounted during his terminal weeks in Ottawa's Tri-Services Hospital, in late 1978.
** Amalgamated in 1959 with the Royal Norfolk Regiment as the 1st East Anglian Regiment.

small men, the regimental depot at Bury St. Edmunds had to tackle their recruiting drive with more widespread efforts, directed by Major A. James. Deputations were sent into Yorkshire and Rutland in search of suitable applicants, and a draft of two hundred Bantams was gratefully received from the Middlesex Regiment. Elsewhere, other regiments were suffering similar problems.

Twenty-three Gaelic speaking fishermen sailed from the Outer Hebrides to the mainland when word reached them that The Camerionians (Scottish Rifles) was forming the 13th Battalion. They arrived at Hamilton Depot in mid-July and were signed up in turn after brief interviews conducted via their one English-speaking member. He was made a Lance-Corporal on the spot, with the sole job of herding his fellow-islanders through their training.

Other bantam recruits included schoolboys and black-smiths, sailors and clerks. The largest occupational group was again composed of miners, who walked in from all over Lancashire to join the new battalion of this historic regiment.

Originally named after the Presbyterian followers of Robert Cameron, The Cameronians was raised in 1698, and for many years afterward each man in the regiment was required to carry a Bible in his haversack. Such religious fervour was coupled with a redoubtable military skill which in modern times is reflected in their custom of carrying rifles during church parades. One of the appreciative recruits was James Robertson, the coal-heaver who had been re-jected by the London Scottish on the first day of the war. Though Cockney-born, Robertson was determined to serve only in a Scots regiment — following the same strong Celtic homing-instinct as had lured Jack Enrique Jones.

The day after he drew his railway warrant and issue bag of cheese sandwiches for the journey from London, he was in Hamilton Depot being happily fitted with Cameron plaid trews. Wisely perhaps, the authorities had decided that kilts somehow just didn't look right on Bantams.

The 13th Battalion was formed in two months, and moved down to Aldershot in September. It was there steadily reduced in numbers by frequent weeding-out inspections. By February, 1916, only Robertson and 200-odd survivors remained, so they were absorbed into the 14th H.L.I., and The Cameronians' Bantams ceased to exist.

The Middlesex Regiment — nicknamed "The Diehards" — was mainly composed of Londoners, and decided to tap some of the large number of undersized Cockneys who were enlisting in various other regiments. Accordingly, the 22nd (Bantam) Battalion was formed at Mill Hill in June, 1915, "There never was a battalion more buggered about than we was," said Tommy Dickson. "The poor old 22nd had no sooner been trained to a "T", when it was disbanded and off we went to the Suffolks. Then back we all came to the Middlesex again, this time in the 21st Battalion."

Several hundred London Bantams thus found themselves in their city regiment after all, members of an unofficially Bantam battalion. Marching in the 21st Battalion was a 34-year-old New Yorker who claimed to be the shortest corporal in the British Army. Four foot, nine inches high, Henry Thridgould had paid his own way across the Atlantic and been accepted within days of his arrival in London. Possessed of a powerful voice and with a demanding grasp of parade-ground drill, Thridgould was a popular figure at regimental ceremonials until he went to France.

In the spring of 1916, Major General Ruggles-Brise faced the reality that his division was unfit to go overseas in its present state. Lacking the uniform hardiness of the Welsh miners, the Anglo-Scots brigades had lost the struggle to obtain enough fit men from the material sent by their parent regiments. In the 120th Brigade, The King's Own and the H.L.I. had rejected over 1,400 men and could muster only one reliable battalion each, while the 121st brigade had disbanded the Sherwoods and Middlesex and managed to form good battalions for the 12th Suffolks and 13th

Green Howards.

The Divisional Commander insisted that he needed at least four additional battalions of fit men before the 40th could go on active service. The War Office agreed to send him the 13th East Surrey, 14th Argyle & Sutherland Highlanders, and the 20/21st Middlesex Regiment. With the exception of part of the 21st Middlesex, these reinforements were regular-sized men, and it was suggested that the fighting-cock divisional sign be discarded. Though retaining its title of 40th (Bantam) Division, the unit sign would now be a non-committal white diamond.

For the remaining Bantams, survivors of repeated medical examinations which were curiously more exacting than those given to men of normal stature, the prospect of active service was suddenly near. Morale soared when orders were given in early June for the division to move towards Southampton for embarkation to Le Havre. The 11th King's Own were heard to march aboard the SS *'City of Benares,'* singing to the tune of 'The Church's One Foundation' with confident self-mockery,

"We are the Bantam sodgers,
The short-arse companee.
We have no height, we cannot fight.
What bloody good are we?
And when we get to Berlin, the Kaiser he will say
Hoch, Hoch, mein Gott, what a bloody fine lot
is the Bantam companee!"

The last units of the 40th Division sailed across the Channel on the evening of June 5th, 1916. That same night, far to the north, HMS *'Hampshire'* hit a mine off Scapa Flow, sinking into the black waters with all hands. Among them was Field Marshal Lord Kitchener, the nation's top military leader and the Bantam's most powerful champion.

The 40th Division was placed in the First Army Corps,

commanded by General Monro, who inspected the 121st Brigade on June 12th. One of his staff aides loudly chortled to a group of Green Howards officers, "I suppose the little chaps will do alright once they manage to get over the parapet." An apple-cheeked captain loyally riposted, "Perhaps you'd like to come along yourself on our first show, sir, and give them a leg up!"

From his youth, rank, and outspokenness, one gathers this officer was back for his second tour of duty in the trenches.

The division had arrived in some of the most pleasant weather seen in northern France in almost a year. The eternal leaden skies had cleared and brilliant sunshine tried to give even the Western Front a more cheerful appearance. "Larks and other songbirds were everywhere," says David Jenkins. "Singing away with no fear of the guns, a beautiful sound they made. Shelling died down for a few days, as if the gunners didn't want to shatter the peaceful sounds. When an officer set off with a shotgun to hunt partridges in the wire, we all actually booed him."

The majority of officers were concerned with bloodsports on a larger scale, as they worked to organize the fresh division into fighting order. The three infantry brigades were marched into position in easy stages, drawing a somewhat more respectful response than their predecessors from civilians who now opined, "Comme ils sont solides."

Concentrated west of Bethune, with their headquarters at Bruay, they were joined by the non-bantam troops and equipment of their support brigades. Three field artillery brigades, the 181st, 185th, 188th, and the 178th howitzer brigade were under command of Brigadier H. L. Reed, who had won his V.C. during the Boer War. The Royal Engineers provided the 224th, 229th, and 231st field companies. There was a Signals Company, and the 135/6/7th Field Ambulance units.

Indications that General Haig's initial opinion that "The

machine gun is a greatly over-rated weapon" had finally been discounted lay in the 40th Division obtaining its own 244th M.G. Company. The 12th (Pioneer) Battalion, Green Howards, was attached for trench working and, unofficially, as a reserve of infantry troops.

While this organization went on, the familiar pattern of training and attachment for front line experience began. Brigades sent sections to Maisnil-les-Ruitz for training in bombing, wiring, sniping, and patrolling. Other groups marched to the Bois-du-Froissart for training in woodland fighting. Each battalion in turn sent cadres into the trenches alongside veteran units. Within three weeks of entering the war zone, the Bantams had sustained 250 casualties, 47 of them fatal.

Eighteen of the Division's first casualties were members of the 18th Welch undergoing trench instruction with the Munster Regiment near Maroc. One of them was Trevor Jones, who observed, "There was no mud to speak of when we first went into the line. The area quite reminded me of home, all slag-heaps and pitheads. I recall we were having a bit of a sing-song in the trench, when an Irish voice shouted, "Look out, toffee apples on the way!" I just had time to see a big round ball with a stick in it come twirling across the sky when there was one hell of a bang. I dug myself out and helped the others recover six dead men lying right beside me. They didn't look dead, really, and I expected them to start singing again the next minute."

Just as the Somme offensive started further south in early July, the 40th Division was given its own sector to hold at Loos.

When the battles first began in 1915 for possession of Loos, the objective had been to gain control of the coal workings there. Soon the area was devastated, the mineshafts blocked, the railways destroyed, and the miners had fled or lay dead under their ruined villages. Both armies then settled down to a mindless slugging match across the bulging salient in the Black Country between Lens and Hulloch, a futile killing ground.

Here the line ran through the dreary landscape called the *Gohelle*, a chalk plain dominated by Vimy Ridge to the west. In peacetime, a few woods and treelined roads had relieved the flat monotony. There had been many small villages, too; ugly *corons* of red-roofed miners' houses in linked rows. Towering around them were huge black piles of stone waste from the coal mines.

Now, only a few splintered tree stumps and piles of rubble marked the sites of human settlement, and the slagheaps took on a new importance. From their summits, even a hundred-foot elevation provided a commanding observation view of the surrounding *Gohelle*.

All these mounds were dominated by the Double Crassier, a mountainous slagheap through which ran the front line of both enemies. Because of their observation value, these mounds were constantly being fought over, men dying every day for temporary possession of a few piles of stones.

At night, fighting patrols circled the heaps at ground level, pausing to listen for the slither of stones above, which betrayed the slightest movement. Then bombs would fly, either the fat Mills grenade or the skimming oyster bomb and stick grenade of the Germans. Bayonet parties would scramble up to finish off survivors, the dead and victors often sliding down together in miniature avalanches.

The Double Crassier was where the first decoration was gained by a member of the 40th Division. Lance Corporal A. C. Handy of the 12th Suffolks received the award of the Military Medal for single-handedly attacking a German patrol.

This desolate environment of rubbled villages, mining equipment, and shale-tips generated its own savage style of roving warfare. The Bantams were sent out day and night on fighting patrols to meet Germans on similar missions. It became a meeting place for war-parties with no more strategic purpose than to inflict death on the enemy. "We didn't really think about the big aims of the war," said Morgan Davis. "All we knew was the job of killing Jerries and stopping them doing the same thing to us."

So many potential strong points to provide cover or observation gave these ruined features a spurious importance on staff commanders' maps, and resulted in the Division receiving a continual series of such fatuous orders as "A show of force must be made to retain control of Fosse 8 coal-works," and "You will send a strong patrol to penetrate beyond Hill 70."

Raiding was a constant activity along the sector as the Division probed through the heavy belts of German wire in search of prisoners or combat. The enemy learned how to turn this aggression to their advantage by strewing the area with booby-traps or simply lying in ambush for British raiding parties.

"We were out one cloudy night covering a raid, when everything went wrong," Jack Jones recalled. "I was waiting with my Lewis gun and two bombers for what seemed like hours. We'd just decided that our patrol had got lost or captured when the bright moon broke through clouds. Clear as day, I could see our officer and his party running forward all crouched over. I could also see three Jerries lying in a shell hole aiming a machine gun.

"I hadn't time to tell the bombers where to throw, so I just loosed off with the Lewis. I fired a short burst, then the Jerries opened up and hit some of our lads point-blank. I fired two drums at the machine gun crew and we sent a few bombs over too. Our officer was just seeing to our wounded when another bunch of Jerries arrived, firing as they came. Most of the raiding party went down in a few seconds.

"Luckily for me as it turned out, I could not fire until I reached the other pans of ammo. Before I had a chance to pull the trigger, there was a noise behind me and about ten more Jerries passed a few feet away. They could have got us for sure if I'd been firing then.

"The two large groups of enemy turned over our lads, looking for prisoners or identification. None of our wounded can have been able to walk, because the Jerries began to finish them off, one by one. Horrible it was; the sound of rifle butts and bayonets, and the odd crack of a pistol. We didn't want to commit suicide, so could do nothing to help. We didn't let them off Scot-free, though.

"When they moved away and were bunched up to pass through a gap in their wire, I fired three pans of .303 into them and the two other chaps emptied their rifles. After a long wait, we crawled over and found eight Welsh dead and some Jerries scattered here and there. We did not go to examine the enemy bodies near the wire, because there would be a Spandau trained on them for sure."

A second raid by the 12th South Wales Borderers had better luck and managed to enter the German lines. They ranged left and right of the entry point, bombing dug-outs as they went. The enemy fought back with grenades, one of which badly injured Captain Pritchard. While withdrawing, this officer spotted a Bavarian attempting to hide and leaped back down into the trench to take the Division's first prisoner.

Though weak from his wounds, Pritchard refused assistance and insisted on keeping charge of the captive. Soon afterwards, he was wounded again, and only then handed over the p.o.w. to Second Lieutenant Wood. The Captain made it back to his own lines, but died from his wounds.

Lt. Wood delivered the prisoner, who was found to carry useful documents, and returned to the German trenches. He saw to it that all the S.W.B. wounded had been evacuated and was the last man to come back. For his actions, he was awarded the Military Cross. Strangely, there is no record of any medal for the resolute Captain Pritchard.

About this time, the 18th Welch Regiment captured a

prisoner who arrived under bizzare circumstances. While retiring from a raid in which they blew up some mines, lost three men missing, and carried back their wounded, leader Lieutenant Salisbury, a German was seen scuttling along the rim of Double Crassier. He was expertly winged and brought back bleeding but alive.

Under interrogation, he proved to be co-operating in giving information about his unit, but vague about how he came to be wandering alone around the slagheap. From what he could recollect, it was deduced that he had been blown up by one of the mine explosions, hurtled across a fifty yard-wide belt of wire, and was dazedly roaming on the wrong side of the line when shot.

The many miners in the 40th Division found they had reached a sector ideal for their talents. The chalky ground was perfect for trench-making, but even more so for mining. Wherever such ground allowed, military tunnelling added another dimension along the Western Front, as miners sank tunnels to lay explosives under each other's lines. So prevalent was this warfare and so feared was its result that front line units detailed men to do nothing else but listen for sounds of mining below. Stethescopes and microphones were developed for this task but, for the most part, troops relied on their own hearing or on such crude devices as an empty petrol-can half-filled with water sunk into the trench floor.

At Loos, underground war was at times more destructive in its results than the bombardments. Time and again, whole sections of trench earth would erupt skyward with bits and pieces of human flesh, then fall back to bury men who had escaped the blast itself. The British Army employed special tunnelling companies to push mining saps forward and tamp ammonal in place for detonation before attacks. Too often, the resulting craters would only form new magnets of death as troops from both sides would rush forward to occupy them and fight duels around their muddy rims.

"We had three shafts going at once in our trench," smiled

Morgan Davies. "It had been a year or two since we'd used a pick and shovel underground, but if anything we worked harder than ever we did down the pit. Officers warned us to go a bit slower, as too much excavated chalk was a dead giveaway of what we were up to. We had to cart it away or dull it down with mud, or Jerry would give us some extra attention.

"Their lines were sometimes only three or four days digging-distance away. Things got tense near the end, as you never knew if Jerry was sinking a counter-mine. We would dig and lay explosives in a mad rush to beat him to it. The worst part was that we had to get permission to blow from the Senior Trenching Officer. If he delayed the okay too long, up we could go on top of a double load of T.N.T. That happened every few weeks."

One German miner worked so loudly underground that he became known as "Old Bill." So long as he clinked his tools, coughed and generally indicated his position, the British could trace progress of the enemy minework. Listeners became so fond of him that they would delay firing counter-mines until his distinctive clatter ended and he was well clear of the blast. Finally, this unseen chivalry had to end, when the opposing camouflets were so close that it was dangerous to delay, and Old Bill was regretfully blown sky-high by his Welsh opposite numbers.

Night raids and mining gave the infantry brigades some sense of being able to hit back at the enemy and helped alleviate the constant strain of artillery bombardment. Shell-fire was the ever present fear. Whether the projectiles came singly to shatter a quiet moment or in thousands during a major cannonade, men's flesh would cringe at each vicious explosion and sense a helpless vulnerability. A lone shell would crack a ranging air-burst, there would be a bowel-churning pause, then the sky would fill with screaming metal and plough earth, mud and humanity alike into a ghastly paste.

The troops devised their own half-comical names for the different types of missiles. There were "minney-werfers" that threw 150 lb. missiles, "screaming-meemies" that howled before they killed, and "daisy-cutters" that exploded in a thousand razor-sharp blades.

There was the slow rumble of "Big Fritz," a railway-gun twelve miles away, and one could follow the sixteen inch shell on its slow way to devastate a five hundred yard radius. Whiz-Bangs and Jack Johnsons were fast, flat-trajectory shells that arrived before you knew it, while fat Rum Jars and Oil Drums sailed over lazily, fuses fizzling to give the alert or the lucky time to run elsewhere.

At Maroc, sentries were permanently detailed to stand, well-hidden, on pit-heads to listen for the "chung" of a trench mortar. They would then blow a whistle and point to each bomb as it curved across the sky, so that its point of arrival could be anticipated well in advance. But no one could anticipate all the shells that hunted men hourly and tore their bodies.

The grim realities of being a medical orderly under shell-fire are recalled by Phillip Brereton Townsend, then a 17-year old private in the 135th Field Ambulance, R.A.M.C., attached to the 40th Division.* "Shortly after arriving in France, I was detailed to be on duty at a small advanced dressing station in the ruined village of Maroc, not far behind the front line in the Lens-Loos Salient. Together with another private, I was detailed to go to the mortuary which was in a partially demolished house. In a rear room on the ground floor, lay eight bodies, two of which had been recently recovered from No Man's Land.

"My comrade and I had been given a bodkin, string, and eight old army blankets. We were ordered not to inspect clothing or pockets but to place in the docket envelope the men's identity discs and then to sew up the body in the blanket, and sew the docket to the blanket.

"When we moved one body, which was green with age

---

* Townsend later flew as an aircrew officer in both World Wars.

after being in No Man's Land for a long period, onto the blanket, I fainted and my comrade had to bring me round before we could proceed on our task. This was my first job as a medical orderly in the theatre of war, and at my young age I could not quite cope. It took us nearly all afternoon and evening to complete the task, after which the bodies were ready to be loaded onto a mule-drawn ambulance for transit to a cemetery behind the lines.

"Later, when we were about to go back to the line, my section of the Field Ambulance was resting near the forward area. We were partaking of a stew concoction from our field kitchen just as a platoon of Gordon Highlanders came marching out of the line. Each man was lumbered with a load of equipment, all covered in mud, sadly in a filthy condition. Suddenly, we heard the whine of a heavy shell, and it exploded very near the platoon, detonating with terrific force.

"The result was that out of about two dozen men, seven were killed and eleven wounded. We rushed over to the casualties, giving instant succour. I with two comrades came on one soldier who's left leg had been shattered by a piece of jagged metal, and the leg was hanging by only an inch of flesh. We were unable to handle him as a stretcher case until I had cut through the inch of flesh with my jack-knife. After which, we were able to lift him onto the stretcher and into a motor ambulance. His kilt was roughly weighed later and we found it to be about fifty pounds including blood, flesh, mud, and water."*

Andrew Gilmour was a sixteen-year-old private in the 14th Argyle & Sutherland Highlanders who served in the 40th Division. "After having one spell in the line, we were detailed to go back to defend some four or five sectors — thinly occupied lines in extended salients like Hulluch and Loos, deadly legacies of the previous partial successes. With all too many casualties, we were still expected to keep up the impression that the trenches were fully manned, with all the usual activities of patrols and raids, trench extensions, repairs

---

* As Marshal Foch once observed, *"Le kilt est bon pour l'amour, mais pas pour la guerre"*.

and saps manned within forty yards of the German lines.

"During these months, I never heard it suggested that the Bantams were not every whit as good as ourselves (a normal height unit) or as any other division, though we in the Argyles did have one grouse. With an average difference in height of some eight inches, it was not unknown to find that the Bantams had pulled down the parapet and used it as a firestep.

"At a place near Loos known as *Fosse Calonne,* on a hot day in August, 1916, the Argyles were in support waiting to take over the front line from the King's Own. Word came down to us via the bombing platoon that a German raiding party had taken away as prisoners the King's Own section manning a sap close to the enemy lines. The sap had been re-occupied, but would the Argyle bombers please come and help take over as soon as possible?

"I happened to be the first to arrive ahead of three or four others who hurriedly made our way into the sap. I stole apprehensively towards the saphead, expecting to find a sentry with a periscope watching the German lines and someone there to give the usual information about bomb-stores and ammunition supplies. Instead, I found one solitary Bantam, half naked, his tunic, rifle and equipment strewn nearby, busily chasing lice along the seams of his shirt.

"He cocked a mischievous eye at me and remarked, 'Ey, Jock, 'ee wants fookin, doos t'Kaiser!'" With that, he grabbed his belongings and scampered away along the sap."

A strong bond of affection and mutual confidence was forged between this Scottish battalion and the little Lancastrians. In September, when the latter were taking over a trench from the 14/Argyle & Sutherland Highlanders they found posted up a piece of paper inscribed with an unsigned poem:

There's a regiment of Bantams, in a place I mustn't name.
Who, for cussedness and courage, stand alone,
You'd pass 'em by in Blighty with a look of mild surprise.

You'd calculate the column was awantin' p'r'aps in size,
By glory on the other side you'd hand 'em out the prize
                                        — King's Own.

With kits abunched around them, and a bushel load of
    bombs,
You'd barely find the owner on a phone,
With picks and packs and Lewis Guns, they get there
    every time,
A-walkin' on the parapet, to miss the ruddy slime,
The stiffer task afore 'em, the cheerier the climb.
                                        — King's Own.

When shells and other trifles scream their passage
    through the night,
And Very lights a-twinkle in our zone,
When snipers pick a penny from our pockets at their ease,
And enemy machine gunners are cuttin' life as cheese,
We ring up reinforcements, and we say to Bisset, "Please
                                        — King's Own.

And when the units muster in the Grand Review above,
When God to every Tommy lad is shown:
With picks and packs and Lewis Guns, you'll see 'em
    swinging by,
Just little men — not giants — but their chins are carried
    high,
And kindly He'll look down on 'em, and whisper
    "They are My

                                        — King's Own."

The weather began to badly deteriorate towards the end of
the 40th Division's stint in the line. Temperatures dropped to
freezing and cold rain turned the coaldust everywhere into a
black abrasive slime. When word arrived of their impending
relief, it was decided to step up aggressive activities to give

the enemy a last salute. Each battalion during its final four day rest in reserve was required to plan for raids during its last four days up the line. As each took its turn in the trenches it was with the knowledge that they had to go out looking for danger, as if the routine shelling was not hazardous enough itself.

Four raids went out on the night of October 8, two each by the 18/Green Howards and 20/Middlesex. The Yorkshires blew gaps in the enemy wire around Long Sap, and sent in two raiding parties led by 2nd Lieutenant L. A. Venables and A. W. Simpkin of "B" Company. The Germans had not been occupying the tunnel and rushed forward along the communications trench into a shower of hand-grenades. Two Germans were captured unharmed and the raiders would have them withdrawn content if more of the enemy had not arrived. A vicious hand-to-hand struggle began, with men leaning over comrades' shoulders to stab or shoot at the shadowy figures within the narrow trench walls. Five Germans were killed with no loss to the 13th Battalion and they returned with their prisoners.

The next night it was "C" Company's turn, under command of Second Lieutenants Hodgson and Perkins. They blew their way into the German trenches and held them for fifty-eight minutes. This time, no prisoners were captured, but twenty of the enemy were killed in a drawn-out fight which raged at each end of the occupied section of trench. Bantams stacked enemy dead at the traverse angles, firing across these human barricades. As intelligence material, they brought back identity discs, maps and unit shoulder straps taken from the slain. The raiding party carried away their seven wounded, one of whom later died. Though wounded himself, 2nd Lt. Hodgson continued in his duties and was the last man to leave the German line.

The raids brought congratulations for the battalion from the Corps, Division, and Brigade Commanders, along with exultation over "the marked increase of success on our side."

The Germans were not to be outdone, and proceeded to shell, gas, and raid the Yorkshire sector with increasing fury. Deaths and wounds increased among the Green Howards but they held their line until relieved. Another battalion was caught during the relief, when a mine was exploded under them, and the Germans temporarily gained possession of seventy yards of the Division's line. Pride was assuaged next morning when the enemy was ejected by the 17th Welch Regiment, though at the cost of losing Lieutenant Colonel Wilkie, who was killed.

On November 2nd, Divisional Order No. 28 detailed the relief of the 40th Division, and prescribed the route march south west towards their new host XV Corps, Fourth Army. The march was a miserable trek through blizzards, sleet-storms, and very heavy rain. Much resentment was caused when the troops were ordered to march at attention, as the easy leadership tightened once the men left the front.

James Pringle, 12/Suffolks, wrote his memories of their withdrawal. "Soon as we weren't fighting their war for them, senior officers started appearing and barking remarks about what slack soldiers we were. We were dog-tired, constipated, in rags and holey boots. We'd been shot, shelled, gassed, scared stiff, and worked like slaves, but now all they could call us was slackers.

"Our own officers and N.C.O.'s hadn't much choice but to crack down, too, and they went at us, shouting "Straighten up!" and "Left-Right-Left!" We had a bit of fun for a while; making sheep-noises, singing dirty songs, and deliberately staying out of step. We kept this up long enough to show we resented being bollocked about, then we settled down to marching as smart as could be.

"Soon, all you could hear was the tramp of boot-heels and the pouring rain. Already our cheerfulness on leaving the line had gone. I marched on, soaking wet, wondering what new hellhole the Gamecocks were being sent to."

Chapter Eight

One Green Howard's War

Before the First World War, the sparsely-settled North Riding of Yorkshire had always found enough men to enlist in the Alexandra, Princess of Wales' Own (Yorkshire) Regiment.

Strongly local in favour and with a valiant reputation, it had originally been known as Howard's Regiment, following the 18th Century practice of naming units after their colonels. However, when the 3rd Foot and 19th Foot Regiment each were led by colonels named Howard, the regiments became distinguished as "The Buff Howards" (later The Buffs) and "The Green Howards." So the Yorkshiremen became known, even after their more official designation to Princess Alexandra and the display of her Danish cross in their cap-badge.

The regiment fought in actions from the West Indies to the Crimea, and garrisoned Ceylon for half a century. It had always been able to keep its county character, until the demands of the Great War called for numbers of men far beyond that which the local population could supply. The regiment then began recruiting throughout Northern England and quickly made up its Kitchener battalions.

Among the rejected applicants had been sturdy little lead miners and coal miners. In early 1915, they and no less stalwart townsmen received a second chance to sign up when the call went out from the regimental depot at Richmond for men to join the 13th (Bantam) Service Battalion. One volunteer was a young solicitor's clerk by the name of Edgar Robinson. He later wrote a personal journal of his experiences which typify those of his battalion. The journal was not published, but quietly kept by Mr. Robinson as a private memoir: *A Teenager In The Great War*. He contacted this writer during research for material about the Bantams, and has generously allowed part of his story to be included here:

"Right up to Christmas 1914, long queues of men and boys waited daily to enlist, but afterwards things quietened down. I was impatient to get in and join my two brothers who had enlisted on the first day, but being under age, I had to think how I could do it. I realized it would be better to wait a few months until the recruiting office at Middlesbrough was left in sole charge of an old soldier sergeant, a type who lived for beer. The sergeant received one shilling (in those days equal to five pints of beer) for every recruit he swore in.

"One day during my luncheon hour, I decided it was time for me to try to enlist. Walking boldly into the recruiting office, I said to the Sergeant, "I've come to join up."

"He looked me up and down and said "How old are you, son?" "Sixteen" I replied. He just shook his head. Seeing the disappointed look on my face and probably thinking of the beer he was missing, he said, "Tell you what to do, son. Take a walk round the Town Hall, see if you have got any older, then come back in."

"I did just that.

"Walking into the office again I said. "I'm eighteen now, Sergeant." "Good" he replied. "I can swear you in now."

"Taking a Bible in my right hand, I repeated the Oath after him. Giving me the 'Kings Shilling' and taking one himself, he shook hands and we parted. Looking back, I saw he was locking the office door prior to going to the pub opposite.

"Next day, I joined The Green Howards at Richmond, Yorks. When I told my mother later, she said that though proud of me, she would try and stop me going. I replied that I would run away from home if she did. On leaving the firm of solicitors where I was employed, they presented me with a silver wrist watch with my name on the back. I carried this watch right through the War, and still have it.

"After a few days at Richmond, getting my uniform, etc., I was sent to Otley, where the 13th Yorks was being formed. I was 5 ft. 4 in. at the time, and was one of the first members of the battalion. We stayed there for about two months until the battalion was made up to strength and did our training in the extensive grounds of a mansion.

"Part of our training was route marching about ten miles or so. During one I shall never forget, I was marching alongside an old soldier who had served in India, where it was a habit to chew plug pipe tobacco. He was chewing away and spitting the juice out as usual. "Give me a chew," I said. "Righto," he said and handed me his plug of tobacco.

"I bit off a good size piece and started chewing. Just as I was about to spit it out, he slapped me on the back saying, "How are you doing?" I swallowed the whole lot and within seconds I felt proper poorly. I thought my tummy was on fire, and consequently had to fall out, as sick as a pup.

"Later on we proceeded to Skipton, 20 miles away over the Ilkley Moors, where we had another enjoyable two months with plenty of good food to build us up. Then on to Inkerman Barracks, Woking, where we finished our training before going to France.

"In those days, we were paid one shilling per day. If we made an allowance to our parents, we had sixpence a day stopped off; the Government gave another sixpence and our parents received seven shillings a week. We received three shillings and sixpence, less sixpence a week to pay for our washing. This left us with three shillings, out of which we had to buy our own blanco, shoe polish, shaving soap, razor blades, etc.

"After saving up, three of us would have a weekend in London on about ten shillings, from Saturday after dinner until 9 p.m. Sunday night. We walked all over London seeing the sights, and slept the night at the Y.M.C.A. paying fourpence for a bed. During the time we were there all we had to eat was sausage and mashed potato at a cheap cafe, on Saturday night, Sunday morning and teatime, filling with cold water. That was all we could afford and we were hungry growing lads.

"When at Woking, and after learning how to use our rifles properly, we had our firing course at the well known Bisley range nearby. I did very well at all ranges, especially the 1,000 yards, where I scored two bulls and three inners out of five shots. The total number of points I scored entitled me to be called a Marksman and to wear a crossed guns badge on my left tunic sleeve.

"Three weeks later, I passed as a signaller, entitling me to wear a crossed flags badge as well. I also passed as a Scout, which entitled me to wear a badge of an "S" inside laurel leaves. I thought this was enough, otherwise I would be walking one-sided!

"When training at Otley, at the beginning, our Company Officer picked me out as suitable to be a Lance Corporal. A Corporal had to bear the brunt of all the mistakes made by those above him and could not be friendly with those below him. He had more or less a miserable life on his own, and so I refused to become one. I wanted to stay with the lads, with whom I got on very well.

"When our training was finished at Woking, we were inspected by King George V on Salisbury Plain.* Men nearest to him said he was drunk. He appeared to me to be hanging round his horse's neck.

"Eventually, came news that we were off to France, causing great excitement. We received all our kit, tin hats, medical examination, the lot. Next morning, we were on the

---

* Laffan's Plain, May 25th, 1916.

move at 4 a.m. entraining for Southampton and thence by an old fashioned paddle steamer, *'The Daffodil,'* to Le Havre in France. We sailed after dark on account of the German submarines being busy in the Channel. The sea was very rough; we bounced all over and nearly everyone except me was seasick. Arriving next morning, we disembarked and marched through the town to the local station.

"Arriving at the station, we were put into dirty cattle wagons and proceeded slowly towards the Loos area of the Front. The train went so slowly that we used to get out and walk alongside to stretch our legs. It took twelve hours to do about thirty-five miles. After more training behind the lines we were ready for the Battle of the Somme. Being new troops, we were held in reserve to support the forward troops. What a din! Seven days and nights of non-stop bombardment of the German positions by our light and heavy artillery. We were billeted in broken-down villages near the Front. We could hardly sleep for the noise – the ground trembled, we got headaches, and could hardly hear ourselves speak. Came the 1st of July, the day to advance, tanks being used by us for the first time and really scaring the Germans. We followed up and occupied the ground our forward troops had gained. Very heavy casualties were suffered on both sides.

"After the battle died down and the thousands of German prisoners and the dead and wounded were removed, the troops dug and settled into trenches. We were moved to the south of Lens to occupy trenches there. Trenches which had previously been occupied by the French, who did not bother much about burying their dead and if they did, they only scooped soil over them, often leaving hands, feet and heads exposed. Those not so buried were left to rot into skeletons.

"The horrible sickly smell of rotting flesh I hope never to experience again. It is like nothing on earth. We all soon became very callous, even to placing army biscuits or a bunch of wild red poppies into a skeleton hand or a cigarette-end between the jaws. The millions of rats, some as big as cats, soon turned a dead man into a skeleton by eating the flesh. When they had nothing to eat, they often attacked us, and we in turn used to shoot, bayonet, and kill as many as we could.

"Entering the trenches for the first time, we were full of curiosity, while getting blown over and spattered with earth, stones, and shrapnel as German shells burst close by. Our Sergeant-Major led the way in and it was not long before we passed him, lying dead with his head blown off. It made us realize that War was not a game and we were rather shaken.

"Arriving at the stretch of trench we were to hold, we were assigned to our dug-outs. Dugouts were holes dug downwards into the sides of the trench nearest to the enemy. Steps went down about twenty feet deep and entered a corridor about thirty feet long, 8 feet wide and six feet high, with an entrance at both ends. They were pitch dark, except for a candle burning here and there, and these were blown out by the blast whenever a shell or bomb burst close by. They were very damp.

"The first night as soon as it got dark, we were formed into working parties, repairing trenches and barbed wire. Another lad and myself were taken over the top between the lines by the Sergeant. Stopping at a certain place he said, "I want a hole dug here," then he left us. In-between having a look round every time a Very rocket went up and with bullets whistling around us, we dug, and unearthed all sorts of things such as pieces of equipment, and tins of food.

"My shovel struck something which would not move, so I reached down in the dark to feel what is was, and what a shock I got. It was a cold clammy hand. I called my pal's attention to it, and we sat there very shaken until the Sergeant returned. We told him about the hand and asked him what we were digging for.

"He said, "Four men were buried alive there this morning when the trench was blown in and we want the bodies

TS - L

digging out again." We were glad when he sent two men to relieve us.

"At other times we used to help the Royal Engineers to dig 'saps' which were shaped like dug-outs and then levelled out forward, close towards the German lines as possible, filled with explosive and then blown up. When blown up, troops from both sides rushed across to see who could occupy the crater first.

"Our rota of duty in the trenches was four days in the front line, four days in the support lines about 200 yards from the front and then four days rest in a broken-down French village about a mile further back. There we got shower baths, a change of underclothes, better food and caught up with our sleep.

"When in support, we had to carry barbed wire and Bangalore torpedoes up to the front line. Bangalore torpedoes were like drain pipe tubing, eight feet long, and four inches in diameter, closed at both ends and filled with high explosive. They were used for blowing up the German barbed wire when going on the nightly raids. We disliked carrying them, because if they were hit by a bullet or got a hard knock they would explode, and the two men carrying one of them would go up with it.

"Our worst times in the front line were at 'stand to' at dawn and dusk when both sides threw everything they had at one another and when many a good pal 'went West.'

"Our food in the front line, cooked and brought from the rest area consisted of — Breakfast, a small piece of cold-fried bacon on a dog-like biscuit four inches square by three-quarters of an inch thick and one pint of lukewarm tea. Dinner, about a pint of cold greasy stew with the same biscuit. Tea, one pint of lukewarm tea, jam and the same biscuits. All liquids tasted of the chloride of lime which was put in the water to sterilise it.

"We got these meals within two hours of the time due, provided they were not blown up or upset on the way. We had similar meals in the support lines, but when out on rest the biscuits were replaced with bread, and the stew and tea were hot. In wet weather and winter months, a tot of rum was added to the morning tea.

"The trenches were from knee to thigh deep in liquid mud and water and, though we knew our legs were there, we could not feel them. We were supplied with whale oil to rub on but we often got 'trench feet,' for which medical treatment was given.

"In our spare time we used to 'chat up.' That meant taking off our shirts and killing, between our thumb nails, all the lice in the seams. The lice were up to an eighth of an inch long, grey and shaped like a crab, and boy! could they bite. I remember the first time I saw a chap 'chatting up' I thought, "the lousy beggar," and told him so. "I bet you have some," he replied.

"Slipping off to a quiet spot, I thought I would have a look and sure enough, I had. I could have cried when I saw them, hundreds of them complete with eggs, in the seams. They bit, sucked blood, and made one itch. To kill them, we squashed them and then ran a burning match or candle along the seams to get rid of the eggs.

"When I was first 'chatting up,' Lieutenant Simpkins came along, "What are you doing, Robinson?" I showed him and he was horrified, but shortly after, I saw him in a quiet corner 'chatting up' too.

"What we had to put up with! – fighting the Germans, mud and dirt all over us, very little and poor food, no sleep, no relief of bowels for four days, lousy with lice, cold, wet and miserable, loss of pals, digging and repairing trenches and being shot at. It was hard to know which was the worst to bear. It was hell.

"While we were in the trenches at Loos, a new replacement Officer came to our Battalion. It was Lt. Hodson, who lived next door to us at home. Before I had time to have a word with him, he was detailed for a night raid on the

German trenches. He was shot in the knee going over, carried on, brought two German prisoners back, was taken to Base Hospital, awarded the M.C. and was invalided out. It was his first time out of England. In, out, and back home with a medal all within two days! Lucky beggar. At this time I was an 'orderly runner,' that is, carrying messages.

"One night about midnight, I had to take a message to Brigade Headquarters about a mile away through communicating trenches. It was a showery night with the moon shining now and again. It was rumoured that German spies were about behind our lines, and that soldiers on their own after dark had been stabbed or strangled to death. On my return feeling somewhat nervous, rats scuttling in front and behind, duck boards clattering loudly when I stepped off them, I turned the corner of a trench just as the moon came out. There in front of me, placed on a board across the trench, was a grinning skull.

"I was scared to death, turned round and ran back so far, then climbed out of the trench. I went back over the top and risked being hit by stray bullets which were buzzing all over. Next day an order came out that we had to go about in twos.

"Daily rations used to come up to us after dark, in ration carts drawn by horses, and were left in sandbags in a shelter in Loos. Also left wrapped in sandbags in the shelter were men who had been killed that day, who were taken back by the ration carts for burial.

"One night my pal and I thinking the rations had come and feeling hungry, decided we would scrounge something to eat. Going into the pitch-dark shelter I felt around, and found a sandbag tied up just like the rations were. I put my hand in and pulled out what I thought was a piece of meat. My pal struck a match to see what I'd got. It was part of a human leg.

"It turned out to be the remains of a Lt. Lewis who had been carrying Mills bombs in his tunic pocket, and had been hit and blown to pieces. These were the pieces. My pal and I did not feel hungry any more.

"Altogether, Loos was a very unpleasant spot and we were glad when we moved down to the Somme. The German trenches were high above us on the shale tips, near Loos coal mine. They could see nearly every movement of ours during the day and were sniping at us all the time.

"In 1916, when we got settled down to the Battle of the Somme, I being a marksman, was put into the sniping section. That meant going out before dawn, in front of our trenches, finding a suitable ruined building or shell hole where one could see the German lines without being seen oneself. The first job was to smear dirt and mud over oneself to match the surroundings.

"I found a broken-down farmhouse, climbed into the false roof and got behind a broken-down wall, got everything ready and sat down to wait for daylight. Our rifles had telescopic sights. After about three hours wait, I spotted something moving, and looking through my telescopic sights, I saw two German Staff Officers followed by a German orderly. (Staff officers had a white band round their hats). They were walking up a road towards the German trenches, side by side, with the orderly close behind.

"I waited until they were about one thousand yards distance, set my sights, and let them have it. The first officer started falling, and quickly reloading, I shot the second officer and he fell. Reloading again, I aimed at the orderly, but did not fire, I thought "poor devil, he is just an ordinary chap, like me." When he saw the two officers fall, he turned and ran back "hell for leather." For nearly half an hour, I watched to see if the officers moved. They did not, and I presumed them dead.

"Then the German guns opened up on my position. Time for me to move, and I dashed from shell hole to shell hole back to our trenches, wishing that I had shot the orderly as well, and so stopped him from giving my position away.

"I reported it to our officer, he said, "Well done Robinson, well done. I wish I had been there to see it, then I could have recommended you for the D.C.M. (Distinguished Conduct Medal). However, I will see what I can do." He did his best but nothing came of it, only a mention in dispatches. Everything like that had to have a witness. But they all knew later that something important had happened because our position was heavily shelled by the Germans the rest of the day.

"When one of our lads was killed and others wounded, I was very upset about it, and felt like a murderer, killing them in cold blood. I thought 'had they seen and being shooting at me, and I had been shooting back, then that would have been fair.' I still feel upset when I think about it; was it worth it — having one pal killed and others wounded through my killing two German Staff Officers?

"I could not carry on sniping, and asked for and was transferred to the signal section. I am not proud at what I did. Even to this day, I tremble and am upset when I think about it, and this is the first time I have let it be known.

"Towards the end of 1916, when we were out for a fortnight's rest, I was summoned to see the Commanding Officer. "How old are you, Robinson?" he asked. "Nineteen, sir," I replied. "You're not, you know," he said. "I've just received a letter from the War Office to say you are under-age. While I admire your guts for coming out here, I'm afraid we have to send you back." He shook hands and wished me luck.

"On this particular day, I was feeling pretty low, as my best pal had been killed two days before and I had not got over it. I'm afraid that the news of being sent down the line cheered me up. I later found out that my mother, who was naturally very worried about me, had reported my correct age to the authorities.

"After saying goodbye to the lads, I was escorted by a Sergeant to Domart-en-Ponthieu, 20 miles back, where I joined about a hundred other under-age soldiers who had been found out. We were called the Young Soldiers Battalion, and were mainly used for junior officers to practice training methods before they went up to the trenches. Being here meant having clean underwear every week, and good riddance to the lice.

"The young officer in charge of the platoon started a competition, the prize being a wrist watch for the smartest soldier picked out on guard parade the most times in two months. I was picked out sixteen times, won the wrist watch, and was promoted to a waiter. The Officers' Mess was in a big French chateau, where I actually had a real bed instead of the ground I had slept on since going to France.

"We had quite a few Australian and New Zealand Officers attached to us and they decided to celebrate "Anzac Day," the landing at Gallipoli. They fixed on a seven course dinner and dance (men only) in a local hall. The head waiter ordered the special food, with fifty ducks, and saw to the preparation of the food. I was in charge of six waiters and had to see to the setting of three long tables and the bar for drinks.

"About a hundred officers arrived, and by ten o'clock everyone was drunk, including myself. The officers kept falling down and rolling about when dancing and goodness knows what the ten-piece band was playing. Thinking to sober things up a bit, the other waiters and I got soda siphons and started squirting the dancers. The next thing I knew was that the officer in charge had me by the scruff of the neck and I was chucked out. What happened after that I neither knew nor cared, I do know that the officers were a sorry sight next day.

"I was with the Young Soldiers Battalion for about five months before the day came when I became nineteen and would return to my unit. Saying goodbye to my pals, some of whom I later heard were killed soon after their return, I set off back to my unit, still on the Somme. It was good to get back to my old pals again but sad to see how many familiar faces were missing – wounded or dead. I soon settled down to the old routine of in and out of the trenches, with the discomforts and lice and the repeated cry of "roll on the end of the war."

"In the Summer of 1917, seeing how exhausted and fed up we were, "the powers-that-be" decided to give us a short rest and sent us haymaking within a mile of the trenches. There was plenty of grass and there were hundreds of army horses to feed. It made a pleasant change for us, though one not without its dangers.

"When forking over the hay we often disturbed live shells and Mills bombs that had been left around. One had only to catch the bomb release pin with the hay fork, pulling it out, and within ten seconds it exploded. It did not leave much time to throw oneself flat out of the way and several lads were wounded. From their observation balloons, the Germans could see us working and often shelled us out of the fields, and of course the haystacks we built were just right for him to get the range.

"One day, two spotter planes flew overhead, circling one another, one British and the other German; only about two hundred feet high; we could see the pilots' faces. They were shooting at one another with revolvers, all that observations planes had in those days. They both must have hit one another at the same time. The planes crashed together, broke up, and the pilots fell to the ground, no parachutes, of course.

"They fell in the field in which we were haymaking and we went across to them. They took some finding, because they had sunk three feet into the ground. The German was on his side and the Britisher was spreadeagled, both dead in graves of their own making. Aside from these excitements, haymaking was a welcome break, but after two weeks the rains came and we went back to the trenches.

"When I heard that after twenty months, I was to go on leave for fourteen days at home, I was overjoyed. After a medical exam, two other lads and myself walked three miles back to Headquarters. We had a shower bath, were deloused, and got fitted with a new set of clothes. It would not do for the civilians in England to see us in dirty, blood-spattered uniforms. We had another four miles to walk to the railhead where we got into cattle trucks for the all-night journey to Calais. Then by boat to Dover, train to London and home. England never looked so good to us, who thought we would never see it again.

"I thoroughly enjoyed every minute of my leave, fourteen days, less four days for travelling, although I shall never forget the first day at home, in January 1918. I arrived at home unexpectedly at 8 a.m. My mother was ill in bed with the 'Flu,' which was very bad at that time all over Europe, but the shock of seeing me put her right straight away. Came bedtime and how I looked forward to sleeping in a real bed again after over two years. I found I could not get to sleep, I tossed and turned, got hot and sweated, it was agony. Eventually after an hour I could stick it no longer. Taking a pillow and putting it on the floor under the wide-open window and wrapping a blanket round me, I lay down, fell asleep straight away and had a glorious night's rest.

"Came the last day of my leave and time to return. I did not want to go back, I wanted more time at home. But how? Then I remembered how a pal had extended his leave. He had reported sick to his local army doctor and had got a few days extra at home. Scabies was a skin disease, a bit like scurvy which every soldier overseas got off and on. So I scratched myself all over until blood showed and dried, and then set off to see the local army doctor. He was a young chap, just called up. I told him I was due to return to my unit in the trenches after the first leave for twenty months and thought I had got scabies. He examined me, then said, angrily, "You have Hell!! What's the game?" I told him my story and that I was too young to have been out there anyway. He softened, then said, "All right, I'll send you to the skin Isolation Hospital on Redcar Racecourse for a few days. Will that do?" I thanked him and returned home with the good news. My family were delighted and off I went to Redcar.

"The hospital was in the Stewards room on the racecourse, and there were twenty of us with beds to sleep on. We were well fed, and every morning we had to attend the slipper baths situated in the stables. A medical orderly filled the baths with very hot water in which he placed a generous supply of carbolic. Under his supervision, we had to scrub ourselves from head to toe. It was very sore and painful. After bathing, we were free to wander around the course and do what we liked, but were not allowed to go outside. Of course we did. After dark, my pal and I climbed the eight foot stone wall into Aske Road. Away we went into Redcar, to the army canteen in Dene Grove and the canteen at the Coatham Convalescent Home, or to chat to the girls on the promenade.

"Being a Sniper when I first went out to France, it had become my habit to carry a spare clip of cartridges in my first aid pocket, at the bottom of the left hand side of my tunic. One night, in jumping down from the wall into Aske Road, I stumbled and fell, the cartridges pressing hard into my groin. Angrily, I pulled them out and chucked them away into the darkness although I had carried them all over France with me.

"There were no houses built in Aske Road then, it was just a field. This clip of cartridges was found forty-six years later, in August, 1964, when a Mr. Beattie was digging in his garden. He reported his find to the local paper and was very interested when I told him all about it.

"For ten years, I had passed that way every day to Aske Road School where I taught from 1929 to 1940. I was on the racecourse for a fortnight, 'swinging the lead' and on the last day but one I received a letter from my mother enclosing a ten shilling note. This was riches indeed.

"My pal suggested we go out that night for a drink at the Coatham Convalescent Home Canteen. Beer in those days was tuppence a pint, and when we got there he said "let's see who can drink the most" and we started off. The result was a close draw, by the time we got to about the eighteenth pint we were both helpless, hanging on to the counter.

"At closing time, we set off back to the course. How we got there about two hours later, I do not know. Arm in arm we sang, staggered, and fell all over the place. Instead of going back in quietly over the wall, we went through the main gates and were caught by the sentry and reported.

"Next day, we were both sent off back to our units. I was escorted by a Corporal to Middlesbrough station. He was supposed to see me off on the train to London. Wanting to slip back home again at Grove Hill, I said to the Corporal, "Look here, take this shilling, and when we get to Middlesbrough station, look the other way."

"He took the shilling, shook hands, wished me luck and off he went. I went home for another two days, then expecting the Military Police to call on me anytime, I decided I had to go back. After heartbreaking, tearful farewells, off I went, with a feeling that I would never see home again.

"Soon I was back in the mud, blood, and glory (?) of Bullecourt. I found that the farmhouse signalling post I'd been in before going on leave had been blown up by a shell and that my five pals plus the lad who replaced me had all been killed. I certainly had a guardian angel with me all the time and realized it must be my dear old Dad, who daily appeared in my thoughts and guided me to do the right thing when in danger.

"My brother Jack was on this front, about five miles away, and spent a whole day trying to find me. He could not, as I was in the front line at the time. I am glad he did not meet up with me as it would have been heart-breaking to part after an hour or so together. It also might have meant the death of both of us, as one always had to keep alert and it did not do to be upset or worried about anything. Many a lad who came back off leave dispirited became so careless he was dead within a week of returning. You needed all your wits about you to survive.

"On the 21st March, 1918, I stepped out of our corrugated hut at dawn, to take a wet. I could not believe my eyes. Germans were coming into the sunken road about a quarter of a mile away. I dashed back into the hut, waking the others and we ran up the road. Although shot at, we got away and no one was hurt. Those Germans were rotten shots. It turned out to be the start of the big German Advance of 1918. Their entire army was able to concentrate on us, as the Russians had just packed it in.

"After retreating for two days, we made a stand near Armentieres. Here I and two others in the signal section were sent to the Middlesex Regiment to learn how to use a new trench radio. We were issued with one of these instruments, a black box weighing about twenty pounds. We were told that it was the first of its kind in France and that whatever happened it was to be destroyed rather than allow it to fall into enemy hands.

"On the night of April 8, 1918, we in the signals section laid down in a ruined farmhouse, not knowing the Germans were beginning to send mustard gas shells across before starting to advance. We were awoken next morning by a Corporal wearing a gas mask. "Quick!" he shouted, "Everyone has cleared off but us." We could not get up and then started to get sick. We were helpless from breathing mustard gas which lies low on the ground. The Corporal dragged us each into the open air, and after about three hours we had recovered sufficiently to move around.

"When shrapnel began flying near us, it dawned on me that we must try to save the wireless set. Leaving our rifles and packs, we set off for Headquarters, carrying the set between us. Unaware that we were surrounded by Germans, we wondered how the enemy could be shooting at us from nearby. Later we realized they had been shooting from very close range and were glad they were such rotten shots.

"We had gone about a half mile down the road when I was astounded to see a platoon of twenty Germans led by an officer march across. "Quick! Throw it in the ditch!" I said. In the radio went, and sank out of sight, but its splash halted the Germans. They turned and pointed their rifles at me. The officer waved us to come to them. During that twenty yards' walk, we expected to be filled with lead, but I acted as cool as a cucumber and cheekily said, "Good morning, sir."

"The officer detailed an escort to take us back into their lines. On the way, we were halted and ordered to carry a wounded German to their first-aid station. He was slung in a groundsheet between two poles; a big heavy man who had been hit in the stomach and his insides were hanging out. We could not be at all careful with him, swinging him about as we struggled along, and everytime a shell burst close by, we just flung ourselves flat. He was moaning and groaning when we reached the aid-station a mile away; a sorry sight, blood all over and breathing his last. There were about fifty dead Germans at the aid post, neatly stacked on top of one another against a wall. Hundreds of German wounded lay about dressed with crepê paper bandages, as they had no cotton.

"During the four days we were marched towards imprisonment, we were kept under heavy guard and given nothing to eat. When we reached Lille prison, we felt very sorry for ourselves, very thirsty and hungry. We were given thin watery soup similar to wallpaper glue, and a guard brought in a bin of water. There was such a rush that the bin and the guards were knocked flying, and fighting like animals we licked water from the dirty floor.

"We were counted off in hundreds, and placed in cells each designed to accommodate twenty people. One hundred packed in each tiny room. At one end there was a barred window and at the other a latrine tub, always overflowing. I made straight for the window and stayed there. It was standing-room-only all day, and at night we all lay on our right side packed as tight as sardines. Each morning, two or three lads at the latrine end were carried out dead, suffocated by the foul air. Our only meal was at mid-day; thin soup and a slice of black bread.

"After two weeks in this Hell-hole (the Black Hole of Calcutta must have been like it), we were taken to the railway station, locked into cattle trucks, and travelling all day standing up, we reached a proper p.o.w. camp in Germany. Now, I was Kreigsgefangener No. 89818. We were showered, fumigated, and our woollen underwear taken away and changed for a thin German type. I was able to share a seven pound Red Cross food parcel. What a good present for me — it was May 4th, my twentieth birthday. Then we went to the taps outside and for the next few days we were never away from those taps, drinking, drinking, drinking.

"Food was very poor from then on, and we were always hungry. The Germans very often punished us for any infraction of regulations by making us line up facing the sun for up to four hours, with guards standing ready to use their rifle butts on us. After even half an hour of this "stillestande" we would sway like spinning tops. It was hellish, and for the rest of my life I have been unable to stand for long before starting to sway.

"We went to Hameln later where we were worked very hard in stone quarries, mines, and sugar factories. Of these, the salt mines were most terrible, where we worked twelve hour shifts underground without food or water. One day while returning from the sugar factory, we saw a ragged party of German soldiers led by an officer on a very thin horse. We were dumbfounded at their looks. The factory boss then explained "They are marching back from the front. The war is over!""

In telling his story right to the end, Edgar Robinson has been allowed to move ahead of other events. Before that glad day of peace dawned on November 11th, 1918, he and his comrades were to endure many more months of a war that also brought two new Bantam battalions from overseas.

THE HIGHLAND COUNCIL, GLENURQUHART ROAD, INVERNESS IV3 5NX

Incorporates: NORTHERN JOINT POLICE BOARD
HIGHLAND AND ISLANDS FIRE BOARD
HIGHLAND AND WESTERN ISLE VALUATION JOINT BOARD

No. 388076

DATE 12-4-00

REC'D FROM ....

In Respect of .... 12/F. Books

The Sum of

Net .... £

VAT @ .... % £

Gross .... £ 80

(CASH/CHEQUE)

Received on behalf of Director of Finance/Treasurer

VAT No. 663 7582 03

Chapter Nine

The Canadians

On Armistice Night, 1936, some two dozen tipsy but still dapper middle-aged businessmen in company with a large grey horse clattered into the elegant lobby of Toronto's King Edward Hotel. Asked to leave by the outraged but understandably nervous manager, the intruders solemnly assured him that all would be well, took long pulls from bottles in the brown paper bags they carried and burst into raucous song:

"When the Bantam roosters crow,
You'll find the enemy lying low,
Though we're not much in height,
Boy, how we can fight!
Just count on the chickens
To give them a licking . . .
When we march into the line,
That's when we show up mighty fine.
Though we're not much in height,
Boy, how we can fight . . .
When the Bantam roosters crow!"

The group bowed to the amused applause of hotel patrons, boosted up one of their fellows astride the puzzled horse, and swayed out in its wake into the snowy night. For the bareback rider, Alex Batchelor, it was a fitting end to the 216th Old Comrades' Reunion and to a night of reliving memories which began when he had finally managed to enlist in the Canadian Army in 1916. Batchelor, whom we last saw two years earlier in this narrative, was among the first to enlist in the newly formed 216th (Toronto) Battalion.

Once more, a Bantam unit was born mainly through the efforts of a single forceful individual, who co-incidentally also dubbed it the "B.B.B." Major Frank Lindsay Burton was already a wounded veteran of France when he returned to his native Toronto in late 1915. Appointed to an administrative post in No. 2 Military District Headquarters, he began to chafe under his duties of helping to document the thousands of recruits who passed through the depot in the Canadian National Exhibition Grounds.

Long before the war, Burton had been involved in the Toronto Garrison Militia, that quasi-social group which nonetheless managed to keep the martial spirit alive in peacetime. That there was more to the militia than the Garrison Ball and the annual "drunk" at Camp Borden during summer manoeuvres was proved when it formed a cadre of trained men for the Canadian Army when war was declared. In the sudden crisis, the Toronto militia officers donated every last dollar in regimental treasuries to aid mobilization, and went fifty thousand dollars in debt before the National Recruiting League was formed.

While still attending Upper Canada College, Burton had been a private in the Simcoe Foresters. He took his reserve commission with the Toronto Light Horse, and later commanded the University Company of the Queen's Own Regiment. Early in the war, he had gone overseas as Second in Command, 75th Battalion, The Toronto Scottish Regiment, and had been invalided home after a year in France. Now, he wanted action again, and he wanted a command of his own. In January, 1916, he saw his opportunity for both.

Though for its part, Toronto had already sent forty

thousand of its men overseas, and the entire country was doing its best to send more volunteers abroad, the Canadian army was experiencing a severe shortage of replacements.

While recuperating in England, Burton had seen the 35th Division in training on Salisbury Plain, and subsequently wondered why Canada was not attempting to raise the same kind of units. When he heard the first murmurings about such a move in H.Q. at Exhibition camp, Burton approached Colonel Mewburn about forming a Toronto unit. He followed this up with a formally written detailed proposal that he be permitted to raise a battalion and submitted it to the divisional commander, Brigadier General W. A. Logie. The major signed himself as still "Second-In-Command, 75th Overseas Battalion," to emphasize his practical experience.

This proposal seems to have sparked into action an idea which had been only talked about in Canadian military circles for some time. The following day, Brigadier Logie sent off his own letter to the Secretary of the Militia Council in Ottawa, requesting permission to organize a Bantam battalion in his division. Burton has suggested a minimum age of nineteen, and a minimum height of 4 ft. 10 ins. The General increased these to twenty-two and 5 ft. He added that if the plan was approved, he would submit the name of an officer to command it.

Militia Headquarters contacted the Canadian Command in London, England, to check on the British army physical standard for their bantams. They reported that the minimum accepted height was 5 ft. 1 in., unaware of the actual elasticity of that rule in Britain. A mandarin in Ottawa leaped upon this one inch difference and Brigadier Logie was informed that as this British standard was "substantially different" from what he had suggested, he should offer another proposal. The General replied by asking that his original proposal stand, as any increase in height requirements might conflict with other existing battalions in Ontario.

In the meantime, Logie had told Major Burton that there

was nothing new about the idea for bantams and that Lt. Col. R. A. Robertson, 13th Regiment — "who is himself a bantam" — was already being considered for the command. Bets were hedged by Colonel Newburn firing off a telegram to Robertson, urging him to take command and to catch General Logie while he was passing through Hamilton that same day. However, that chosen officer was still on sick-leave and was unable to accept the offer. Burton's name was submitted to Ottawa by Logie after all.

Two weeks later, February 17th, 1916, the Ministry of Militia authorized the formation of Number 216 Overseas Battalion, Toronto, to be organized and commanded by Major Burton only in the City of Toronto and County of York. The minimum height was set at 5 ft. 1½ ins.; chest minimum 30 ins.; twenty-two years minimum age. Along with the job, Major Burton was promoted to the temporary rank of lieutenant-colonel.

Demonstrating the instinct for publicity he was to display throughout the whole of the recruiting campaign, Burton promptly called every newspaper in the Toronto region; explaining the new unit's formation. The result was a gratifying volume of press coverage, which helped draw three hundred applicants within a matter of hours.

"I was feeling poorly that day and had taken the day off work," says Alex Batchelor. "Then I felt restless all of a sudden and got out of bed to walk across to Bay Street for a newspaper. The Bantams story hit me straight away and I realized I was only a few blocks from the recruiting address given, 16 Adelaide Street West. There were dozens of short chaps like me hurrying along the street towards a big cloth sign that said "Join Up Here — Burton's Bantam Battalion." I went inside almost in a daze. Half an hour later I was in the army, walking down the street to quit my job, proud as a peacock of the white band on my arm that read 'BBB'."

It was this proprietary use of initials which first raised the hackles of Burton's superiors. Lacking his sense of publicity, and not a little hostile to the entire enterprise, some of them resented his high-profile personal indentification with the unit. The banners and armbands annoyed conventional officers who were further incensed by the new Lt. Colonel's use of bilious green stationery headed "BBB — Burton's Bantam Battalion." On this paper, the O.C. 216th Battalion fired off a volume of memos and letters pressing the unit's cause to Ottawa, military commanders, newspapers, and politicians. General Logie took offence at all these "unsoldierly flamboyances," and they were the source of continuous friction during the next twelve months.

Though recruiting for the 216th moved with great smoothness during March, with a steady flow of recruits and repeatedly favourable press coverage, the Brigadier began to respond with increasing choler. He finally instructed Burton to "discontinue forthwith" use of any title other than the officially designated 216th Overseas Battalion, C.E.F.

This problem had no sooner been resolved when Burton was on the carpet again. His men were out on the streets of Toronto selling tickets for a unit concert, and he himself had outraged the chief recruiting officer of Hamilton by seeking men there for the Bantams. Logie was not sure which was the worse offence — soliciting money or soliciting recruits in another unit's territory. Burton was told off about both.

Burton cheerfully responded by once more applying for permission to have the unit name changed to Burton's Bantam Battalion, "as the slogan has become recognized by the public." This received a one-sentence refusal, but the sub-title "Bantams" was officially added to the unit designation.

Men were accepted at the average rate of fifteen a day, but this did not satisfy the impatient Lt. Colonel who cast about for fresh attractions. In mid-March, a man fully uniformed as a German officer from pickel-haube to jackboots marched through the streets of Toronto to lure the curious to a recruiting drive. When the inevitable outraged telephone call came from Exhibition Camp, the 216th's Adjutant, Lt. Norman Williams, hastily assured H.Q. that the stunt would not be repeated.

By now, the unit had a full complement of officers, led by two acting majors Lieutenant Stanley King Bennet and Lt. Alexander Cameron Lewis, previously Secretary of the Toronto Harbour Commission. The Assistant Adjutant was Lt. Malcolm McCallum, and the Quartermaster was Lt. H. A. Coach. All of these and the other eight senior officers would receive promotions of two or three steps up the ladder before year's end. As well, the 216th eventually took on strength a further eighteen lieutenants who transferred from various other Canadian regiments.

Examination of the nominal roll of the 216th reveals that most of the recruits had been born in either Canada or Britain, but that ten other countries were also represented in the ranks. Americans and Russians, Italians and Anzacs, Poles and French, even a lone West Indian, had signed up. Among them was a South African-born youth named Billy Butlin. He was later to serve as a sixteen-year-old stretcher-bearer at the Front, then settle in Britain, where his innovative holiday-camps enterprise earned him great wealth and the eventual title of Sir William Butlin, M.B.E.

An even more exotic and warlike quality might have been added if Burton had had his way. He was approached in his office on Saturday morning March 11th, by a Japanese gentleman formally dressed in striped trousers, black cutaway coat, and a grey top hat. The visitor stated he could bring in close to one hundred Japanese young men if a place for them could be found in the unit. The understandable excitement with which Burton put forward the prospect of such good fighting material was dampened by General Logie. His frigid reply was that the proposal to raise a company of "Japs" had not received favourable consideration, and that Lt. Col. Burton would confine his efforts to men of York

County.

By May, the battalion had reached a strength of five hundred and thirty-eight than half the target goal, and Colonel Burton again pressed for more leeway in recruiting. He approached General Logie to allow the 216th to recruit throughout the whole of the 2nd Division area. He showed he had as usual been active before asking formal permission, by outlining a plan to recruit two platoons in Hamilton, one platoon each in St. Catharines, Niagara Falls and Brantford, and another entire company throughout the northern part of the Division, from the Sault on down.

He got his permission to enlarge his recruiting mandate, but "only on the distinct understanding" that he adhere to the age and height minimum in future. He was ordered to parade his men before a medical review board, which discharged six on physical grounds and questioned the age of thirty-three more. "Some of these appear to be somewhat younger than the minimum age of twenty-two years." Fortunately for the volunteers, this point was not pursued, as about one quarter of their number were really of such tender age they were eight years below the official minimum.

The Toronto Bantams' H.Q. staff was repeatedly confronted by overwrought mothers of boys in their early teens who had contrived to join up. "It was quite a sight to see a uniformed soldier being dragged off by the ear, taken home by his mother," says William Leyland, only sixteen years old himself at the time. "My father had managed to enlist in the Ordnance Corps by using his Boer War experience to offset his age of forty-six. I wanted my father to see me in uniform, too, before he left for overseas. Besides, I was looking forward to getting into the scrap myself. As I wasn't very tall, my best bet was the Bantams. They were suspicious about my real age – I'd told them I was nineteen – so they challenged my claim to be a bugler. I just played a few calls for the bandmaster, and I was in; no more questions asked."

Lt. Colonel Burton then came up with yet another recruiting gimmick. He had manufactured a miniature silver brooch engraved with a bantam rooster and the words, "I also serve." He organized a reception party and invited all wives and mothers of each man in the 216th to meet the officers and be presented with a brooch. It was a good morale booster for the unit but was pointedly not attended by any of the invited District H.Q. staff.

Further irritation was communicated to 16 Adelaide Street West, when Burton inaugurated a canvas of the city for names of men of military age. Of the eighteen thousand five hundred men contacted in a house-to-house approach, only one thousand four hundred were found eligible as bantams. The direct line from Exhibition Camp jangled again, and the aggressive door-step recruiting was halted.

However, by mid-summer, the battalion had reached its full strength of one thousand men. A late recruit was John Taylor, who travelled north with a final draft of one hundred men to join the 216th in the desert sands of Camp Borden.

"It was over 90 degrees at the Infantry School there," Taylor remembers. "We marched and drilled until we dropped from the heat. Then after a half-hour rest, we'd go off for firing practice. The Senior Musketry Officer at Borden told Colonel Burton that the Bantams had excelled any unit in camp, so we were given that Saturday off duty."

The battalion struck tents on October 23rd and was entrained aboard fourteen C.P.R. coaches back to Toronto. Never one to miss a chance for favourable exposure of his unit, Burton led the men on a parade up Bay Street to billets in Jesse Ketchum School. It was here the unit spent the winter keeping up their marksmanship by shooting with .22 rifles at hordes of rats in the cellars. In time, they would find that this practice was strangely prophetic.

Had it not been for administrative delays, the first Canadian Bantam battalion would have been formed in Victoria, British Columbia. Mobilization was authorized for the 143rd B.C. Overseas Battalion (Bantams) on November 29th, 1915, but recruiting work did not begin until February 20th, 1916. The driving force behind mobilization was Lieutenant Colonel Bruce Powey, a returned front-line veteran of the Canadian army. After he was appointed C.O. of the battalion in December 15th, 1915, he found it difficult to find quarters for the thousand men he hoped to sign up, and also ran into a certain amount of obstruction by people seeking recruits for other West Coast regiments.

By February, Lt. Colonel Powey had been given part of Sidney Camp on Vancouver Island, along with enough tents and huts to house a battalion. From the outset, the 143rd did not lack for applicants; civilians in the coalmining areas of British Columbia applied by the hundred, as did bantam-sized men already in other units of the army. The battalion did not have much luck in obtaining transfers of such troops, as warm bodies in Canadian uniform were then too prized to relinguish.

At this stage of the war, Canada had two hundred thousand men under arms, all volunteers. The nation had been quick to send men after the outbreak of war. On October 3rd, 1914, the First Contingent sailed from Gaspe Basin in a convoy containing one thousand four hundred and twenty-four officers twenty-nine thousand one hundred and ninety-three other ranks. Of them sixty-two percent had been born in Britain, and another two percent were from other British possessions. Over two-thirds of the officers were Canadian-born and had trained with the militia.

By early 1916, Canada had sent three divisions to the Western Front and a fourth division was training in England, together making up the Canadian Corps. They had been the first troops to experience poison gas in April, 1915, when the Germans released the contents of five thousand seven hundred and thirty cylinders of chlorine in the Ypres Salient. That day, the Canucks had wrapped wet cloths around their mouths and held the line despite appalling casualties. When the Algerians fled from this horrible new weapon, vomiting green foam as they ran, the Canadians had to close the gap left in Allied lines. German troops braved their own death-dealing vapour to attack the division's horse artillery, and Lance Corporal Frederick Fisher won Canada's first Victoria Cross in helping to successfully repel the enemy.

A day later, the gas came again at St. Julien, where choking soldiers of Sir Arthur Currie's 2nd Brigade wept from effects of the acrid fumes and the frustration of having their Ross rifles jam during rapid fire. The Canadians scavenged the battlefield for Mausers and Lee Enfields from German and British dead to continue to fight with, but in the end had to fall back from their positions. Here, the 8th Battalion's C.S.M. Frederick W. Hall won the V.C. after rescuing a wounded trooper under point-blank artillery fire. By the time the battle was over next morning, two more V.C.'s had been won by Canadians — Lieutenant Edward Bellew and Captain Alex C. Scrimger.

The British C. in C., Sir John French, sent his personal thanks to the Canadians for holding the Salient only six hundred yards further back. The price for this foul yeast of mud and blood was six thousand killed, wounded, and missing. "These splendid troops averted a disaster," said Sir John. The question was, how long could they endure without a constant flow of reinforcements?

The heavy fighting at St. Eloi had since butchered thousands more Canadians. Six giant mines had been exploded by the British, throwing up mountains of earth with a roar that was heard as far away as in Kent, in South-Eastern England. Again it was Canadians who held against the German counter-attack, tussling for thirteen days to control the craters. One of these giant mudholes alone was the grave of one thousand three hundred and seventy-three soldiers. Where were the young men to replace them?

With the political balance in Canada hanging on the Conscription Debate, and with much of Quebec opposed to sending its sons abroad, every single volunteer was valuable.*

---

*   Eight French-Canadian regiments fought with distinction on the Western Front.

In such conditions, Lt. Col. Powey found that officers commanding other Overseas Battalions containing bantams refused to transfer them, maintaining that the small men did not want to leave. Despite his documenting lists of hundreds of such applicants, Powey was blocked in his attempts to take them into the 143rd Battalion.

"We only got fifty men from the 6th D.C.O.R., and twenty from Colonel Vickers' 102nd R.M.R. Kamloops," he complained to Ottawa, "The 11th Irish in Vancouver railroaded their bantams into the 121st, notwithstanding many of them protesting. Other overseas Regiments have Bantams and one battalion after another went away with them."

The battalion's main hope lay in the direct entry of civilians, though this source had already been drained off to some degree by the recruiting efforts of other regiments. The sparsely settled Province of British Columbia, which then probably held little more than a half-million people, had responded wholeheartedly early in the war. Intensely loyal, and with a high proportion of British immigrant stock, B.C. had virtually shot its bolt by early 1916 in its capacity for manpower for war. The coal mining towns on Vancouver Island and of the mainland interior provided the likeliest source of strong bantams.

One of them was Benjamin Barnes, a red-haired Cornishman who volunteered from his well-paid job as fire-boss of Coal Creek Mine. Another was Peter Campbell, an office worker from Sidney, who joined "B" Company in camp just down the road from his home. Allan Bell came over from Vancouver, on the same ferry that brought Humbert Campbell from his job on an Alberta ranch.

"It seemed the greatest adventure in the world," says Bell. "The sun shone on the water and the mountains stood out against the sky as we sailed across that day, and I felt my chest swell as if we were all setting out on a great crusade. My comrades proved to be such happy chaps, forever telling jokes, with never a cross word, and I never felt so happy in all my eighteen years."

Despite such enthusiastic recruits, Lt. Colonel Powey could not enlist enough suitable men at the pace he needed, He regretfully reported to Ottawa on October 15th, 1916. "We were finally forced to take in some larger men, with a view to later exchanging them for smaller men of other units. But exchanges in Canada are not easy, and the result is I have a battalion of over half Bantam and the balance of larger men, though their average is below 5 ft. 6 ins. They are training very fast and I hope to proceed overseas with a smart battalion if not wholly a Bantam Battalion."

When the trained battalion returned to Victoria, it was so outspokenly impatient to be sent to France that they became known locally as "The Fire-eaters." Their attitude may be thought all the more remarkable in view of the high proportion of older, married men in the ranks. The 143rd was a sober, well-behaved unit with few if any brushes with authority. They went about their preparation for war with a serious competence, trying to befit themselves for front-line service.

Among those who chafed to go overseas, was Ben Barnes, who, as an accomplished cornet-player, had found himself in the battalion band. In January, 1917, he wrote to his brother in immaculate penmanship from the Dominion Hotel in Victoria, "We are all classed as soldiers, and though bandsmen do not put in much time now with a rifle, we are all prepared for the firing-line. Each of us in the band has learned machine gun drill or signalling, first aid, and stretcher-bearing."

He wrote again in December, excited by news of embarkation, but depressed by feelings of foreboding. "I get a little downhearted when I dwell too much on my home, but I shake it off as best I can, and will be content when I get a little more excitement at the front. If I get a bullet to put me to sleep, I will only be beside my comrades so I should not worry."

The 143rd Battalion sailed from Halifax aboard S.S. *Southland,* on February 17th, 1917. Ten days later, they were in the Canadian Holding Depot at Purfleet Camp, Shorncliffe. "We felt like cattle, the way they treated us there," said Allan Bell. "The Canadian Corps needed more men in France in a hurry and made no secret of the fact that we were viewed as potential cannon-fodder. One could not but notice that while ordinary soldiers were getting this treatment, there were over five hundred lieutenants lounging around camp, many of whom had been there since the previous summer.

"But that was the least of our irritations, because it didn't take long to figure out that the B.C. Bantams as a unit were going to be broken up forthwith."

Unaware of this future, the Toronto Bantams had received word of their imminent departure for overseas. The first signal that this was coming had been on November 27th, 1916, when the battalion paraded at the University Avenue Armouries. The ceremony packed the galleries and an estimated four thousand people were left outside, unable to gain admittance.

The Armouries were decorated with patriotic bunting and clusters of Union Jacks adorned every wall. Promptly at 8 p.m., the battalion marched in behind their brass and bugle band, and amid cheering crowds. The men formed up three sides of a square, gratified at the worthies grouped in front of their drums and colours.

Lieutenant Colonel Burton was a member of the prestigious Timothy Eaton Memorial Church, and had already obtained it as the 216th's garrison church. He had further gained status for his battalion by having on hand Mrs. Timothy Eaton, one of the country's wealthiest women, to personally present the King's Colours to the unit.

Flanking her was Major General Logie, who was probably gratified in more ways than one by the embarkation news, and a clutch of the city's establishment, the clergy, and the military. There was Hon. Colonel Sir John C. Eaton, Hon. Colonel Reverend Dr. Chown, Mr. W. C. Bolus, Secretary of the Board of Trustees, a bevy of Lieutenant Colonels and various society ladies.

When Mrs. Eaton had presented their King's Colours, consecrated by The Reverend Dr. James Henderson, the unassuming Bantam rankers were bemused to realize they were now in a "social" battalion. Chests out, they marched away through cheering crowds, the words of the reverend gentleman ringing in their ears — "These colours send you off to assist in preserving the British Empire through what we feel is a holy war . . . "

Their actual departure was all too ordinary a military event in that it was a foul-up. On April 13th, 1917, hundreds of friends and relatives of the embarking 216th arrived as they had been told at Bayside Park Station to make their last farewells. At 3 o'clock, they were informed that the men were being entrained miles away at Exhibition Park Station and a frantic rush of women and children surged across the city. They arrived at the last minute for tearful farewells, and the Grand Trunk train pulled out at sundown "with the Bantams singing lustily on their way to war."

When they disembarked from the S.S. *Scandinavian* on April 28th, 1917, the 216th were sent to Dibgate for the same treatment received by the British Columbians. Lieutenant Colonel Burton found out that there was no intention to use his battalion as a whole. Despite his vigorous protests to Militia Headquarters in Ottawa, the 216th was broken up within days of its arrival in England.

The Brigade Headquarters at West Sandling found that six hundred and sixty-six men and twenty-three officers were in A.ii condition, and rejected eighty-nine as below standard D.iii class. The medical report ended with this peculiarly contradictory comment: "Although we have classified six hundred and sixty-six O.R.'s as fit, these men are short in stature being of rather poor physique and in my opinion they would be of more use in Railway Construction or Labour Units."

On May 4th, 1917, Lieutenant Colonel Burton was given a copy of Divisional Orders which described procedures for winding up "depleted units" and was told to act on them immediately. Thus without ceremony, the 216th Overseas Battalion (Bantams) next day ceased to exist. The dazed men were sent off in small groups to various units being formed by the 1st Canadian Reserve Brigade.

Most of the Toronto men were transferred into a number of artillery units, where their identity as "Bantams" was lost. Bill Leyland spent the rest of the war as a camp bugler in England. Billy Butlin went off to take up his dangerous job as stretcher-bearer in Flanders. Alex Batchelor and John Taylor were among the 225 "Bants" who joined Canadian infantry units along the Vimy front. Giant trench rats were the first targets they fired at there with the newly issued Lee Enfields which replaced their flimsy Ross rifles.

Lieutenant Colonel Powey was not given the opportunity to even say goodbye to the unit he had formed despite many obstructions. Peter Campbell recalls how it was for the crestfallen Victoria battalion. "After spending a brief landing-leave in London, we were called before a medical board. The 143rd Battalion was abruptly broken up, many going to the 47th Regiment, some to the 2nd Canadian Mounted Rifles, and many more, including me, to the 3rd Battalion, Canadian Railway Troops."

Transportation was ever a big problem in France during the war, as roads were often impassable with mud and shellfire. Eventually, the Allies realized that the German secret of rapid movement of troops and supplies was the use of a network of light railways. Because of Canada's experience in building railroads, General Stewart was asked in late 1916 to organize the Canadian Railway Troops. Before long, there were 13 battalions of them, responsible for all railway construction throughout the British sector, and they proved to be vital to the conduct of the war.

Their work was to build light narrow-gauge railways beyond the standard gauge lines, right up to forward artillery batteries and reserve trenches. The Canadians' skill enabled troops and supplies to be quickly moved along the front and revolutionized the Allied ability to wage war.

Campbell and his fellow ex-Bantams were thrust into their new job in a matter of days. "We crossed the Channel in mid-March, and wound up at Poperinge in the Salient, in brand-new tents which Jerry enjoyed shelling. After a short time, we went to Three Trees Camp behind Messines, where we put in some light railways for the new operation. Then on to the south-east of Vimy Ridge, and we took over the maintenance of existing railways."

The four hundred and eighty-nine decorations awarded to Canadian Railway Troops is some indication of the dangers they faced. The Germans kept a jealous eye on railway movements, and shelled the construction gangs daily. Their shellfire was accurate, as usual, so that casualties were frequent and repairs to broken lines had to be repeated as often as a dozen times every twenty-four hours.

In late 1917, light railways found a new role when they began to be used in gas attacks. Many ex-Bantams were employed at this, which involved night-time building of rail lines parallel to front line trenches. Then carriages containing cylinders of poison gas were quietly brought up through the darkness, dragged by men using long ropes, as engine noises would draw artillery. The spectacle of hundreds of tiny men hauling their deadly juggernauts inevitably brings to mind Lilliputian imagery. One's instinct to grin at this picture fades at reading a report of how at Passchendaele on October 18th, German shells bracketed a gas train, moments after the nozzles were opened. Thirty-one of the little soldiers died there from enemy shrapnel or from the strangling fumes of their own cargo of chlorine.

Nearly all the British Columbians who had been chosen as infantry replacements were shipped direct to France. They arrived in early April, just in time to take part in the Canadian Corps' most historic assault.

The modern traveller who follows in their trail leaves Arras and heads northeast over the gently sloping countryside. You have no sense that the ground has gradually risen until you reach four hundred and seventy-five foot summit of Vimy Ridge. Suddenly, the escarpment edge drops away, and a magnificent view opens wide in front of you. The horizon stretches across the Flanders Plain, clear to the Belgian border; but one's eye is drawn to the towns below, glowing redly in the sunset and in their own sinister aura of tragic memories.

Just down there is Lens. Then there's Bethune, and Lille, and Armentieres of the oft-importuned mademoiselle. Messines lowers far off beside Mt. Kimmel, so grisly Passchendaele must be just beyond. They look strangely small and close together, to have been fought over for four years at the cost of millions of Allied and German lives. You avert your eyes, looking back the way you came, and realize then what a commanding position this gave the Germans. From here, the backslope of the ridge falls away, providing an uninterrupted view westward of what was once the British lines. You can see well beyond the towers of Arras, along the shining Scarpe River, and even survey the wrinkled *rideaux* of terraced hills to the southeast. From here, the German observation posts looked over the entire British sector, providing direct control of artillery fire against roads, railways, and troop movements. No wonder they fought hard and long to hold Vimy Ridge.

The wind rises chill and damp as the sun dips out of sight. The slope goes dark and you look down, half-expecting in this ghost-ridden aerie to see thousands of gun flashes winking below as they did on the night of Easter Monday, 1917.

For a whole week before, three hundred and seventy-seven

heavy guns and seven hundred and twenty field guns cease-lessly pounded German positions on and behind the ridge. A rain of shells fell on fortified villages, supply points, and trenches, pulverizing defences which had been built up during the three years the Germans had held the position. Since 1914, the slopes of the hill had been the dying place of two hundred thousand men, most of them French. Now, the Canadian Corps had the job of storming up over their graves.

The assault here was part of a wider move which pivoted on a massive French attack further south. The handsome young General Robert Nivelle had supplanted General "Papa" Joffre, and promised dynamic new methods of gaining quick victory. His plan for attack in the Champagne was soon known by the Germans, who countered it in advance by retreating to the Hindenberg Line.

They left behind them an area of complete destruction, systematically destroying every town, village, and farmhouse. They slaughtered cattle, chopped down fruit-trees, and poisoned every well. Thousands of booby-traps lay among the ruins to trap unwary souvenir hunters, and time-fused mines exploded for weeks after.

Nivelle's offensive into this desolation failed, but Field Marshal Sir Douglas Haig decided to plunge ahead anyway with the British support plan, despite the fact that its original purpose of drawing off enemy reserves from the French attack was no longer needed.

Three of his army corps were allotted to open the Battle of Arras along a twelve mile front. On the extreme left of the drive, stood Vimy Ridge, dominating the objective, a German Gibraltar swathed in barbed wire, honeycombed with deep machine gun posts and line after line of trench-works. It was under the personal command of wily old General E. von Falkenhayn, who kept one Prussian and two Bavarian divisions in place to hold the bloodsoaked ridge.

His adversary was Lt. General Sir Julian Byng, a practical

1. New Yorker Henry Thridgould paid his own way across the Atlantic to join the Middlesex 'Diehards'. At 4 ft. 9 inches he claimed to be the shortest Corporal in the British Army.

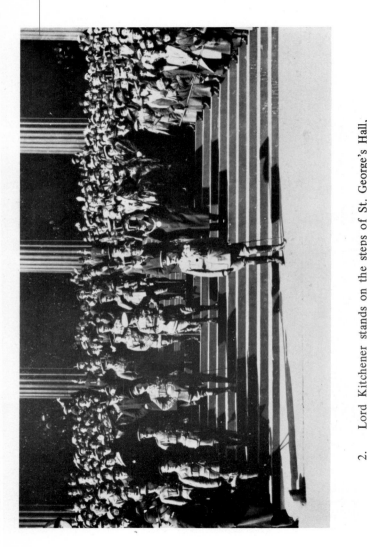

2. Lord Kitchener stands on the steps of St. George's Hall, Liverpool, March 21st, 1916, to take the salute as Bantam battalions march past. Their founder, Alfred Bigland MP, stands modestly back in the crowd, upper left.

3. Marching song of the 216th Toronto Bantams was composed by Captain Stanley Bennett (left) shown here with part of the battalion's band. Youth standing in centre next to Captain Bennett was later to be celebrated as Sir William Butlin, MBE, developer of popular Butlin's Holiday Camps.

4. Fatigue at the end of a long route march is evident in the casual shouldering of Long Lee-Enfields carried by these members of the 17th Battalion, Royal Scots. The unit went to France shortly after, where they were issued with more manageable Short Lee-Enfields.

(Photo: Royal Scots Museum.)

soldier who alone amongst "Imperial" staff officers was able to hold the respect of his subordinates in the Canadian Corps. His demonstrated military common sense along with his personal modesty was a refreshing change from the pompous ways of the General Staff, and he in turn respected the hell-for-leather fighting style of the Dominion troops. Since their arrival, Canadians had shown an aggressive spirit, tempered with a reluctance to be considered mere Colonials. By early 1917, the Canadian Corps not only had a hard-earned reputation as shock-troops; they had been forged into what was in fact a National Army of Canada.

Their Canadian-born leaders were Major-General Sir Arthur Currie, 1st Division; Major-General E.W. Turner, V.C., 2nd Division, and Major-General D. Watson, 4th Division. The commander of the 3rd Division, Major-General L.J. Lipsett, was British-born, though he had served with the Canadian Army for many years. These men were as determined to take their objective as they were to avoid the wasteful tactics of bad generalship imposed on them in earlier battles.

Among the thirty thousand Canadians who started up the hill at 5.30 a.m. on April 9th, was at least a company of ex-members of the Victoria Bantams. One platoon was attached to the 7th (B.C.) Battalion which picked its way through the forward trenches guided by stakes daubed with luminous paint.

"I remember the hundreds of dead horses which lay everywhere in front of our jump-off position," said Allan Bell. "There was heavy wet snow falling so we could not see well, and kept falling over the poor beasts' carcasses. We had practiced the attack time and again and now we were doing the real thing it was hard to believe it. Then the German counter-fire started and there were no more doubts. We were not wearing our greatcoats, but the minute the shells began to fall, I felt actually hot all over and did not notice the cold all during the fight."

T3 - N

As Bell said, this was an attack which had been planned with a thoroughness rare in Great War battles. Aerial photography, trench models, and practiced assaults had prepared the Canadians well. Even more unusual, the attack itself was pressed forward with clockwork precision, and the men found themselves taking one objective after another exactly as planned. The hill was divided into Black Line, Red, Blue, and Brown Line, matching stages in the enemy trench systems.

Bell's section saw little of the enemy until the Red Line was reached. "We got rid of our bombs into some dug-outs there, when Heinie refused to surrender. None of our guys had ever fired a shot in anger before, yet there we were coolly shooting at men as if it was a gallery in a fairground."

The 7th Battalion rolled past the Kiegel Stellung, leaving a party of sharpshooters to watch tunnel-mouths. Too many Canadians had died before in battle from eagerness in over-running enemy machine-gun crews who arose to shoot them in the back. By 6.45, the 1st Division had got in amongst the Bavarians, driving them back beyond La Folie Farm. All along the line it was the same, a relentless, steady advance through the blizzard that rolled the Germans back off the hogback ridge like a flayed animal's skin.

The Bantams tried to stay together, watching each other's fortunes. When a machine gun ripped through their ranks, the dead and wounded received prompt attention from comrades, while others fanned out for vengeance. "We went after that gun with our blood up," said Allan Bell. "We fired and fired our rifles in a volley so they had to keep their heads down. A lucky bomb killed two of the crew and the third one stood up to surrender. It didn't do him much good. We left the crew all dead. Funny thing was, each one of them was an officer."

By 7.30, the 3rd Division had reached Brown Line, the crest of Hill 145, and the entire ridge was in Canadian hands by 9 o'clock. For the battalion including the Bantams, the fight went on for hours more, as they helped mop up groups of Germans who held out until killed or captured. "The idea was to refortify the trenches at the top," recalled Allan Bell. "So when we finally got up there, I was handed a shovel and told to lower the parapet's back wall, to face it the other way. The sun came out late that afternoon and you could see far down, where the enemy were running away below. Some of our men tried pitching grenades onto them, but the bombs went off long before they could do any damage."

As reinforcements settled in to the splendidly-built fortifications, German dominance of the Douai Plane was ended. More significantly, the victory that day gave the Dominion its final step towards nationhood. So it was on April 9th, 1917; three thousand five hundred and ninety-eight men of the Maple Leaf died while an independent Canada was born on Vimy Ridge. A few years later after the war, the crest of Hill 145 was ceded in perpetuity by France to Canada, a shrine to more than valour.

Meanwhile, the remaining Victorian troops were sent for toughening up at a battle school prior to service as infantry in France. In early May, Ben Barnes wrote of the "quite hard training they put us through here at Shorncliffe. But we all have been picked for different drafts and are having final inspections, so we shall be going at any time. We are not sorry, as we came over here to do our bit and cannot stand this hanging around. We all feel very good, and expect to make a name out there."

Barnes was among a draft of six hundred and sixty-seven men from the B.C. Bantam Battalion which went to the 24th Canadian Reserve Battalion in France on May 11th, 1917. Barnes' group was joined by Alex Batchelor and other Toronto Bantams who were immediately thrown into the hideous meatgrinder that was the Battle of Lens.

This affair was yet another brain-wave of Field Marshal Haig, who despite having earned a nickname of "The

Butcher" was still kept on as British commander-in-chief. The more impatient French had thrown out the briefly-hailed Nivelle and replaced him with General Petain, fresh from the bloodbath of Verdun. Haig did not like his new opposite number and expected little aid from the now-demoralized French Army, so he decided to increase British pressure on the Flanders front. As part of this grand strategy, he threw the Canadian Corps against Lens as their first objective.

The Canadians surveyed the black slag heaps, the broken, churned graveyard of so many troops before them and were not inspired. "If we have to fight there at all," said General Currie who now commanded the Corps, "Let us fight for something worth having." His eyes were on the country beyond; why not try to sidetrack Lens and Hill 70 and burst into open mobile warfare? But Haig was adamant. Lens had to be taken by assault.

On August 15th, the Canadians took Hill 70; little more than a low mound, really, but riddled with concrete pill-boxes and concealed artillery. In a single morning, they captured the hill which had defeated the British Guards Division in 1915, and pushed on through the smoke and poison gas and shrapnel into the mining hamlets on the outskirts of Lens itself. The ruined suburbs, called cités – St. Emilie, St. Pierre, Calonne – were made up of clumps of miners' cottages and pithead workings, and had been fortified in an interlocking maze of German defences over the past two years.

All Lens was like that – street after street of rubbled buildings hiding blockhouses and m.g. posts interconnected by miles of passageways knocked through cellar walls. Alex Batchelor recalls an officer telling him, "Fix your bayonet soldier, we're going to have to winkle them out."

Batchelor found his small size to be an advantage during the next ten endless days and nights. "I could pop through those tunnels easy as could be, you see. We left our packs off, stripped down to undershirts and went crawling around with a bagful of bombs and a revolver. Find a hole, bung a bomb through, and then nip through after it before the dust settled. After a while, I could tell if no bomb was needed in the next cellar. The smell would tell me when the Heinies had been dead in there for a time."

Allan Bell fought here too, attaching himself to some Nova Scotian machine-gunners to keep them supplied with ammunition. He would make repeated trips back through the hellish streets, casually employing his Lee Enfield on stray Prussians who tried to stop him. On one such journey, he stopped to aid the wounded Humbert Campbell, the English clergyman's son he first met an age ago on a British Columbian ferry.

Street by street, the 4th Prussian Guards were forced back, dying hard for every cellar and crossroad. On the third day, reinforcements came in; two more Guards Divisions, the 11th Reserve, and the Saxon Brigade, until there were forty-six German battalions battling to keep the Canadians from capturing the battered compost-heap that used to be Lens.

Ben Barnes told a little of this to the folks at home. "Had a busy time of it," he wrote in his flawless copperplate on Y.M.C.A. stationery, "but we all went forward and accomplished our objective. It was mostly all street fighting and we worked hard for protection from gunfire. When we got settled in our new ground, Fritz did not give us much rest as he had our range down pretty fair.

"He tried to come back but we were always ready. We had quite a few casualties but not so bad. We are all very thankful to God for his protection as we had no time to think what would come next. I had a very close shave with his heavy high explosives. They nearly split your head when they came anywhere near your trench. There were three of our old band boys wounded and sent back to Blighty.

"I saw some of my old chums fall and it only gave me more grit to dash ahead, and believe me there was not a man but who was anxious to get a score. We took quite a few prisoners and they told us that the Canadians were a hard class of men to fight. Little do they think that the majority of us here in my outfit are Englishmen.

"We are resting for a short time after some hot street-fighting in the ruins. We even went quite ahead of our objective to make sure we had cleared them up good. Our officers acted well and we got pretty fair treatment. It was one of the biggest affairs that has been pulled off by us.

"The Bantams certainly made a name for themselves this time. We are all of British stock here and fight with British spirit, and the Canadian Bantams are not going back without a name worthy of being set down in history for future generations to take notice."

He was never to know the eventual irony of those words he wrote on the battlefield, minutes after being in close combat. Yet the belief sustained this modest, dedicated soldier, whose letters were filled with loving messages for nephews and nieces he had met only for a few precious days. Though he had already seen so many friends cut down six thousand miles from homes they left in beautiful British Columbia, he retained his generation's simple faith in posterity's appreciation. It was a faith which sustained so many men through that last bitter winter of the Great War. For Barnes, and for most of his comrades in the platoon, time was running out.

During the next few months, they were in constant action — now a wild-eyed crew of trained killers whose steady drain of casualties only served to hone the survivors' skill at their dreadful trade. From the letters written home, it seems they seldom knew exactly where they were, dully accepting higher authority's orders which flung them here and there along the desperate front line.

In October, the Canadians went north to Flanders again, summoned there to help break the deadlock on a vile, mad place called Passchendaele. Though the General Staff's neat, colourful maps of this region in the Ypres Salient showed green patches of woodlands surrounding a quaint little village, all that existed now was a desolate swamp of shell-pocked mud, stinking with high explosives and the ripe putrefaction of four hundred thousand dead. For four months, British and Australian and New Zealander regiments had been plunged into this foul mire, losing whole battalions in a matter of days. Now it was the Canadian's turn.

Torrential rain mingled with the sleet of steel and lead from German guns when the Canadians went forward on October 26th. There was no cover available – no trenches could be dug there, and to lie down was to invite suffocation in minutes – so they waded forward at a painfully slow walk. "We just chucked everything away but rifles and ammunition," said John Taylor. "It was a hard job on to even walk fast, let alone run, so we lost a lot of men from the shelling and sniper on the way across. But when we finally got to grips with Heinie, well we paid them back in kind."

The site of what had once been the village of Passchendaele was on top of a low ridge, and the key to its capture was the Belleview slope. All along it, was a string of concrete block-houses which had directed machine-gun fire to cut down every previous attack. The Canadians concentrated here, knocking out the pill-boxes one by one, and by late afternoon they had a toehold. At dusk they set about reforming, sending down their wounded and even sending troops to relieve the New Zealanders nearby.

George Marr was an infantryman with the 4th Battalion of the New Zealander Division that held Abraham Heights since taking it by storm three weeks before. "We were successful in taking the strongpoint, after some fierce fighting and losing a good number of killed and wounded on both sides," he recalls. "After digging in just down from the top of the ridge, we held out for days. One night at dusk, our relief arrived, and at first glance I honestly thought that they were just young boys. When I got a better look, I marvelled that they were really the small Bantam soldiers we'd heard of.

"One of them was sent to take over my possie in a shell-hole. I said in a joking way, "Those fellows out in front of us are a pretty tough lot, Tommy." His reply was simple and to the point. "We'll fix the bastards, don't worry, chum!"

After four days of desperate fighting, the Canadian 3rd and 4th Divisions managed to cross the Ravelbeekstream, storm the ruins of Meetscheele village and take the high ground at Crest Farm. They held on there and opened the way for the final assault by the 1st and 2nd Divisions to attack during a violent gale and rainstorm, capturing Passchendaele at last on November 6th, 1917.

The day after the battle ended, Sir Launcelot Kiggell, the chief of staff, arrived to take his first look at the battle zone. When his Daimler limousine began to lurch through the mud, the general stared out unbelievingly at the endless quagmire, then burst into tears. "My God!" he moaned. "Did we send men to fight in this?"

One of the men who had was Benjamin Barnes. On October 29th, during a lull, he wrote home in despair. "Moved to another area after quite a long journey. Had a busy time of it for eight straight days and nights. I am sorry to say that my pal Alf Patterson got napooed * yesterday. He got hit with one of Heinie's high-explosives. He was on an M.G. and 3 of his 5-man crew were hit. I had many narrow escapes myself. Two men were in a dug-out and a heavy came over and killed the man by my side. Another time, one burst outside the dug-out, buried 3 of us — one blinded, one wounded, and all I got was shock. When I came out and heard about Alf it brought tears to my eyes. I have the painful duty of writing to his aunt in Cumberland . . . Kindly excuse scribble as I am quite upset. Au-re-voir."

Fresh replacements were getting scarcer every month for the embattled Canadian Army, and veteran troops of any kind were kept in the line until death or a lucky Blighty-one

---

* Killed.

released them. Barnes managed to get letters home past the indulgent censorship of his officers, telling that "Not many of the originals are left now." On January 22nd, 1918, he wrote, "In trenches. If we did not get our rum ration, we would be laid up very often, as we are subject to wet feet and chills all through our system. Disappointed at no leave; anxiously awaiting a square deal, as we can't see why we have not had it yet. There are quite a few of the boys had their leave who have not been in the line so much as your humble servant."

There were only a couple of more letters from Ben Barnes that spring, in which he made no further mention of warfare, other than the address, "In trenches." He poured out a stream of suggestions about how to make his nieces and nephew happy, and sent them what small amounts of money he could afford.

His last letter from the front was devoted to this same theme, "Whenever you feel like making up a parcel for me, fix things fine, then let the children have a party of their own and enjoy its contents. I know you are kindhearted, but rationed in England, and I would be the last one to see those dear little ones go short for my sake. Not much time to write. Continually on the alert. We last Bantams are in a Battle Platoon, so we are not here as ornaments."

A week later, he heard his C.O. read out a commendation for his gallantry in rescuing a wounded comrade. The same day, August 11th, 1918, Ben Barnes' luck finally ran out, and he was killed in an obscure skirmish near Amiens.

Chapter Ten

Along Death Way

The wet streets of Amiens teemed with British and Dominion soldiers as they roamed in search of diversion from thoughts of what they must soon face under the guns which boomed less than fifteen kilometres away. A shilling a day paid by a grateful British government did not buy much, and Tommies enviously noted the greater number of dollar-a-day Canadians and Anzacs who had girls on their arms. But there was little to spend their meagre pay on in the line, so survivors arrived with pockets relatively full after the enforced savings, eager for a few hours of relaxation.

Two years later, the Germans would push back the Allies and occupy this area; but now, in mid-1916, Amiens was a boom-town, the nearest that most non-commissioned men ever got to the storied fleshpots of Gay Paree. Even junior officers seldom reached the French capital, but took their leave in Amiens, where they were well served by certain "officers' houses" identified by discreet blue lamps, and by dozens of elegant establishments such as Godbert's Restaurant (which prospered so well that it stayed in business for another forty years). The only places open to the troops were either drab canteens serving "char and wads" – weak tea and tasteless buns – or riotous bars, cafes, and bordellos.

One of these places, known as Estaminet Caze's, was popular with the Bantams who had recently moved over to this sector of the front. The place provided a variety of rough entertainments. At the side door, a bold red lamp advertised the services available upstairs, and cast a warm glow on the pale faces of soldiers who stood in a long line to shuffle slowly forward in turn.

However, the majority of soldiers did not frequent the *poules*. The youths and men in khaki were only a few months away from their own largely respectable homes, where their upbringing instilled a morality which shrank from prostitution even after the brutalization of trench life. For them, a night of boozing was desperate enough. They jammed the bar downstairs, to swill beer or "van rooge" and blot out hideous images.

Singing and drunken laughter filled the smoke-laden barroom of Caze's one memorable night in July. Standing at the zinc counter then was Victor Lill. Near him was Second Lieutenant William "Titch" Cook, of the Lancashire Fusiliers, who had donned an elisted man's tunic so as to be able to drink with his troops.

Two years before, Lieutenant Cook had been selling newspapers aboard a Mersey ferry. He had walked off the boat at Liverpool with a group of would-be volunteers and successfully enlisted in the Bantams, despite a cherubic choirboy look and an actual age of sixteen. After reaching the rank of sergeant, he was awarded the Distinguished Conduct Medal, and gained a battlefield commission. Despite this, he remained unaffected and had a democratic way with his men which horrified more haughty superiors.

A buxom barmaid peered at his shoulder-flash of a red rooster and expertly identified the 35th Division. Having overheard his men address him as "Sir," she remarked, "Your officers are very small." "Yes, Madam," Titch replied gravely, "But we have big privates."

His words brought down the house in a bellow of laughter and became the Division's favourite joke forever after.

"It might seem like a hoary old tale now," said Mr. Lill,

"But at that time we had precious little to laugh about, and an officer who would crack any kind of a joke with us was rare indeed."*

After assembly at Doullens, the Division had been moved to a new sector of the line, running north from the riverbank at Moulin Fargny, up through Maricourt Wood to the edge of German-held Guillemont. This was the lower end of the bloodiest ground in British Army experience, where sixty thousand of its men had fallen in a single morning on July 1st, 1916 – opening day of the Battle of the Somme.

Throughout history, the River Somme has provided a military defence line. A glance at a map of northern France shows that it is one of a number of rivers which slice the landscape inwards from the seacoast, protecting Artois and Picardy. At the apex of these natural barriers lies the ancient fortified town of Doullens, said to trace its name from *vallum dolens,* "vale of sorrow," because of its long-suffering guardianship of the Authie defence line. Germanic tribes, Roman legions, and the Spaniards rampaged here, and the Somme also had an eerily repeated link with British armies over the centuries. In 1346, the English victory at Crecy was as much credited to King Edward III's cunning deployment of his forces in Maye ravine near the Somme as to the skill of his archers.

Seventy years later, Henry V led another invasion, and again it was the Somme that acted as the French defence line, which had to be forded before the English could win at Agincourt. Now, in 1916, the river formed the British main bastion. The much-vaunted "breakthrough" of early July had withered under German machine-guns and settled down to a series of wasteful attacks which would last until late autumn.

The 35th (Bantam) Division had inherited French trenches which were in bad repair and contained fearsome momentoes of battle. One officer wrote in the war diary, "Trenches full of liquid mud. Smell horrible. Floors and walls contain many

---

* Lt. Cook went on to serve with the Burma Rifles between the wars. He disappeared in the jungle while fighting the Japanese invasion in January, 1942.

dead Frenchmen, too bad to touch. Our men quite nauseated." Other war diaries tell the same story, "Clay, muck, and mud rather bad here. Men have to pull each other along to walk. If you stand still, you sink, and have to be hauled free with horrible sucking noises. To be wounded, is certain to die in the mire."

Having to struggle to even walk through such cloying mud made the crushing load of standard issue equipment bad enough when piled on soldiers of average height. When carried by Bantams, it became almost grotesque, making them look like moving mounds of luggage. Before the 15th Cheshires left for France, Lt. Colonel Harrison Johnston recorded, "Paraded with everybody in full kit with all our Christmas Tree decorations on. As we officers are only allowed to take one valise weighing thirty-five pounds, we all took as much as possible on our persons. Luckily, being mounted, my pack was on my horse. The men's total weight of stuff including packs, clothing, rifle, and one hundred and twenty rounds of ammunition each, averaged seventy pounds. The men's weight, stripped, averaged one hundred and twenty pounds. Yesterday, we weighed several as a test."

Though such a load bore heavily on those men who had joined straight from school or from sedentary occupations, it was generally accepted that Bantams should be treated the same as other troops. J. J. Hutchinson maintains, "Our equipment and Lee Enfield rifles were no trouble to us at all, and we carried the same weight of pack as any other regiment on the Western Front.

"Today, a lot of people must think that the Bantams were a bunch of little Boy Scouts. Well, we had miners, shipyard men, men who worked in the lead works carrying heavy metal all day, and bakery workers used to carrying two-hundred-weight sacks of flour, and we also had some pretty sturdy dock workers from Liverpool and Birkenhead. None of these men were exactly weak."

It is difficult today to trace the adventures of Bantam units during the summer of 1916, because the 35th Division was seldom used as a complete unit during its service on the Somme. Brigades, battalions, even companies and platoons were broken up in penny packets for work anywhere they were needed along the front.

Two such units were the 15th Sherwood Foresters and the 16th Cheshires who were sent to a sector northeast of Maricourt. Moving up at night, they made their way through the maze of trenches which straggled in all directions to no particular plan. Hastily dug in minutes for dire convenience, the trenches would be later reinforced and finished until they were accepted as permanent. As thoroughfares, some trenches bore names which commemorated their original inhabitants, like Scottish Trench and Cornish Alley. Others echoed past tragedies like Deadman's Ditch and Machine Gun Alley, while more flippant others were Beer, Hops, and Pint Alleys.

The Sherwoods took over Maltz Horn Trench, relieving a badly-punished regiment. "On July 14th, we are rushed to the front line," writes J. E. Taylor, who had just that day returned from sick-leave in England. "Some of Y Company are in Trones Wood and Z Company is in the chalk trenches. Just outside the wood, 16 Platoon of Z Company join up with the French soldiers who are on our right. In a short communications trench are the Signals Officer, Mr. Dexter, and three signallers, including myself. On entering the trench at dawn, my eyes are gazing into those of a dead soldier, his body leaning over the top of the trench. On his tunic shoulder is the name Buffs, the battalion here before we took over."

A new draft of Cheshire Bantams arrived in time for the battle. One of them was Nelson Spencer. "Silently that night we followed our guide into the trenches, unaware we were about to be baptized by fire. Indeed this night soon proved to be a horror. No sooner had I spoken to my new platoon officer, the darkness was split by the multiple explosions of Hun rapid fire. One shell burst on the left of this officer, with me to his right. Both of us were blown over a sunken road into a field. The officer was found dead and I was taken unconscious to a field hospital for ten days. Later I realized that the officer killed was a business acquaintance of mine in civilian life."

The Cheshires travelled along Chimpanzee Trench in chaotic conditions. Somehow, the unit managed to arrive at dawn more or less intact. Two platoons which had scattered down side trenches during a bombardment were reunited with the rest of their comrades in time for "stand-to" around four o'clock in the morning.

As the darkness faded, the Bantams looked across the short desolation of No-Man's-Land towards their objectives. Straight ahead was a low mound of bricks and rubble which marked the site of Waterlot Farm, a strongpoint which had repeatedly changed hands. Far to the left lay the pulverized village of Guillemont, which the Germans had stubbornly held against a score of attacks to dislodge them. A sunken road called "Death Way" led to the village through the stumps of shattered trees – daring more British troops to join the numberless others who had been slaughtered there.

"Death Way" was now no more than a churned mud track, pitted with countless shellholes, and flanked by limbless poles which once had been luxuriant trees. The wrecks of wheeled transport were strewn along the road, attesting to the accurate ranging of the Germans. Wafting along the track was the stench of unburied men, and dead horses and mules, hundreds of whose bloated, stiff-legged carcasses lay beside the wagons.

This was the hazardous route taken by "W" Company of the 16th Cheshires when they advanced to relieve the Cameron Highlanders at Waterlot Farm. The position was a pulverized heap of bricks which once had been a historic* old building typical of fortified farmhouses in the area. Now it was so

---

* From here had originated the Royal Academy painter famed under his Anglicized name, Sir Ernest Waterlow.

flat and pitted with muddy shellholes that it made an ideal defensive site for infantry wanting a commanding view of the German trenches between Delville Wood and Guillemont.

The company moved out shortly after midnight on July 17th, 1916, groping their way through flame-stabbed darkness. At dawn, the men were able to begin shoring up the broken trench walls and prepare for visitors. Their commanding officer, Lieutenant H. D. Ryalls set out with 2nd Lt. R. MacLaren to see if the Camerons could be somehow withdrawn despite the bombardment.

In minutes, Lt. MacLaren was mortally wounded and the isolated Camerons lay pinned down under intensified shellfire. The Cheshire's own position was in danger also as shellfire boxed them in and strong parties of the enemy were spotted darting forward along the deep railway cutting leading from Guillemont Station.

Ryalls sent Private Hoare back to Battalion H.Q. with an urgent request for reinforcements. Lt. Colonel Johnston tells why they could not be sent. "We got a request from our brother Battalion (the 16th) to send them two Companies as reinforcements, but as they were in one Brigade and we in another this was impossible.

"Furthermore, we were each holding a wood, they run parallel, with instructions to hold it to the last man. If we sent two Companies, we could not be sure of doing our job — fact, we couldn't risk it.

"The wires were all cut and we could not get Brigade except by messages carried along a heavily shelled road by runners. Requests came from the same source for ammunition and bombs. The large dump had been cleared during the afternoon and we had few to spare, but we fished round and sent them all we could — about 20,000 S.A.A. and some bombs."

The hard-pressed Ryalls sent a Lewis gun team to a brick wall south of the farm to hold off the advancing German infantry. A hand-to-hand fight raged here until the enemy

5.   Poet Isaac Rosenberg returned from South Africa to serve in the King's Own. Killed in 1918, his work has steadily gained popularity in recent years.

6. Far British Columbia raised a Bantam battalion despite poaching of volunteers by other regiments. Lt. Robert Ely led this company, which included 46-year-old Joseph Daniel (extreme right, second row) who eventually served with the Railway Troops in France in spite of age and

7. Welsh Bantams included many sturdy miners who were often employed between battles in carrying up supplies to the front line. Note the covers over rifle muzzles and

8. The war is over for this wounded Bantam and for the helpful German prisoner he is escorting back to the POW cage behind the British line on the Somme, Summer 1916.
(Photo: Imperial War Museum.)

was thrown back. They were observed to join up with about three hundred Germans who came forward pulling two Maxims on sleds. The plucky Private Hoare went off with another request for help, while the Cheshires attacked as best they could.

Private Harry Barlow was the sole survivor of a six-man Lewis gun team. He picked up the weapon, which had a shattered butt, and two pan magazines. As the forward slope was under direct fire from the enemy, he crawled on hands and knees across it until he reached the crest. A methodical man, Barlow tapped out three-shot bursts at each of an enemy rifle squad in turn. He had knocked over all but four of the Germans when a sniper killed him with a shot between his shoulder blades.

This time, Colonel Browne-Clayton was able to send help. It arrived in the form of a Vickers gun team led by Lieutenant G. Frazer of the Machine Gun Corps. The team set up in a shellhole west of the farm and began to drop harrassing fire among the attackers. The Germans fell back and made no more advances from the south.

Then, right in front of the farm, an entire battalion of the enemy suddenly rose up from a trench whence they had infiltrated from Delville Wood. The Germans charged in six rows, over nine hundred determined opponents to the one hundred-odd Cheshires. It was high time for the company to spring their one ace in the hole.

An apparently wrecked trench had been secretly occupied by two platoons against this very eventuality. They were commanded by 2nd Lieutenant R. B. Schofield, who waited until the last minute before he ordered his riflemen and two concealed Lewis gunners to open fire at almost point-blank range.

The fat Lewis barrels spat .303 bullets at 550 r.p.m. into the packed target, and miraculously did not jam at the crucial moment, as they were often prone to do. The l.m.g fire was so devastating against the close ranks that the attackers fled, leaving many casualties.

The fight for Waterlot Farm was costly to the Bantams, too. At the moment of triumph, 2nd Lt. Schofield was fatally wounded, and lieutenants MacLaren and A. C. Styles were already dead, along with thirty-two other ranks. Other casualties were one hundred and ninety-four wounded and seven missing presumed dead. Before the survivors went into rest, Colonel Clayton called Lieutenant Ryalls in front of the battalion, thanked him, and announced his immediate award of the Distinguished Service Order.

Next morning, it was the Sherwood's turn. General Pinney showed his redoubtable style by coming forward to Brigade Headquarters in Stanley's Hole, "an evil-smelling dug-out" only four hundred yards from Maricourt. He personally gave the orders that the 105 Brigade should regroup and go forward to capture the German trenches between Arrowhead Copse and Maltz Horn Farm.

The attack was scheduled for next morning, June 20th, so the job was handed to the 15th Sherwood Foresters who occupied trenches right opposite Pinney's objective. They had only a few hours to prepare, and so things rapidly began to go wrong. There was no clear observation available for artillery support, and storming parties had to go out in two separate groups. This pronged attack was dictated by the one thousand-yard wide target which was really too extended for assault by a single battalion. The rushed plan was to lay down the best artillery support to be managed under blind conditions and to have the infantry attack the far ends of the enemy trench then bomb their way towards each other.

Shaky as these arrangements were, matters worsened when Major Cochran reported that the Sherwoods were in no shape for an attack even under the best of circumstances. They had been under direct shellfire for two days and had been wearing gas masks all day in trenches drenched with phosgene. He could recommend only two companies for the operation. As a result, two companies of the 23rd

Manchesters were brought up the line to help, and the attack went forward at 5.00 a.m., June 20th.

They didn't have a chance. Sunrise limned the troops, perfect targets for Spandaus and many fell before they got across No-Man's-Land. The Manchesters did penetrate the enemy line but were quickly driven out into shell-swept open ground. What was left of them straggled back to their own trenches.

The right hook of the attack went in anyway, launched at 10.45 a.m. Manchesters and Sherwood Foresters rose up from their parapets into the steel teeth of German machine guns which had been waiting expectantly. One entire company of Mancurian late-arrivals literally ran down the communication trenches and carried on straight over the top into the attack. Their zeal stopped short at the empty fire-swept line which the Germans had prudently abandoned. An avalanche of explosives came down and the newcomers ran for their lives.

Somehow, they managed to stand firm in their own trenches and the expected German counter-attack fizzled out. Later that day, the two battalions staggered out of the line, on relief.

The 23rd Manchesters left behind nine dead officers, including Lt. Colonel E. L. Maxwell, and one hundred and sixty-two slaughtered Bantams. The 15th Sherwood Foresters, which had been shelled and gassed for four days, lost ten dead officers and thirty-nine Bantams, and carried away one hundred and forty-six wounded. Another thirty-six were missing, presumed dead.

General Pinney received a letter next day from General Magnan of the French 153rd Division. He congratulated the courage of the 23rd Manchesters whom he had witnessed advancing "as if on parade" against heavy fire. It was a panache the 35th could ill-afford. There were frighteningly fewer Bantams every day and their reservoir of fit replacements was drying up fast.

The 104th Brigade had remained intact as a unit and found much to occupy its Lancashire grit, any deviance from which received short shrift.

"I found myself sharing a shellhole at Guillemont with several lads," says Frank Heath. "We were all afraid, but the youngster the French girls called "Piccanini" completely lost his nerve. Sergeant Pregnall brought over Captain Crooks who said, "What's the matter with you, Felton?" The boy lay in the bottom of the hole and sobbed, "I have heart failure." The Captain said, "If you don't stand up, my boot will give you arse-failure!" It had the desired effect immediately."

This happened at dawn on July 22nd, when the 18th Lancashire Fusiliers were withdrawing from an ill-planned attack which had begun at 1.30 a.m. Brigade Headquarters was then in the process of moving its position, which may account for the last-minute dispatch of orders from Brigadier Sandilands for a strong raid to go forward within six hours. The 18th Lancs were to destroy wire across a five hundred-yard front to open the way for an advance against Guillemont by another regiment.

Detailed orders were not ready until midnight, with the result that the raiding parties were only in position ten minutes before the attack was set to begin. They were forced to huddle in open ground in front of the parapet, instead of in a gully as was originally intended. Their movements alerted the Germans, who sent up dozens of Very lights and star shells to illuminate their wire. Just as the Bantams began to advance, the enemy sent up red signal rockets. Their artillery responded in seconds.

"I recall thinking what a bloody silly business this was," says Ronald Marsden. "Here we were walking along as if it was broad daylight on the Promenade at Blackpool, while the Jerries were plastering us with every gun they had!"

The raiders went forward in two columns, five hundred yards apart, hoping to destroy wire across as wide a front as possible. The right-hand column was under heavy fire from the start and suffered their first setback when the Bangalore torpedo was touched off. This long explosive-filled pipe had been intended to blow a gap in the wire, now it was gone, along with the two soldiers carrying it. Soon, the column was forced to retire.

Marsden was with the left-hand column, which got into the German front line and bombed its way back into the support trenches. They settled down to hold the position, hoping to aid the expected follow-up attack, though in fact this did not arrive. Although wounded, Lieutenant M. R. Wood retained active leadership and kept his platoon together as a fighting unit. They set up two Lewis guns on each side of a shellhole and continuously engaged the enemy for five hours.

After inflicting numerous casualties and breaking up a counter-attack, Lt. Wood and Corporal A. Pattie began to collect their wounded. They fought their way out through a ring of enemies and returned to their own lines in mid-morning. Their losses were ten killed and ten wounded. Cpl. Pattie received the Distinguished Conduct Medal for his bravery in dressing wounded men under shellfire and carrying six of them to safety. Lieutenant Wood was awarded the Military Cross for his leadership.

All three Lancashire Bantam battalions endured heavy shellfire during the next week, with little opportunity to hit back. Then on July 25th, they sent up companies to prolong the line at the Eastern end of Trones Wood, under the command of Captain R. A. S. Coke.

"When we went to help at Trones Wood, we found the front line was just a jumble of shell holes under heavy German gunfire," recalls Fusilier Heath. "What a sight! mangled bodies, arms and legs and bits and pieces everywhere, and about a hundred and fifty Royal West Kents lying dead in No-Man's-Land. While coming along the wrecked communications trench, we passed an officer carrying a soldier on his back. The soldier's leg was hanging almost severed at the knee. Somebody said, "The poor devil," The wounded man heard and said, "There are dozens up there worse off than me." We tried, but the fire was so heavy it was impossible to bring in the dead and wounded lying beyond the front line."

The enemy saw this activity as being the prelude to an attack and laid down a heavy bombardment of high explosive and gas. "You could always tell a gas shell by the funny 'gobble-gobble' noise it made," remarked Ronald Marsden. The troops had to dig their own new trenches as the perfectly-registered German artillery destroyed the front line within an hour. Not for the first time, the miner's skill of many Bantams was the difference between life and death and freshly-dug earth flew to give them sanctuary.

"At Trones Wood, I did a foolish thing," explained Fusilier Heath. "We had been without water for twenty-four hours, and I spotted that a few yards from our position was an iron lattice gantry with a round tank on top. Hoping there might be some rain water in it, I climbed up the girders. Right away, bullets whizzed around me and punched loudly through the tank. I didn't climb down, I fell down, trembling at my lucky escape."

Captain Coke was unearthed from a destroyed trench which had temporarily buried him, and he proceeded to organize rescue parties to dig out the other men. He devotedly dressed wounds of his troops, and occasionally noted down the last messages of dying men. When his company was relieved thirty hours later, he had been awake at his post the entire time although badly wounded by a shell-splinter. His men heartily approved of his subsequent award of the Military Cross.

The 104th Brigade was thankfully ordered into rest on August 1st, a suitably appropriate date. They paraded in the miscalled "Happy Valley" near Bray-sur-Somme with other units of the Lancashire Fusiliers for a combined Minden

Day Parade. This event goes back to 1759, when the regiment marched forward 'at beat of drum' across Minden Heath to Hanover, against massed French artillery and cavalry. As they passed among the wild rose briars, Lancashiremen snatched up blossoms and stuck them in their hats. Thus bedecked, they plodded forward, delivering musket volleys that cleared their way to victory. Ever since, the regiment has celebrated the event wherever they are stationed.

This time, someone saw to it that enough roses were available to enable three battalions to wear them on their steel helmets for Minden Day, 1916. The troops were reviewed by Brigadier J. W. Sandilands, who read a message to the 35th (Bantam) Division from Major General Shea, G.O.C. 30th Division: — "In the name of my division, I wish to thank you and yours most sincerely for all you did for us. You gave us all help you could, and it is our earnest hope that someday we may be able to repay you. We much deplore your losses, but will always remember the gallantry of your men."

The troops took more comfort in being given a real rest behind the lines at last without the expectation of carrying supplies up the line each night. They were moved to Corbie, a quiet spot untouched by war, at a junction of the Somme and Ancre Rivers. Glorious hot weather encouraged the men to enjoy bathing naked in the river below the beautiful old town, under the giggling appreciative gaze of local women.

"We all went a bit mad that month. Lads who'd been too tongue-tied to say so much as "hello" to a girl before were dragging them off into the woods after five minutes acquaintance," smiles Ronald Marsden dreamily. "From all the threshing in the bushes, I'd say there must be a fair number of people with English blood in their veins around Corbie to this day!"

While the 104th Brigade unwound, the 106th was suffering a dangerous and unglamourous time along the Montauban front. The West Yorkshires, Durhams, and two Scottish battalions supplied carrying and road-building parties under heavy shellfire without being able to fight back. Some idea of their martyrdom can be gained from the brigade's fatal casualties — two officers and one hundred and eighty-three other ranks lost between the 15th and 20th July.

The 19th Durham Light Infantry took no part in attacks, being occupied with trench-building and the escort of prisoners-of-war, yet they lost twelve officers and two hundred and fifty men during the last two weeks of July. It was the same for the 17th Royal Scots and 18th H.L.I. — hard labour with all the danger and none of the stimulus of actual combat, "Lost seven men this morning to shellfire," wrote a Royal Scots officer. "We buried them within ten minutes of their death and went back to digging trenches."

The 17th West Yorkshires had a particularly bad time at Bernafay Wood. While working as burial parties and ammunition carriers, they lost seventy-one N.C.O.'s. One company paid a toll of three out of four sergeants dead in an hour. One entire platoon was reduced to one officer, a lance-corporal and six men.

The casualties of the battalion since the 13th of July was ten officers and three hundred and four other ranks, a remarkably high percentage considering their so-called "purely support role." In one operation on July 30th, it received this commendation from Brigadier H. O'Donnell: — "I consider that the O.C. of the 17th West Yorks did well in firstly proceeding himself to the front line trench at Zero Hour and, secondly, in pushing his battalion through the troops ahead of them, and occupying the front line at a time when it would otherwise have been left vacant; more especially as his battalion had, during the early hours of the morning, suffered from the effects of gas shells."

When the battered remnants of the battalion marched back for a "rest" in a wrecked trench less than one mile behind the line, they still wore the canvas hoods that passed for gas-masks but were heard to be singing in muffled tones the

Yorkshire 'anthem,' "On Ilkley Moor, Bar T'at." This was the battalion a Leeds Ph.d in military history would in 1978 dismiss as "a total failure, no more than a recruiting gimmick."

The Leeds Bantams would endure for another year and see one of their men awarded with Britain's highest award for valour. How William Boynton Butler of the 17th West Yorkshire Regiment earned his Victoria Cross was described by the London Gazette of October 17th, 1917.

"For most conspicuous bravery when in charge of a Stokes gun in trenches which were being heavily shelled: Suddenly one of the fly-off levers of a Stokes shell came off and fired the shell in the emplacement. Private Butler picked up the shell and jumped to the entrance of the emplacement, which at that moment a party of infantry were passing. He shouted to them to hurry past as the shell was going off, and turning round, placed himself between the party of men and the live shell and so held it 'till they were out of danger. He then threw the shell on to the parados, and took cover in the bottom of the trench. The shell exploded almost on leaving his hand, greatly damaging the trench. By extreme good luck, Private Butler was contused only. Undoubtedly his great presence of mind and disregard of his own life saved the lives of the officer and men in the emplacement and the party which was passing at the time."

He returned home in December 1917 to be invested with his Victoria Cross. On the day before his investiture, he travelled up to Leeds to visit his parents, but owing to a misunderstanding his parents had travelled to London already for the investiture, and this Victoria Cross hero found his house locked up and had to sit on the doorstep until some-one recognized him. He was in London on the next day,

December 5th, 1917, and was invested by HM King George V at Buckingham Palace, and returning to Leeds on December 6th, he was recognized this time by a civic reception.

If the individual Bantam persevered, the drain of casualties and strain of service was beginning to mount for the division as a whole. This was again brought out in a critical commentary following an abortive attack by the 14th Gloucesters and the 16th Cheshires on August 21st. Their brigade had suffered twenty-eight killed, two hundred and forty-four wounded, and twenty-four missing within four days. Nonetheless, the troops kept up their assaults and raids from a forward trench dug in advance of the line by the 23rd Manchesters and proudly named Bantam Trench. Shelling and gas attacks by the Germans threw back the exhausted Gloucesters who had been sent over the top despite their commanding officer's opinion that the men were in no condition to make the attempt.

The word came down from Brigade H.Q. that the enterprise had failed because short-falling British artillery had demoralized the troops and that the class of new recruits were no longer proper Bantams, but were either half-grown lads or degenerates.

General Pinney was unique in that he personally visited the trenches the following week to see for himself why a last-minute order for an attack to support the French had failed. General de Fonclare was even more understanding and wrote to Pinney "L'oeuf est dans la coque, et la victoire est dans la preparation." It was a wittily appropriate play on words to remind the Bantam's superiors that it is not always the private soldiers who cause grand military strategy to go awry.

There is no question, however, that the 35th (Bantam) Division was at this stage in trouble so far as replacements were concerned. In addition to casualties, endless punishment by artillery, fragmented employment as infantry shock-troops, and gruelling physical work in trench-building and carrying parties had worn out many of the surviving Bantams.

There seems to have been an ambivalent attitude of "work the little buggers harder" – as expressed by a Royal Engineers Lt. Colonel at Montauban – and at the same time an expectation that such outwardly cheerful troops had little need for rest out of the line. The result was steady attrition of the original men with scant official ability to provide suitable replacements.

In retrospect, it is obvious that the Bantam's problem was part of a larger malaise affecting the British Army as a whole in late 1916. Already, unsettling thoughts were being expressed. When the concerns of front-line commanders reached the calcifying levels of London-based review boards, the worthy aims of military or medical men fell into the trap of rigid categorization. At the War Office, troops were seen as "sound" or "unsound" types. The Southborough Committee, which did much good work in striving to ensure that more care would be taken with medical examination of recruits, itself oversimplified the human consequences of battle.

"We are of the opinion," reported the Committee, "that adoption of the measures we recommend would result in the admission of a much smaller percentage of recruits mentally and nervously unsuitable for military service. Such types of men are likely under the strain of war to become the subjects of varieties of hysteria and neurosis commonly called 'shellshock'."

While it is obviuosly true that nervous or unfit men make poor soldiers, even the bravest warriors could and did crack under the hideous conditions of the Western Front. No amount of earnest committees could mitigate against what the "soundest" of men faced month after month in the trenches.

The official line at the time was that shellshock (recognized as battle-fatigue in later wars) was at best "fiddlesticks," and at worst deliberate treason. Generals in comfortable chateaux would despatch orders stating that "malingerers claiming shellshock must be treated with the utmost severity." Even regimental fighting officers, compassionate in most things towards the men with whom they shared danger, felt an obligation to be stern against anyone giving in to nervousness.

"The Brigadier gave us his views of the officers and men who 'take ill' when things get hot in trenches," wrote Lt. Col. Harrison Johnston, 15th Cheshire Regiment. "I agreed with every word he said. I am truly thankful that our battalion has been so free of this 'shellshock' business, but regret that isolated cases have occurred. Revolvers will stop any men leaving in future when funk is their trouble."

During the entire four years of war, when the death penalty could be awarded for the offences of desertion and cowardice, the total number of officers and men officially executed in the entire British Army was three hundred and forty-six. Of these, eighteen men were shot for cowardice, two hundred and sixty-six were executed for desertion in the face of the enemy. Incidentally, no Bantams were among them.

Considering the millions of men involved who endured a relentless war of unsurpassed savagery, this is not a large number to fall victim to court-martial, even when taking into account the unknown total of unofficial on-the-spot executions by officers and Military Police which also took place in the trenches. This summary form of execution became euphemistically known as "being sent behind Dickie's bush," evidently a play on the name Dickebusch, a village in Flanders.

"Battle police, M.P.'s, Redcaps – the ordinary soldier regarded them as his natural enemies, more so than the Jerries," recalls Harry Hurst. "Though I was not an eye-witness, others who were told me that a few Tommies wandering behind the line did not live to face court-martial, receiving on-the-spot execution from battle-police."

Though such drastic action was fairly uncommon, the

threat of punishment was there, a nagging fear which the men had to consider whenever their nerves were close to breaking under the strain of constant warfare with little hope of rest or escape.

"The first time I saw a man on Field Punishment Number One, I couldn't believe my eyes," said Edward Scales. "A youngster of less than eighteen by the name of Barton, who had been in the thick of the fighting, disappeared soon after. When the Military Police found him, he was sent back to face Major Yatman. This officer had just arrived from India and he was very strict. "Shellshock is cowardice, and will not be tolerated!" he told us on parade.

Young Barton was the first one to be punished. We were marched in single file so we could see what to expect. The poor lad was spread-eagled across a gunwheel, his wrists and ankles tied with rope and a sign "coward" on his chest. He was kept like that in the pouring rain for hours at a time. We Bantams were all volunteers from Tyneside, and we could not understand how anybody could treat one of our own men so badly. We would never ill-treat German prisoners like that, and certainly not torture them. Yet after being marched past Barton, we were told by Major Yatman, 'He got off lightly. The next coward will face a firing squad!' We private soldiers began to wonder who our real enemies were."

A "Blighty one" – a wound serious enough to send the soldier back to England – was considered the height of good luck. Once a wounded man was seen to be in no danger of dying, the bloody recipient of a Blighty would be congratulated by his comrades and be watched enviously as he was carried away. John Hutchinson of the Cheshires laconically tells, "We went out on a big raid one night. I had a spot of bother with a Jerry. I got him with my bayonet and he got me with his rifle butt on the head. I was sent home to hospital, and when I came out I was sent back to the shipyard as I was an apprentice riveteer, and that's how I ended my days with the Bantams."

Self-inflicted wounds were a temptation to men to whom even the deliberate loss of limbs was preferable to having to endure any more torment in the front line. Pain and mutilation was less of a fear than the knowledge that "S.I.W." was a capital court-martial offence

"Not everyone was able to stand up to the conditions without cracking," points out H.L.I. Bantam survivor George Cunningham. "As the war went on and on, with a few of your mates dying every day, life in the filthy trenches seemed a purgatory, so good men would do anything to escape. One of our young officers walked around one morning saying, "I've got to get out of this." A bit later on he was found dead with his revolver still in his hand.

"Another time we were bringing up supplies at night to a stores inside a big factory. The Engineers had carefully blacked out the doors and windows, but somehow forgot to cover the glass roof. A Jerry aeroplane came over and dropped a bomb right through the roof and killed a lot of horses and men. Some of us got behind a nearby wall when the raid happened. Next thing I knew, one of my pals was moaning, holding his leg and saying he's been hit.

"You couldn't have been" I said. 'We were safe behind the wall.' But I pulled up his leg and found a ragged hole right through his calf. I knew right away what he'd done. He'd fired through a sandbag into his own leg. "You crafty bugger," I said. "You've finally given yourself a Blighty one."

"We got him away to an Aid Station and I kept my mouth shut about it when he was sent home as wounded. But that same night, I threw away the special bullet he'd asked me to keep for him a few days before. He had made a Blighty-round — by taking out the bullet and sticking pieces of shrapnel into the cartridge. I didn't want to be caught with it, as having a doctored round was a court-martial offence."

For the Great War private soldiers serving in the line, there was little prospect of the relief of home leave. They stayed there continuously for months on end, even years, in a grinding routine of six or eight days in the trenches, a week in reserve, and another week of rear-line labour. The unofficial period between leaves for the troops was about twelve months, but as the average life expectancy was six months at the most for front-line troops, the only relief to look forward to was a lucky "Blighty-one" — a disabling wound or serious illness — or death itself.

No consideration for length of active service was given to soldiers, even after being sent back wounded. As soon as they recovered, they were sent back to France again, reducing their statistical odds of survival even more.

One Gloster Bantam tells of the fear-laden atmosphere aboard the boat trains carrying once-wounded troops back to France. "It was all smiles and laughter at the railway station in London, as men wanted to keep loved ones from feeling too bad," recalls Graham Ormsby. "But once the kisses stopped being blown and the train pulled out, a terrible quiet fell over the carriage I was in. You could tell from the songs and skylarking where the first-time soldiers were sitting. We old sweats — I was twenty at the time — knew what we were going back to and we were scared to death. The best song we could raise was,

> Send out the Army and the Navy
> Send out the rank and file
> Send out the brave old Territorial
> They face all danger with a smile
> Send out my Mother and my Father,
>   my brother and my sister
> — But for Christ sake, don't send me!"

In Ormsby's case at least, he was saved from repeating his ordeal by what seemed a miraculous whim that suddenly whisked him into an atmosphere of glittering luxury far from the filthy realities of the common soldier's experience.

"When I was getting off the boat at Boulogne, I was all spiffed up with shiny boots and a beautifully pressed new uniform. My mother and sisters had even tailored the jacket and trousers so they actually fitted me, instead of looking like potato sacks. Anyway, I was marching along the docks, saluting like an idiot every few seconds because there were so many officers there. One of them stopped me, asked my name, and complimented me on my appearance. Then he turned and called out to another, "Major, here's a smart-looking little chap. Just the ticket for the mess!" Next thing I knew, I was in the back of a motor lorry on my way to base headquarters to start work as a waiter. I just couldn't believe my luck!"

Ormsby's delight at being saved from returning to the front line was tinged with fear that the sudden transfer would be countermanded by his regiment. "I daren't mention it to anybody, in case they changed their minds. But I needn't have worried, because when I arrived at H.Q. I found out that they could get away with anything they wanted, including taking squaddies off front line drafts!"

"I'll never forget how different it all was there in the senior officers' mess – like one of those smart West End clubs you saw pictures of; all lights and chandeliers and music and officers laughing and drinking, even French waitresses in little white aprons, and silverware on snowy tablecloths. No wonder the General Staff never understood what the war in the trenches was really like. It was like paradise after what I'd expected to go back to.

"I thought about my mates on the draft who'd be settling in at that very minute to face mud and rats and shelling, and I felt guilty to be missing it – but not much!"

Few of his comrades in the 35th would have begrudged his luck in avoiding return to the Somme. The three brigades had each suffered a high turnover of men from casualties and illness throughout their first nine months of service. This was, of course, a common-enough experience for all front-line units during the First World War, when an average of four thousand men died every single day. But the problem was worsened for Bantam battalions in that their replacements were required to conform to set standards of height and chest measurement.

Divisional medical officers were by now so concerned at the low quality of replacements that they recommended the division should evacuate back to the depots every man of poor physique who had arrived in recent drafts. It was decided by G.H.Q. that though rejecting sub-standard men was a good idea, the division should wait until they had left Fourth Army and moved to their new sector.

The brigades were sent by train and bus north to the VI Corps, Sixth Army, and began to arrive at Arras during the first week of September. Here they found they would be fighting a different style of warfare. At their back was the ancient city, resting on a system of catacombs hollowed out in medieval times and which now provided safe, dry quarters during rest periods. The trenches also promised to be a great improvement over the wet ditches and precarious above-ground embrasures of the Somme. Miner-like, the Bantams set to digging, shoring, and revetting their lines, while sending out reconnaissance patrols to get to know the territory.

Very little was seen of the Germans, despite the closeness of their lines. The opposing troops were believed to also be recent veterans of the fierce fighting on the Somme. They contented themselves with continual trench-mortar fire but otherwise showed a marked preference for a quiet life. The feisty Bantams resolved to change this condition as soon as possible.

Chapter Eleven

The Bells of Hell

The troops of those days were fond of singing, and what they lacked in technique they made up for in lusty volume. Born in a less sophisticated time than today, they had few entertainments other than those they provided themselves. This may be the main reason why they now seem to us to have been so relentlessly cheerful; marching into battle with songs on their lips.

Even those of us who are barely aware that the Great War occurred at all are familiar with the lyrics of *"Tipperary"* and *"Pack Up Your Trouble."* These and a dozen other popular melodies were sung with heart-breaking buoyancy by troops under the most trying of circumstances. Less familiar to us may be one doggerel verse which the men would sing repeatedly over and over in a mind-numbing mantra against the fearful reality they endured.

"The bells of Hell go ting-a-ling-a-ling,
For you but not for me.
The angels they all sing-a-ling-a-ling,
They hold the goods for me.
O death, where is they sting-a-ling-a-ling,
O grave, thy victory?
The bells of Hell go ting-a-ling-a-ling,
For you but not for me . . . "

In early September, 1916, Lancashire Bantams were heard chanting it as the 104th Brigade swung along the slate-tinted road to Blangy, entering the trenches which would be the division's graveyard in more sense than one.

The village of Blangy was a suburb of Arras, the nodal point of their new front which stretched from Faubourg St. Sauveur below the Cambrai Road and northward to Roclincourt. The area was crisscrossed with trenches notable for being well organized in a system of named streets and avenues.

The 104th Brigade took over "I" Sector which ran up from the banks of the Scarpe and included trenches named Iceland Street, Iron, Imperial, Infantry, and Ivory Streets. Next to them, the 105th Brigade got "J" Sector with trenches named after months, centred on January Avenue. At the far north of their turf were three mine craters named Claude, Cuthbert, and Clarence. The 106th Brigade flanked them in "K" Sector, fronted by Kick, Kent, and Kate Craters and backed by a maze of derelict trenches known as The Gridiron.

While the trench improvements had been underway, there was also a number of other activities to occupy the division. In the face of more complaints about the poor quality of Bantam replacements, a series of medical inspections began to examine new men and veterans alike. These resulted in several hundred recent arrivals being sent back to Amiens as unsuitable. The rejects included men with both physical and moral defects who should never have been sent up the line in the first place. Less fortunate escapees from front line duty were those combat veterans whom authority decided were in need of "battle training and a general smartening up." They were sent to the Bull Ring.

In those days, a series of training camps had been built along the French coast south of Boulogne. The worst of these was Infantry Base Depot Number One, situated near the fishing town of Étaples, just across the bay from the fashionable resort of Le Touquet-Paris Plage. Now, Étaples is the site of one of the largest of British war cemeteries, where 11,000 men lie buried amidst lonely sandhills in a silence broken only by the scream of seagulls and the Atlantic wind. Most of them died in nearby military hospitals once so busy trying to patch up gassed and mutilated bodies brought an agonizing distance from the front lines. Also buried here are the unknown hundreds of victims of the most notorious training camp in the British Army – the Bull Ring.

Every soldier who passed through this hellish travesty of a training camp looks back on "Etaps" as being among his worst experience of the whole war. God only knows what rationale was behind its brutal treatment of soldiers, who were after all volunteers, but Étaples was staffed by screaming, bullying sadists who pounced on fresh-faced youths and bronzed old sweats alike the moment they arrived and subjected them to two weeks of unrelieved humiliation, abuse, exhaustion, and outright torture.

The camp staff, dignified by the title of instructors, were senior N.C.O.'s who wore yellow armbands and have thus ever after been hated for their nickname, "Canaries."

Harry Hurst says of them, "All that you have heard is true about the horrors of the Bull Ring. Those "base-wallahs" were absolute sadists in their treatment of the front line troops. Their hatred for us was only equalled by our contempt for them."

These hardbitten louts were evidently hysterical with fear that they would be sent to the front line at the first sign of humane treatment of their charges. The Canaries were simply threatened with this fate by their cold-eyed officers, who then turned over the running of the Infantry Base Depot to the N.C.O.'s and like the Base Commandant, Brigadier General Andrew G. Thomson, lived in fastidious isolation inside the Commissioned Officers' Compound.

Thomson would only be dismissed in September, 1917,

after the I.B.C. finally erupted in a mutiny by one hundred thousand troops. The mutiny was put down with the utmost severity and hushed up so successfully that little is known of it in England to this day. Unfortunately, these events occurred too late to help men of the 35th (Bantam) Division sent to sample the Bull Ring.

Cyril Wright remembers Étaples with clarity after sixty years: — "Every minute of the day, instructors shouting "Nip to it, short-arse! Move! Move!" The Canary points a long, ringed cane at me. I'm supposed to stick my bayonet through it while we both run . . . We lie down in the mud and crawl while they fire live rounds from a Lewis gun just over our heads. One man gets shot in the foot and is sworn at all the way to the first aid post . . . We polish our boots like mirrors every night, then right after inspection next morning we are marched into ankle-deep mud again. And all the time, the Canaries shouting filthy names at us, bullying us, abusing us, and even hitting us with their canes when they feel like it."

The brutish treatment never varied at Étaples. Awoken before dawn, given a quarter of an hour to bolt down sausages and tea, new arrivals from various regiments were paraded on the barrack square. A careful inspection of brasses, boots, and rifles brought the inevitable flurry of men being "put on a charge" for later trial and punishment. Then, the troops were marched off behind a small pipe band, bound for the distant sand hills.

It was a routine the fledglings would be subjected to for the next fourteen days. Laden with sixty pounds of full equipment, they were marched at attention, rifles stiffly at slope arms. Tired already after the long uphill march, they would be put through every imaginable type of battle-drill — and every humiliation — the instructors could devise.

The loathed Canaries drove the men with frantic savagery. Assault courses, trench digging, bayonet charges, went on by the hour, to the obscene screaming orders of the instructors.

The brutalizing two-week course was supposedly intended to prepare men for what they must soon face at the front. Live ammunition was used; this along with high explosives and shellfire caused frequent accidental deaths and injuries, and gave the men a taste of the danger to come. At the end of two weeks, they were grudgingly told they "were as ready as they'd ever be," and sent off to join their regiments.

Drafts of the 15th Sherwood Foresters had an equally hard time in the Bull Ring, as J. E. Taylor writes. "It was a very tough camp. Talk about jumping to it! Bayonet fixed, you run at stuffed sacks, screaming as you stab them. Then, "On the hands – down! Knees bend! Arms out – in – out!" On and on with no letup. I could have wept. How I wanted to get away. I actually wanted to be back in the line with my little Don Three telephone, shellfire and all. When our time is up at Étaples, almost happily away I go to fight the foe."

There would have been plenty of need for Taylor's skill as a signaller on his return to Arras. The Germans had brought up a strong concentration of heavy trench mortars against the British lines. These monsters hurled fat shells known as "rum jars" with enough explosive power to wreck twenty-five yards of trench at a time. As well, the Germans fired off salvos of smaller mortars and thousands of rifle-grenades. To avoid insupportable casualties, the front lines had to be cleared of all but suicide-squads of holding troops for days at a time.

Such constant damage required endless hard labour to dig out trenches and repair the parapets. Harry Hurst was guiding a fatigue-party bringing duckboards from the rear up to the front line at Arras. "Leading the way, I happened to glance backward, and saw a lot of lengths of duckboard sticking up well above the parapet. The Germans had seen them too, for as I expected I noticed a flock of "toffee apples" in the air. I evacuated hurriedly, and I'm sure the survivors of that fatigue party didn't carry duckboards in that manner again."

The casual finger of death could tap a man at any time. Lancashire Fusilier Frank Harris tells of his narrow escape while working behind the lines. "Our party of twenty men was coming back after a trip up the line with a load of empty sandbags and concertina wire. We were just jogging along (amazing how fast one can travel on the way back) when swish-bang! a mortar shell dropped just behind us. After going another hundred yards or so, we all pulled up. I was shocked to find that instead of having five men behind me I now was the last in line.

"We went back and found only two of the five still alive, and they badly wounded. I never will forget passing the same place the next morning. Although the bodies were gone, I saw three steel helmets lying there, and knew from the stencil badge they had belonged to my pals."

The infantry troops found themselves mainly employed as mortar artillerymen, their only way of hitting back at an enemy they scarcely ever saw. The Stokes mortar was a simple tube which lobbed a shell at high trajectory into the German trenches as close as fifty yards away. The 104th Brigade tested their skill at this when a sniper shot an enemy and some of his comrades came out to his assistance. A Stokes bomb was dropped neatly right into the centre of the luckless group.

More effective counter-batteries had been set up by the Divisional Artillery guns in the ruined *faubourg* hamlets ringing the town to try to silence German mortars which threatened to soon destroy the entire front line faster than it could be rebuilt. The artillery began to be able to at least discourage the enemy when Heavy Trench Mortar Batteries arrived on September 12th. The Bantams grinned apprecia- tively even though half-deafened when the four 9.45 mortars of V/35 H.T.M. opened up to give Jerry a taste of his own medicine.

On the night of September 10th, the Germans came across

The Gridiron to raid what they hoped was a thinly held sector. However, the Durhams were expecting them, and manned the rim of Kate Crater. A salvo Lewis gunfire and grenades fought off the Germans that time but it was the first of a series of probing moves by the enemy all along the front. They had been alerted either by aircraft or espionage agents that large shipments of poison gas were arriving at Arras and were not unnaturally curious to learn where the cylinders would be placed.

About nine hundred and sixty deadly containers arrived, their red nozzles soldered tight, and were brought forward by nervous carrier parties of the Cheshire Regiment. Colonel Johnston recorded, "Our men had an important job at night, carrying gas cylinders for the Brigade on our left. The gas is worked by a special battalion who go about for the job; most of the men are chemists, generally over military age, and wear spectacles. They are a very intelligent lot of men and do nothing but look after our various forms of frightfulness. It may interest you to know that the British have made one hundred and twenty-two gas attacks this year and the Germans have made four. It is nice to feel that the Boche, having invented these pretty things, is getting some himself, and being beaten at his own game."

The gas cylinders were lined up in specially dug pits and aimed towards the German positions. Several times, elaborate plans were made for their employment, then cancelled at the last minute. The cylinders lay in their pits for weeks, unused, pregnant with death, and an ever-present threat to the British troops stationed nearby.

Two weeks of trench digging and dodging mortar shells began to tell on the Bantams' nerves. They impatiently asked when they might get a chance to pay a visit to the German lines. It was an aggressive attitude which needed the outlet of raiding. The 15th Cheshires were the first to go over, on the night of September 14th.

Their target was the enemy line between Claude and

Kate Craters, where three smaller holes were known as Three Craters Salient. It was a badly shelled area which would be difficult to cross even during daylight. "The salient looked devastated," said Nelson Spencer, "Water, mules, and dead men covered in foam caused by gas could be seen everywhere."

A well-planned support programme involved rehearsals at Duisans against replica trenches, and a co-ordinated attack by artillery and diversionary mines being fired between Cuthbert and Clarence Craters to distract the defenders. The guns opened up at 8 p.m., their shells forming a box-barrage to fence off the point of entry in the German front line. Sixteen minutes later, four large camouflets were touched off with such force that they shook Arras. By then, the Bantams had reached the enemy trench and suffered a dozen casualties from "shorts" of their own artillery.

Despite the fourteen hundred rounds fired by the 159th Artillery Brigade, the German defenders showed their typical bravery under fire by popping up along the parapet to shoot at the bayonet-waving Cheshires. Hot work at point-blank range enabled the raiders to get into the trench, and they began to bomb their way along in both directions.

One of their purposes was to enable a party of New Zealand miners to search for a suspected mine shaft, so there was even more need for speed. The Germans resisted so vigorously that Captain Bertie LeMesurier led his men up outside the trench to bomb it from above. They fought in this way for about forty minutes, then sounded the recall at 9 p.m., and retired with a loss of five men dead and twenty-seven wounded. Whey they reached their own trenches, it was found that one New Zealand officer and his sergeant were missing.

Three search parties went out for them without success. The mystery of their fate was probably solved at 9.45 p.m. when a huge crimson flame, which looked like a charge of ammonal, shot up in the German trenches. The determined

Kiwi had found his target after all, and its destruction formed his own funeral pyre, for he was never seen again.

The enraged Germans intensified their mortar fire, to discourage further invasions. In this they were disappointed, as the Bantams began to send over raiders virtually every night all along the Arras front. Manchesters, Scots, Lancashire men took their turn at what a later war would call commando raids. They suffered relatively few casualties beyond the wire but paid a steady toll inside their own trenches.

One night, three men were killed and six wounded by one rifle grenade which landed among a party of 20th Lancashire Fusiliers. Moments later, another grenade dropped into Iodine Sap and killed two men of the 18th Lancs. They were revenged the following dawn when Sergeant Tinsley shot five Germans at a range of seven hundred and fifty yards.

Sniping was a constant danger to men on both sides throughout the war. A moment's carelessness in passing an open space or in raising one's head over the parapet could bring a bullet from marksmen who lay patiently waiting for just that opportunity. Aside from the casualties, the very threat of snipers wore down men's nerves, adding to the terror of trench life.

Early in the war, the Germans enjoyed superiority in this mode of killing. From 1914 on, their snipers were specially equipped with Mannlicher hunting rifles and Leitz telescope sights which gave them a murderous accuracy. However, when British snipers were finally equipped with Ross telescope sights tapped onto standard-issue Lee Enfields, it was found they had a weapon every bit as good as the enemy's and the menace of snipers was balanced. Men with good marksmanship scores and the required implacable temperament were taken out of the line and given special instruction in the personal art of murder. The Bantam Division trained their snipers at ranges along the French coast near Le Havre and at the Sniper School near Arras. There, men were shown the arts of concealment, the needs for patience, observation, and ruthlessness, then sent back to play their lonely trade of killing.

These deadly duelists were not always officially trained. The official war diary records that a sniper of the 106 Brigade killed a German staff officer who was accompanying his general around the line. This officer's death was a very personal act of vengeance by a young Bantam.

Private David Hammond of the 17th Royal Scots was a stores clerk who, because of his job seldom had to stay in the forward trenches. For weeks, he spent a dangerous enough time dodging shells as he would bring up supplies to his fellows in the front lines. "I had a particular mate," he said, "A Cornishman called Jamie Smith, who was a proper fire-eater of a lad. Forever going on raids, he was. But he was a happy-go-lucky sort of fellow, too, and many's the night he would sit singing and cracking jokes with us all down in the trench as Jamie would give us a song.

"I had just said 'so-long' to him one morning and turned away along the trench when I heard a "Crack!", and heard his mates cry out. I turned back, and there was Jamie with a little hole through the side of his head. He had stood up once too often and had been sniped by a German.

"I don't mind saying I cried that day," said Hammond. "I picked up his rifle after a while and climbed up on the bank behind some wagon limbers. I waited there for a long time, watching Jerry's trenches. A bit later on another one of the lads was sniped, but this time I saw a puff of smoke and knew where the killer was. I put ten rounds rapid into a pile of wreckage where I thought the man was, though I never did know whether I had hit him.

"The trench mortar retaliation was close enough to warn me to never fire more than one shot in future, but this experience started me off. Every day after duty either in the morning or twilight I would go off to near where Jamie had been shot, and I would watch for a Jerry. The very first morning I got down to being a sniper, I bagged a senior German Officer and a Sergeant, one after the other.

"After a while, my officer got to hear of this and called me into the dug-out. "You're not supposed to be a sniper," he said. "What are you doing this for?" I told about what happened to my mate, and how I used to shoot a lot on the farm. "Good luck to you," said the officer, and gave me permission to take time off from my regular duties every second day, just to hunt Jerry.

"Soon it was my full-time job and I put paid to over forty Jerries in the next two years by sniping. It was a rotten business, but they started it and by God, I wanted to help finish it."

The Germans also developed special camouflaged equipment for their Jaeger (hunters), including flash-eliminators, false tree-trunks made of concrete, and porthole shields. One innovation was discovered by H.L.I. Private Peter Cassidy, "While on patrol in No-Man's-Land, we learned of a dangerous trick of Jerry when we found a dead cow which had been hollowed out and steel plate put in for use as a sniper's post."

The discovery of another well-concealed sniper's post on September 20th, earned the personal congratulations of the new Divisional Commander. Major General A. J. S. Landon that day replaced the popular General Pinney, who left to command the 33rd Division. Sergeant H. C. Bolton of the 20th Lancashire Fusiliers became suspicious of an old chimney in No-Man's-Land.

Carefully carrying a small pack, he went out in daylight to examine the ruins and came under frequent sniper fire. Dodging bullets, he finally managed to enter the brickpile and found a ladder placed below a shellhole in the wall about twenty feet up. Iron spikes had been set aside the chimney to enable a sniper to climb up to the top.

Noting traces of fresh mud on the ladder, Sergeant Bolton decided to use the explosives he had thoughtfully brought along. Blowing up the chimney earned him the Military Medal.

There were many opportunities for acts of individual bravery during the next couple of months while the 35th Bantam Division held the line at Arras. Daily bombardments and nightly raids took away a few more familiar faces each week and the survivors hardened into professional soldiers ready to follow a good leader anywhere.

There was a strong bond of comradeship among officers and men in the front lines, where death was always so close that caste and position were rendered meaningless. Many who were there spoke of how this levelling influence would be quickly felt soon after experiencing the continual shelling and trench raids. This was particularly marked with good-quality troops who had served together for a long time, among whom mutual confidence reduced the need for rigid differences in rank. However, officers and N.C.O.'s in charge of less familiar replacement troops felt greater need to keep an iron discipline.

Whatever posturings were fashionable at O.C.T.U.,* the front-line officer learned how to adopt a friendlier and more easy-going manner with the rankers under his command — men whom he would have to order to follow him into deadly danger; men whom he might one day need to rely on to save his life; and men calloused to killing, whom he would have to present his back to when he led them over the top. A harshly unpopular officer could risk grievances being settled permanently by a bullet during the handy confusion of battle.

"Our officers were gentlemen in all things" still maintains George Palmer, late of the 14th Gloucesters. "We all understood that there was the Book of Army Regulations to be followed, and we would do anything for a leader who was fair to us. But the officer or N.C.O. who was a real bastard to us never tried his Vernon (nastiness) twice, as many a one was shot in the back."

---

* Officer Cadet Training Unit.

Though British troops usually endured much hard discipline without taking reprisals, it would be surprising if they did not occasionally turn on their tormentors. Brutalized in battle and constantly exhorted during training to "Kill the Boche, even prisoners!" the Bantams frequently became creatures of their hideous environment.

Sgt. H. T. Crook was an instructor in musketry and sniping. In 1916, he went overseas and found himself with the Birkenhead Bantams, "A more blood-thirsty lot I never met," Sgt. Crook would long recall. "They were of course embittered by six months of unrelieved fighting service in the front line, and when I arrived, I was seen as someone who had been skulking behind in England. They were so hostile to me and behaved so badly towards me that I had to fully explain my position before I even dared go up into the line with them.

"I observed they killed everyone they did not like — and took very few prisoners. It took some time to convince the Bantams that I was worthy of being followed and obeyed. Once accepted by them, I couldn't have had better troops to lead.

"They had seen so much bloody fighting, that many were quite deranged, as indeed were some soldiers of other regiments. The result was that once they were in the line, killing was the order of the day, and woe betide the German who faced the Bantams and woe betide any N.C.O. or officer who did not act towards them in a way that they approved of."

Many Bantams who went "trench-happy" displayed this somewhat fearsome attitude towards their trade of soldiering. Moved constantly from one regiment to another, with little regard for their own group pride, continuously thrown into trench raids and suicidal assaults, some Bantams became a collective band of battle-hardened troops who fought ruthlessly and fearlessly with little expectation of surviving.

Asked how smaller Bantams would fare in personal combat against larger enemy soldiers, George Palmer replied simply,

"Use your loaf! The bigger the German, the bigger the target. One could always put the butt in or a knee in the groin. One thing we were taught was when it was light was to spit in his face and when he shut his eyes, which most people will, then was the time to give him clobber – in, out, and away. We always kept a .303 up the spout for such times, too. Not very sporting tricks, but I came back.

"Many of our officers were Regular Army types, kind if stern," George Palmer continued. "Some of the taller fellows in charge were inclined to say us small chaps suffered from "duck's disease" – our backsides too close to the ground. Be that as it may, I never regretted my lack of height since the time a sniper's bullet hit the tree just above my head while I was making water. I was soon down in the latrine pit, clean boots and all!"

Nelson Spencer had the same sentiments, and told how, "One time whilst leaning against the trench-wall, a whiz-bang exploded right above me, burying a lump of hot shrapnel in the wall not three inches above my head. My short stature saved me, as it must have done on many occasions unknown to me."

Their views on this were not always shared by taller troops. Captain Richard Peirson was commanding a company of the Northumberland Fusiliers when they went into the line to relieve a battalion of Bantams. "A little while after the relief operation was completed, my company sergeant major came to me in a great state and said, "Sir, them bloody little dwarfs have built up the fire steps so they could see over. Now when my lads stand up, half their bodies are above the parapet." Soon afterwards, standing orders on trench relief procedures were read aloud to the 104th Brigade: – 'Two sandbags per man for filling and placing on the firestep are provided. Parapets are not to be lowered.'

These orders were doubly important by early November when a combination of very heavy rain and bombing kept trenches and parapets in an almost permanent state of damage. It became dangerous to sleep in the funk-holes dug in trench walls which could suddenly collapse to bury the unwary. This happened in "I" Sector where most of the gas cylinders had been moved, and gave troops the ticklish job of digging out the containers by hand for fear that spades broke the seals.

"J" and "K" sectors received a heavy bombardment just as a raiding party of the 17th West Yorkshires set out on November 9th. Despite the mortar bombs, they reached the enemy, killed six Germans, and brought back identification of the 89th Grenadier Regiment. Later that night, a patrol of the 15th Cheshires captured a German near Clarence Crater. He was wearing a gas mask. The Cheshires eyed the red-tipped cylinders squatting near them. Jerry was definitely up to something.

At dawn that day, firing was heard overhead and a British aircraft crashed into the wire south of the Cambrai Road in "I" Sector. Several Germans fatally exposed themselves to division snipers when they curiously peered over the parapet to watch the wounded pilot crawl to safety in the British line.

Another of his squadron was not so fortunate, as Nelson Spencer witnessed. "My officer looked upwards and said, 'What is that?' I looked up and there was something like a large cross dropping from the sky. As it came nearer, one could define it to be a man with outstretched arms turning and turning head over heels, and I heard my officer quietly say, 'Poor man.' The body dropped some distance in front of our trench but we could not bring him in then because of enemy fire. That night, we recovered the body of a young British airman who we concluded had been in an aerial dogfight and lost."

Officers and men alike began to increasingly sense that an enemy attack was in the offing. It was little things, like a German calling across to a Royal Scots sentry of No. 1 Sap in "K" Sector, "It's cold tonight, Jock," Though they had not raided for identification, Jerry knew exactly which regiment was stationed there. Signs that the enemy was preparing a major attack was perceived when they began to bombard the division's front in massive strikes; aerial torpedoes, rum jars, and petrol shells pulverized February Avenue, "K" Sector, and the Pope's Nose in "I" Sector. More fighting patrols came out along the enemy front, and a German officer was even discovered in an empty British listening post. Perhaps it was because the British Command was planning to loose a major gas attack at last that these signs of German preparation were mainly ignored.

On the night of November 26th, 1916, the front line of the 104th Brigade in "I" Sector was ordered cleared as a gas discharge was to be released. The men had been battered by very heavy mortar fire all afternoon and thankfully retired down Iceland Street, leaving only a few Lewis gun parties in forward saps. Using a confusing series of codewords – Duncan and Jack, and Rubber and Gravel – the gas was ordered used or not to be used in a manner which Brigadier Sandilands later called "a perfect nightmare." The gas was ordered released at 11.45 p.m., cancelled for an hour, then cancelled again. Finally it was ordered to be released at 2.35 a.m., although the scattered defenders knew nothing of this and had been wearing masks for over four hours.

"The first type of gasmasks was just a bag saturated with chemicals," says George Palmer. "By then, we had better ones with two eyeglasses, a nose-clip, and a rubber spout like a duck's bill. You could only blow out and suck in a little air, so the glasses steamed up. All you could do was breathe shallowly and hope for the best. Not very useful during a raid, though."

A German raid – three of them, in fact – was what hit the divisional line around 2 o'clock that morning. Large parties of the enemy had advanced under cover of the massive two-way bombardment and arrived at exactly the weakest section of trenches before the gas had been released. General

TB - Q

Sandilands had ordered Lt. Colonel Mills of the 17th Lancashire Fusiliers to take special precautions to defend a number of bombarded trenches just vacated by men of the 12th Division further along, and this move further depleted the defenders. The pleased Germans jumped into the trenches unopposed and purposefully fanned out, hefting stick-grenades.

The second enemy party encountered a Lewis gun section at the top of Hulluch Street, which emptied four 47-round pans of ammunition into them and then withdrew. Two Lewis gunners at 16 Street were shot before they could go into action. This firing alerted a lone Stokes gunner in his emplacement near 19 Street. This spirited man, whose name we regretfully don't know, fired off all his ammunition and had one bomb still in the breech when called on to surrender. "You voss my prisoner," a German shouted. "Oh, voss I?", the Bantam replied and pulled the lever. The German went up with the bomb and the Bantam escaped with his gun.

Not all the troops were as valiant. Most of the men at 16 Street had fled without firing a shot. One of them was lucky in that he reached a rear first-aid post commanded by a sympathetic Canadian doctor, Captain W. O. Whitman. Ernest Quickenden was there and describes what happened.

"Down the dug-out steps staggered a terrified trembling teenager, poor kid. 'Witty' asked him, "What's up, lad?" The boy said, "We have run away." "Who from," the Captain asked, "Your mother?"

"Shaking, the kid answered, "No sir, we were in the front line and the Prussian Guards came over, so we ran away."

"The Captain said to me, "Hell, if they are sending these kids up here, what hope have we got? Give him a red ticket." That was a four-by-three card with large, red letters NYD, meaning 'not yet diagnosed.'

"I tied a card to his tunic and Witty made sure the boy would be passed straight down to base, away from the firing line."

The third German raiding party met no resistance either when they came into "K" sector. Again, luck was on their side. The usual sentry groups holding King Crater had been withdrawn in expectation of retaliation shelling after a raiding party of the 19th D.L.I. went across. The Durhams reached the German wire only to be hit by short-falling British shells, which wounded Lt. Welbourne and killed two men. Pinned down by their own barrage, the D.L.I. patrol did not encounter the German raiders, and returned after they had left.

At about 2.15, Lieutenant Mandy left "I" sector with a sergeant to patrol the crater edge. They met a German raider group in the crater itself and Lt. Mandy was shot and fell. The sergeant took to his heels with such speed that he had reached the junction of Bogey and Wednesday Avenues before he was stopped by battle police. In the meantime, Corporal Stevenson from the other side of the crater had rescued the wounded Mandy and bombed the pit free of Germans.

The sentry group left by Mr. Mandy, consisting of a corporal and two men, fled at first sight of the Germans. Only Private Hunt stood his ground but he was quickly made a prisoner and hustled back to captivity. His less-plucky comrades reached the sentries at Cecil Avenue and shouted, "Run – the Germans are here!" The fleeing private then decided to go back to his post, but the N.C.O. ran on, right into the ungentle hands of the battle police on Bogey Avenue.

By this time, it was realized through the din of bombardment and the movement of troops moving up for raids that the Germans had broken into the line. Grenades were heard exploding amongst the forward trenches and troops in the reserve trenches began hurrying forward despite the shellfire. By the time they arrived, the Germans had gone, taking with them at least twenty-five prisoners. Two Bantams had been killed and six more were wounded. The loss of so many prisoners shook the commanders and an enquiry was in session before dawn.

Several of the men swore that they had only pulled back when they heard blasts of an officer's whistle and shouted orders in English to withdraw. Their statements were accepted by Brigadier Sandilands who remarked that, "As bad luck would have it, the enemy finished up their bombardment by raiding the line at exactly the same zero-hour as our own gas was discharged lower down the line. On account of this gas discharge, orders had been issued to vacate most of the front line, which made it all the more easy for the enemy to get in. The raiding party was composed entirely of English-speaking men; this added to the general confusion and resulted in some of our men being taken off as prisoners."

However, he and the other Brigade-commanders were less inclined to let the opportunity pass to demand a drastic evaluation of the division's ability to continue to hold the line. The successful German attack was soon to end the Bantam composition of the 35th Division. Immediate action was ordered for a review to be made of all personnel on the Arras front and hurried conferences about reorganization were held at Divisional Headquarters.

On December 6th, Lt. Col. Johnston sadly wrote, "A circular letter had just come round which states that we are not to be known as the Bantam Division any more and that our reinforcements in future will be normal-sized men. I'm sorry, as the little men have done so well, but I suppose there are no more, as all regiments now take small men."

There was a certain amount of reluctance by regimental officers to let go men who were for the most part good soldiers even though their physique was not up to standard. Too, in the front line, experienced troops of any quality were in such short supply that junior officers were more concerned with keeping what troops they had for day-to-day fighting. Army regulations also impeded any action being taken to remove more than the most obviously unfit soldiers.

The final knell for the Bantams as a distinct unit was

sounded by the roars of Lt. General Sir A. Haldane, then commanding VI Corps. He had already sent two directives aimed at "weeding out undesirables" without much response, when he arrived at a parade of one of the battalions near his headquarters on December 21st, 1916.

Seizing the opportunity, General Haldane began to tear through the ranks, followed by red-tabbed aides wielding notebooks. Prodding his leather-covered swaggerstick at the most undersized, deformed, or sickly-looking troops, he barked, "Take his name – out! . . . You can go . . . you can go . . . Out! Out!"

While weeding out unfit tiny men, the General suddenly came upon Sergeant Benjamin Peirson. He stared up at the towering 6 ft. 5 in. N.C.O. for a long moment, then exploded to an aide, "Ridiculous! Send this man away, too." He moved on down the line in search of other rejects.

Far from feeling humiliated, Peirson gleefully looked forward to being sent behind the lines. With any luck, it would be weeks before he was transferred to another unit. He began to make farewells to his friends in anticipation of the reprieve.

That night, he and part of his battalion was sent into the reserve trenches on yet another fatigue party. Many of the officially rejected troops were included in the job, as the paperwork had not yet been completed for their release. The supply-laden Bantams were caught in a heavy counter-barrage, suffered casualties, and scattered for cover.

Sergeant Peirson found an empty dug-out and crawled to the back, followed by a dozen of his platoon. Even above the barrage, he heard one of them jokingly shout, "Get out, Peirson. We can get six in where you are!" He remembers nothing more until rescuers reached him with their shovels the next morning. Only two of the twelve others buried in the dug-out survived what had been a direct hit by a Jack Johnson shell. He was dragged out of the charnel hole, and confessed that his main concern was the fact he had been wounded in the hand. He was terrified of being accused of causing a self-inflicted wound.

Thankfully unaccused and alive, he walked to the light railway for evacuation with two thousand seven hundred and eighty-four of his tiny comrades. As the open train pulled away, one of the rejected Bantams looked back at the smoke-wreathed battlefield of Arras and said to Peirson, "I wouldn't have minded staying, you know. I must be daft."

The three Lancashire Fusilier battalions were least affected by these arbitrary dismissals or medical inspections. The 17th battalion lost one hundred and seventy N.C.O.'s and men, the 18th had about one hundred and ninety rejected, and the 20th sent away one hundred and thirty-five men. Though the units were then still essentially composed of undersized men, orders were received that "the Bantam standard must be disregarded for good and all." New drafts were of regular-sized men and the units gradually became a mixed bag of no particularly uniform level of stature.

Brigadier Sandilands paid them tribute after the war, "It is a matter of common knowledge within the division that until the Armistice in 1918, we never attacked without one of the old original Bantams distinguishing himself, and there had never been a medal parade in this brigade without at least one of them being present."

However gallant their motivation, the very uniqueness of the Bantams had all along contained the seeds of inevitable problems. Lt. Col. H. M. Davson, who later wrote a superb history of the 35th Division, commented "Those who had knowledge of the Division when first formed unite in describing the original drafts as a fine body of men, whose shortness of stature was compensated for by breadth of chest and physical condition, and if the supply of such could have been continued, the arguments of those in favour of the employment of small men would have been proved.

"As it happened, it was found no more possible to support

a Bantam Division consisting of well-developed men below the average height of the nation than it was to fill up the ranks of the Household Cavalry with men above it. The result in the former case was that the type of recruit deteriorated. Many who joined were immature and with the laudible intention of serving their country when enlisting become somewhat hazy about the actual date of their birth.

"Others who were conscripted later, were weaklings who would never be fit for the strain of active service, and who were passed to the Division as the supply of men of the original Bantam standard had failed. These later men had not the fortitude to endure fatigue and hardship and although possibly a long period of training might have given them the mechanical discipline which would have to some extent counterbalanced the failing, this was denied them. The complaints of battalion commanders became frequent, and the efforts of the Division Commander to have the weaklings removed were only partially successful.

"Whilst in training at Masham, a certain number was withdrawn, but the recruiting authorities refused to have them discharged and instead sent them to the depots and kept them there. The result was that, but half-trained and as yet unsubordinated to habits of automatic obedience, they rejoined at a critical period of the war and took their places in a series of battles which tested the courage and endurance of the most highly trained soldiers of the three nations. The result was not only disastrous to these men themselves, but harmful to those who fought alongside them."

The Bantams lasted until losses in battle had decimated their ranks; and the Bantam Division continued to exist some six months longer, until it was recognized that there was not a sufficient number of small Bantams in Britain to supply so large a unit. So in the spring of 1917, the 35th (Bantam) Division passed away. The 35th Division took its place and the rooster divisional sign was replaced with seven fives in a circle.

It was a period of regret, for great expectations had been entertained in the success of the enterprise. The ultimate result was not the fault of the officers and men of the original battalions, who all went into battle with high hopes and desire for action. As one of their officers once remarked, "they were little men but had big hearts."

But war is no respecter of hopes or theories, and it was to war, and war alone, that the settlement of their case was entrusted. The project failed, but the failure was not due to the men who gave their lives in early battles, or to their comrades who survived and took an honourable part in the succeeding years of warfare. For them, the bells of Hell kept ringing.

Chapter Twelve

Butchery at Bourlon

Joy-bells rang all across Britain at noon on November 23rd, 1917. For hours before the stroke of twelve, huge crowds had gathered on the steps and in the churchyard of St. Paul's Cathedral in London. When the clock struck noon, one of the small bells in the campanille rang out, followed in slow time by others. Then there came a loud crash as the carillon began tolling in great chords. At the first note, the thousands of pigeons feeding on the pavement in front of Queen Anne's statue rose fluttering up in a silvery cloud and circled high above. There was a burst of applause from the listeners, and a white-haired man with a powerful voice began to sing the National Anthem. The crowd joined in the words — for the first time since the end of the South African War, the bells of St. Paul's were ringing a joy-peal.

The Cathedral chimes signalled the whistles of steamships along the Thames to join in, as did bells of other city churches. The cheerful sounds spread across the country, echoing from belfries in towns and villages across England and Wales, and reaching to dioceses in the far north of Scotland. The idea had been suggested by 'The Times' newspaper, taken up by the Bishop of London, and arranged by Canon Holmes, Archdeacon of St. Paul's. That day, the whole country gave itself up to tintinnabulant triumph over the announcement of a great victory at Cambrai, which seemed to herald the end of the war within weeks.

As events of the next few days proved, the celebration was bitterly premature. The initial British success was reversed by the German counter-attack which actually gained them seven square miles of new territory. However, though it could not be then seen, the new open-warfare tactics with massed armoured vehicles which the British employed did eventually pave the way to ultimate victory one year later. But in the meantime, the nation nursed its sheepish disappointment over Cambrai and the War Office sent letters of condolence to the next-of-kin of more than four thousand Bantams who had been butchered there.

Exactly a year before, the 40th (Bantam) Division had left the Loos Salient. It was then employed continuously in the Somme country, putting in a winter of almost unendurable cold in trenches between Rancourt and Bouchavesnes.

"Our division finally reached the Somme battlefields at their worst climate-wise in the deadly 1916–17 winter when both sides were completely immobolized," reminisced Andrew Gilmour of the 14th Argylls. "We suffered cruelly unnecessary losses, manning trenches up to the waist in mud. Judging from our own casualties from trench foot, frostbite, pleurisy, nephritis and so on, I should imagine that the Bantams must have lost up to thirty percent of their effectives. This is where I myself finally dropped out from frostbite, twenty-three degrees below zero in trenches on the slopes before Peronne."

Another casualty from frostbite was the diminutive New Yorker, Henry Thridgould, whose hands were afterwards crippled for life.

The troops had to hold the line in these appalling conditions against a very aggressive enemy, the 104th Infantry Regiment. In one of their attacks, a large party came across to raid a listening-post manned by six Green Howards. After a heavy barrage of mortar bombs and tear-gas shells, twenty-five Germans arrived, led by a "powerful and loud-tongued non-commissioned officer." He was one of the first to be wounded in the hand-to-hand fight, which may be why the enemy began to lose heart despite their superiority of numbers.

The pugnacious little Yorkshiremen flailed away with sharpened entrenching spades – a favourite weapon of theirs for close combat – while the wounded German leader kept shouting orders even as he lay dying at their feet. His opposite number, Lance Corporal Smith, was killed, as were two more Britons, while another ran away.

The surviving two Green Howards fought on desperately back to back in the dark. They were saved when the man who had left returned well-armed. Private W. Cooke had braved the barrage to grab a satchel of Mills grenades from an adjacent trench, and bomb his way back into the listening-post.

When the raiders retreated, leaving four dead comrades, the wounded *feldwebel* gamely refused to tell his captors anything more than that he was with the 20th Company of his regiment. Though Private Cooke and Evans carried him to an aid-station, the man died soon after. For this act of valour, Private Cooke received the D.C.M., but he was killed at Villersplouich in May, 1917.

Because of constant rumours that the enemy was about to withdraw, British troops went out on nightly raids to test his strength and obtain prisoners. Sniping became a vicious game on both sides, their task made easier by the slower reaction and dulled alertness of miserable, half-frozen men. Every day, two or three would die this way in the division's trenches, plus the steady trickle of victims from shellfire and periodic volleys from fixed rifles clamped to cover vulnerable open spots in the support lines.

The carnage in the line tore at all men's minds, though most were unable to express it so well as could Private Isaac Rosenberg of the King's Own. He left a scene of horror clearly illuminated as if by Very lights in his poem, "Dead Man's Dump."

THE BANTAMS

"A man's brains splattered on
A stretcher-bearer's face;
His shook shoulders slipped their load,
But when they bent to look again
The drowning soul was sunk too deep
For human tenderness.

They left this dead with the older dead,
Stretched at the crossroads.

Burnt black by strange decay
Their sinister faces lie,
The grass and coloured clay
More motion have than they,
Joined to the great sunk silences.

Here is one not long dead;
His dark hearing caught our far wheels,
And the choked soul stretched weak hands
To reach the living world the far wheels said,
The blood-dazed intelligence beating for light,
Crying through the suspense of the far torturing wheels

Swift for the end to break
Or the wheels to break,
Cried as the tide of the world broke over his sight.

Will they come? Will they ever come?
Even as the mixed hoofs of the mules,
The quivering-bellied mules,
And the rushing wheels all mixed
With his tortured upturned sight.
So we crashed around the bend,
We heard his weak scream,
We heard his very last sound,
And our wheels grazed his dead face."

BUTCHERY AT BOURLON

Few surviving veterans of the 11th King's Own are now aware of Rosenberg's reputation as a war poet, yet they still remember him as a comrade. They speak of him as an untidy, polite but painfully reserved man. "I vividly remember one morning sitting on a step in the support trench trying to talk with Private Rosenberg," said the late Corporal Harry Stansfield. "He always was a shy sort of fella, very quiet and seemed to keep to himself. He was writing and paid little attention to me. I wanted to show friendship because I think he thought he was often shunned because he was Jewish. Believe me, we didn't think much about a person's background one way or the other. When you were in the trenches, all we wanted to know was if you were a reliable comrade or if you weren't.* Religion or race had nothing to do with it.

"I also well remember the other Jewish member of our platoon, Lt. Sternberg. He was from Manchester, where his parents had a large business. He was a very good and herioc officer, well-liked by us all. Unfortunately, he was killed while meeting a raiding party. That night we were out on the raid cutting wire, and things were going well, when suddenly a Very light gave an enemy sniper the chance to shoot. Lt. Sternberg was shot in the spine, and we abandoned the raid right then but we dragged his body back to our trenches.

"That same night, it was my duty to take rations up the line, and collect Mr. Sternberg's body to take it back on the same limber cart for burial at Marizincourte Cemetery. I found it a difficult task," said ex-Corporal Stansfield. "It was hard to hold the body on the limber, because of the rocky roads and of course, his rubber ground-sheet got in the way.

"Each man was issued with a rubber cape. This was first a raincoat, second a ground-sheet, and finally your coffin, should it be needed for such. The ground-sheet had lace holes all round, and laces to tie up the corpse for burial. Somehow, I managed to shove the limber back through the darkness,

* Isaac Rosenberg was killed by a German raiding party on April 1st, 1918, near St. Quentin.

253

and felt very sad the whole time as he was such a good officer."

Just as the weather began to slightly improve in mid-March, 1917, the division found it could leave the icy mire of their trenches and advance across a suddenly deserted No-Man's-Land. The Germans had decided to shorten their front by withdrawing to the immensely strong Hindenburg Line. They left behind a systematically destroyed wasteland of ruins, ingeniously strewn with booby-traps. Troops of the 40th Division moved gingerly forward to occupy a still-burning Peronne and the dozens of brick mounds which once had been villages. Just as they were beginning to enjoy themselves, the Bantams were withdrawn from the advance across open ground and put to work as labourers on road-building and railway construction.

"This was a heartbreaking and back-breaking job for raw-boned youths of eighteen years," a Bantam newcomer wrote. "I rather think we were not particularly sorry when the time came for us to join our company for a spell in the trenches."

His first sight beyond the division's new front line at Gouzeaucourt was the spires of a city eight miles away across the open plain. It was Cambrai, headquarters of the German Second Army. Over to the left, rose a high ridge covered with oak trees – Bourlon Wood, which the 40th (Bantam) Division would not be able to reach until six months later. First, they had to fight their way through the ravines and fortified villages west of the Canal du Nord.

All three brigades tested themselves in battle by successfully taking Fifteen Ravine and Villers Plouich and destroying blockhouses at Beaucamp. This grim work cost nine hundred and sixty-four casualties, a quarter of which were fatal. If the price was high – about twelve percent of infantry effectives – the lessons of open warfare had been well learned, and the division settled down for a long summer of raiding the Hindenburg Line.

Edgar Robinson was with the 13th Green Howards when

his battalion moved in to occupy Villers Plouich. They were heavily bombarded and lost eleven men killed, but Robinson still declined alternative employment. "About this time, we were asked if any of us would like to transfer to the new Royal Tank Corps. They wanted small men ("bantams") like we were. I was expecting my fortnight's leave at home to be given me any day now, otherwise I would have transferred. Had I done so, I would not be alive here now."

Small stature was a useful factor in manning the newest weapon of war, the tank.* This British invention had been introduced during the Battle of the Somme but had not then been successful because of being used in too few number. Now the Tank Corps was being rapidly expanded and crews were at a premium. The cramped quarters inside the first primitive armoured fighting vehicles left little room for their wretched crews jammed in the hot, noisy, fume-filled interior amidst driving controls, weapons, and all manner of ill-designed corners. Small men were seen as logical crew members to function in this hellish environment.

The Mark IV tank was a steel rhomboid in which was crammed a crew of eight men, one of whom was an officer. He and the driver sat on raised seats in the nose of the tank. The rest of the crew huddled in two narrow gangways, one foot wide by eight feet long, which ran the whole length of the vehicle on either side of the engine. These narrow corridors were only five feet high, making it even more difficult for average sized men to move about.

The 100 h.p. engine reached to the roof and behind it was a small platform with a starting handle which required four men's strength to turn. Two gearsmen squatted here in deafening closeness to the motor; their job being to manipulate two secondary gears plus neutral to steer each track.

Between the officer and gearsmen on one side and between the driver and gearsmen on the other, were the gunner, two in each gangway. A "male" tank had two sponsors with a

* The Soviet Army's new T–72 Main Battle Tank, brought out in 1977, is specifically designed around a 3-man crew of small size because of space requirements; their height officially ranging from 1m.55 to 1m.60 (5ft. to 5ft. 4ins.).

gun-layer and gun-loader for each 6-pounder, a cut-down naval cannon. The "female" tank was armed with machine-guns only, usually five or six Hotchkiss .303's inside and top mountings. Both types of tank also had a forward-firing Lewis 1 machine-gun operated by the officer. Crewmen were armed with Webley revolvers for use through pistol-ports against enemy infantry who might climb aboard.

Even egress to the cramped interiors was difficult. Door hatches were only two feet by three feet; vertical in the male tank and horizontal in the female version, so that crews had to wriggle inside on their backs.

While smaller men found it easier to function inside the hulls, they were by no means the only types to appy for tank training at Bovington Camp in Dorset. Soldiers of all shapes and sizes volunteered from infantry and cavalry units and the Service Corps, as did men from the Navy and Royal Flying Corps. Though volunteers were preferred, the need for personnel was so great that drafts of veteran soldiers were transferred from their battalions and sent for tank training.

One of those chosen for this new role was Private Len Marks of the Middlesex Regiment. He first learned of his new role when taken out of a party of men about to board a troop transport at Folkestone. "There were two of us London lads picked out that morning," he recalls. "Sam Pearlman and me had grown up together in the East End and joined up on the same day in 1915. We were among a group of six Jewish boys from the same neighbourhood who volunteered together for the Bantams. A bit over a year later, Sam and I were the only two left alive.

"I'd been wounded just seriously enough to get sent back to Blighty for three months. Sam had been in hospital for trench-feet, and we weren't feeling too good about trying our luck in the trenches again. Then out of the blue, this RTO comes along and tells us to report for special training. He signed us off the regimental rolls, there and then, and

,ave us railway warrants to report to Bovington Camp.
When we got there and found it was the tanks for us, we
couldn't think why we'd been chosen for the job. Neither
one of us had ever so much as ridden a bicycle."

Alan McKenzie was a volunteer with a group of Manchester Bantams who became tankers after the 35th Division
was reorganized. "After being trained at Bovington in driving
and machine guns, I did 6-pounder gun training at Chatham
Naval Barracks. Our gunnery practice was at sea in the
English Channel on naval gunboats; the motion of ships
being supposedly similar to that of a tank on rough terrain.
We were classed thus: − Lewis-gun 1st Class, Hotchkiss 1st
Class, 6-pounder 1st Class, Tank driving 2nd Class, also
trained in revolver-shooting, signalling and pigeon-handling.
For all this, we got paid a few more pence a day."

After their training, crews were sent to France for collective tactical exercises at Tank Corp. H.Q., Bermicourt, near
St. Pol. Unknowingly, they were intended to lead one of the
most ambitious attacks yet devised by the British High
Command. The enterprise had not begun in that form. On
August 4th, 1917, Colonel J. F. C. Fuller presented a plan to
the General Staff for a large tank raid south of Cambrai.
He was an enthusiastic proponent of tank weapons,* but was
maddened at their being mis-employed at Ypres, where they
all too often sank in the mud and became easy targets for
German artillery. Fuller believed they would be better used
on the Cambrai front where there was firm open ground with
room for tanks to manoeuvre to best advantage.

Fuller's plan called for a local raid 'to destroy the enemy's
personnel and guns, to demoralize and disorganize him, and
not to capture ground.' As the covering letter stated, "The
duration of the raid must be short, eight to twelve hours,
so that little concentration of the enemy may be effected
for counter-attack." If these original time restraints had been
kept, the joy-bells which ran in November may not have

* Major-General Fuller's later writings on tank warfare were adopted by German
panzer units for their brilliant blitzkreig tactics in the Second World War.

been as premature.

Haig's staff were intrigued. Here might lie the chance for that elusive master-stroke, the massive breakthrough that could take Cambrai, and even keep rolling all the way to Berlin. Excitedly, they began to revamp and enlarge the plan, which had proposed a raid by two tank battalions across an eight thousand yard front. General Sir Julian Byng of the Third Army went to see Field Marshal Haig and suggested a major surprise attack to capture Cambrai. A large success was needed by the Commander-in-Chief; any kind of success would be welcome to erase criticism of the costly failure at Passchendaele which was still grinding whole divisions into the mud. His staff set to devising a new campaign, based on Fuller's tank raid plan.

By mid-October, Haig had approved General Byng's proposal for a major offensive against Cambrai, with a target date of November 20th. The project had grown to a massive effort involving three hundred and eighty fighting tanks, a thousand guns, two Army Corps, three infantry divisions and three Cavalry Corps. There was no longer any room for Fuller's preliminary vision of a few score tanks setting off to "advance, hit, retire." Nor, by the time the attack had been finally approved, was there the volume of manpower to sustain it. Most of them lay dead where they had been slung into the Ypres Salient. All available men would have to be used to take Byng's ambitious objectives.

These were threefold: − to penetrate the Hindenburg Line between Canal de l' Escaut and the Canal du Nord, to capture Bourlon Wood and Cambrai, and to cut off the enemy south of the Sensée River. As students of military history knew, the Germans around Cambrai were well protected on all sides, being in the naturally fortified quadrilaterial known through centuries of warfare as Caesar's Camp.

On three sides, they were moated by the Scheldt and Sensée Rivers and the Canal du Nord, and on the fourth side lay the wooded heights of Bourlon. This dominating feature not only commanded the surrounding plain and the Agache Valley carrying the Canal du Nord, it also overlooked the Scheldt and territory as far as Bouchain. If Bourlon Ridge could be taken, the Germans would have to pull back from their carefully prepared defence systems for a considerable distance to the north of it.

This vital objective was later earmarked for the 40th (Bantam) Division, one of the thirteen support groups which would follow the mere six divisions put at Third Army's disposal for the initial attack. When General Franchet d' Espery arrived at British Headquarters in Albert, he was puzzled to learn that offers of French army support had been refused. "But where are your reserves?" he asked. He was languidly told, "Mon General, we have none." The French-man turned on his heel to leave with a disgusted "Mon Dieu!"

Code named 'Operation GY,' the assault remained a close secret while troops were quietly assembled behind Bois d' Havrincourt. The tanks' noisy engines posed the biggest problem to security, so several old Mark I's were kept running up and down just behind the lines to obscure from the Germans any tell-tale indications of an unusual build-up of the machines.

All the tanks going over the first wave had been specially modified so as to be able to bridge the wide trenches and canal ditches they would encounter. Huge fascines made of about seventy-five bundles of brushwood compressed by steel chains were hoisted onto the nose of each vehicle. A simple releasing gear would enable tank commanders to drop their fascines into a trench when required and so allow them to roll forward over the obstacle.

Each bundle weighed a ton and a half and required twenty Chinese labourers to roll on to its tank. Many of the workers at the Central Repair Workshops at Teneur belonged to the 51st Chinese Labour Company. Their skill and capacity for hard work which they brought from the other side of the world was taxed to the utmost during early November.

One thousand Chinamen managed to make and fit over three hundred and fifty fascines within three weeks, often working twenty hours at a stretch. They laboured also at engine maintenance, gun-fitting, and hull modifications to help prepare the tanks for the assault. In mid-November, the tireless Chinese began "tank fills," the final touches to their clanking charges. Each vehicle was loaded with sixty gallons of water, ten pounds of grease, and either ten thousand rounds of s.a.a., or two hundred 6-pounder shells. When the British tank crews swung aboard, they found Chinese good wishes chalked inside the doors.

"We drove away with all the coolies smiling and waving," recalled Len Marks, "We shouted back the only words in their language we knew — "Shi-Shi," which, as far as I could make out, means everything from 'yes' to 'very good luck.' We certainly needed lots of the latter."

Early on the morning of November 20th, 1917, Marks' tank was one of hundreds which waited, engines ticking over, at their point of assembly near Beaucamp. Somewhere among them too, was Alan McKenzie, in the right-hand gun sponson of the tank 'Blair Athol.' Soon after 6 a.m., the sky began to lighten and it was possible to see the rolling expanse of greyish dead grass that offered such a promising arena for the armoured attackers. Low clouds dipped curtains of mist and rippling rainsqualls across the sea of grass. It was uncannily quiet for a few minutes, then precisely at 6.30 a.m., a single gun roared. Far to the right, came an answering roar and a flicker of flame, then link by link the whole line broke into a chain of explosions.

Through the grey half light, the German lines were seen to erupt in shell bursts, signal rockets, and fountains of golden sparks from smoke-shells. Machine-guns began yammering from each side but were drowned in the roar of hundreds of tank engines at full throttle as the armoured giants slowly moved off like monsters into the mist. The infantry followed them in waves, fixed bayonets glowing coldly in the dawn, while squadrons of British, Australian and Canadian fighter-planes flew low above them to strafe the opposing trenches. The Battle of Cambrai had begun — and the 40th (Bantam) Division had not much longer to exist.

The German Second Army of General von der Marwitz was taken by complete surprise and was further thrown off balance by being in mid-transfer of front line units to two divisions which had just arrived from Russia. In the first few hours, the 54th Division was destroyed and the 107th Division and the Pomeranian Grenadiers were particularly hard hit. Only their artillery was able to enjoy any success. For the German guns, it was like target practice; being able to "brew up" British tanks as fast as gunners could pull their lanyards. Soon, the battlefield was strewn with the hulks of wrecked tanks, but the others kept driving forward regardless of their vulnerability.

Tank commanders exposed themselves with reckless bravery to press home the attack, as Alan McKenzie attests, "We were ordered to patrol a ridge to draw fire so that the Cavalry could ride over and get the German gunners, which they did. During this, we received a direct hit on the left sponson, disabling the tank. The order came, 'abandon tank.' The other R.H. gunner was a Bantam named Clapton. He threw open the door and jumped out into direct fire, shouting, "Follow me! Follow me!" I was a bit dazed, but managed to get out. Clapton saw a shell land and make a big hole, so he headed for it, dragging me with him, saying, "A shell doesn't land in the same place twice".

"There we stayed until the barrage lifted, and went back to the tank which was now riddled. The other Bants were dead or wounded. Murray had taken a direct hit and the man behind him did not live long. Taylor, the driver had a foot missing. Clapton had saved my life for sure."

When the Germans recovered from the first shock of the tank attack, they began to fight back with characteristic courage and ingenuity. Many of them remembered they had been recently issued with a 5-round clip of new "K" bullets — high velocity rounds with a tungsten-carbide core able to pierce armour plate. Tank crews began to feel their effects, and one nearly ended Len Marks' life.

"The heat inside our tank must have reached a hundred degrees by mid-day. Shrapnel and small-arms fire rattled on the walls like rain, and two or three times we had to poke revolvers through portholes to shoot Germans who'd climbed onto the hull with grenades. We were all pretty badly cut about from bullet-splash coming in through the ports and from being thrown against sharp edges of equipment. We were issued with padded leather clothing and steel-mesh face-visors against this, but nobody wore them because of the heat. The only man who always did wear a visor was our driver, whose name I can't recall.

"The moment we rolled over a high bank, there was a noise like Big Ben striking one o'clock, then metal buzzed around my head like a swarm of bees. An armour-piercing bullet had punched through the raised tank nose, hit our driver underneath, passed all the way up through his body, and went ricocheting around inside the tank."

There were sixty-five tanks destroyed or disabled during the first day of fighting, with another hundred and fourteen out of action with mechanical troubles. The vehicles had helped win the first phase however, and the infantry had thrown back the hard-fighting Germans all along the line. The British 6th and 12th Divisions had secured their objectives, then let the 20th Division pass through to capture Masinieres and Marcoing. This was the picture all along the front from Gonnelieu to west of the Canal du Nord, which had been cut by tough Northern Irishmen of the 36th (Ulster) Brigade. The British Army had advanced four and a half miles in a day. It was the receipt of such news in Britain which called for celebrations.

The field commanders were less exultant, for half the

objectives still lay in enemy hands, the most important of which was Bourlon Wood. On the second day, the entire thrust of the British attack began to focus on the all-important Bourlon hill which guarded the door to Caesar's Camp. Repeated assaults by the 51st Division were broken against the bottom of these heights; and regrouping there was impossible with the Germans firing down upon them from the slopes and the village of Fontain Notre Dame. The exhausted 51st were pulled back after three days of vainly fighting here, and the 40th (Bantam) Division was brought forward from reserve to take their turn at storming Bourlon Wood.

The division was now part of IV Corps, and had a new commander, Major General J. Ponsonby. After six months continuous service in the line, they had been relieved in October and sent far back to Doullens. They entered camps in the Forest de Lucheux and were given training in woodland fighting, a fortuitous preparation for what then lay just a month ahead.

Now, rushed orders had brought them back to the Cambrai battlefront, and on November 22nd, the brigades were grouped around Havrincourt awaiting final instructions for their first major battle. General Ponsonby's written orders arrived at Brigade Headquarters in the catacombs below Graincourt Church at midnight. The 119th Brigade would send in the 12th South Wales Borderers and the 19th Royal Welch Fusiliers to assault Bourlon Wood across the Cambrai Road, between Anneux Chapel and Fontaine. The 17th Welch Regiment were to act as support from positions along a sunken road leading from the cemetery at Anneux, while the 18th Welch waited in reserve south of the Sugar Factory on the Cambrai Road.

This factory has been rebuilt in the same place, so that the visitor today can stand in the exact vantage point of 1917 and see across the open fields bordering the wood, with the edge of Bourlon village beyond. These buildings mark where the 13th Battalion, The Green Howards, formed the 121st Brigade's left flank. The 20th Middlesex Regiment were assigned to the section east of there, next to the Welsh Brigade. The 21st Middlesex and the 12th Suffolks would provide support from trenches behind the Sugar Factory. For a while, the entire 120th Brigade was held in reserve at Havrincourt.

Zero-hour was set for 10.30 a.m., so the two assault brigades had to move into position overnight. They marched up through the darkness, along tracks reserved for them past Flesquieres and Graincourt. The Commanding Officer of the 13th Green Howards recalled, "The morning of 23rd November came in with a blustering north-east wind, sending cloud shadows chasing over the undulating ground. An occasional scud of sleet made way for spells of sunshine in which Bourlon Wood to the east glowed in ragged autumn finery."

Their objective was formidable – six hundred acres of dense forest, fir, oak, and ash trees choked with thick underbrush which hid machine-gun nests and snipers. The ridges and paths were under constant shellfire, drenched with poison gas, and garrisoned by the German's crack 3rd Guard Division.

At 10.30 a.m., Saturday, November 23rd, 1917, the Welsh Bantams went forward behind sixteen tanks, while just ahead of them the barrage crept up the wooded slopes, splintering trees, setting fire to the undergrowth and wreathing the hill in smoke. On their left the Londoners and Yorkshiremen loped towards Bourlon village, straining to arrive before the Germans had time to recover from the bombardment.

The South Wales Borderers drove into the forest and spread out through the trees as they had been taught. One group made the mistake of following along the pathway itself and ran into machine-gun fire immediately. The Welshmen faded into the trees and began to creep forward "like a blood pack of Red Indians," as Jack Jones put it. They sniped the guncrew and pushed on until they reached a sunken road and encountered more Germans face-to-face. These were tackled with the bayonet and the survivors forced back into the woods. "Nothing could stop us," said Jones. "We were laughing and yelling and firing at anything that moved. When a Jerry popped up, a half-dozen of us would run at him with bayonets and jab him to tatters."

This exultant mood swept through the men; Private Plummer single-handedly attacked a strongpoint, killed several Guardsmen and took eight prisoners. He ran on to repeat the performance twice again, capturing a machine-gun, an officer and fifteen more prisoners.

Battle-fury was no protection against shells, machine-guns, and poison gas, however, and casualties began to mount as the Borderers got deeper into the forest. The Prussian Guard were as tough a group of soldiers as any on the Western Front and adapted themselves to the rushing tactics of the little Welshmen who popped out of the trees on all sides.

"Soon, we dropped any resemblance to platoon advance," said Jones. "It was every man for himself, and we scattered to go hunting Jerries, just as they were doing to us. Now and then, you would hear some poor, wounded devil scream as he was caught by the blazing underbrush, but you just had to ignore him and go on regardless."

The 19th Royal Welch Fusiliers moved north-east, fighting their way across difficult broken ground and under constant shellfire from guns along the railway embankment at Fontaine. The stubborn German defence of that village eventually proved to be a key factor in the outcome of the battle. In the meantime, it was the source of much execution among the Welsh.

"The Jerries started to lob fire-shells over about mid-morning," observed Trevor Jones. "These caused the Christmas trees to burst into flames in a moment and made it so dangerous that many of my oppos were so busy watching the treetops, they missed seeing snipers and got shot instead."

Despite this enfilade, the Royal Welch drove their opponents back, and by 11.40 a.m. had reached the road from Fontaine to Bourlon which ran through the wood. To their left, the rattle of Lewis guns and crish-crash of grenades signalled the presence of the South Wales Borderers, who were still moving ahead despite the fact that many of their officers had become casualties. After only an hour of fighting, the 119th Brigade was halfway through the wood that had defied the previous British attacks for three days.

Things did not go as well for the 121st Brigade. They had moved across open ground with orders for the 20th Middlesex to capture a long wooded spur north of Anneux Chapel while the 13th Green Howards kept pace with the 36th Division on their left and attacked Bourlon village. The 21st Middlesex were to advance in support of the Yorkshiremen and cover their left flank where the enemy was known to be strongly entrenched. Even before they advanced, the Green Howards began to suffer heavy casualties from enfilade fire from guns in Quarry Wood to the north, when Second Lieutenants Stanford and Walton were killed along with nineteen other ranks. The battalion was glad to leave their death-trap when at 10.30 a.m. whistles blew for them to advance.

"At that time, I was a signaller," Edgar Robinson recounts. "I was in the second wave to go over, with a portable set on my back and a revolving spool of thin telephone wire in my hand. It was my job to run out the wire and when we got to our objective to report our progress to base. All went well when we began to advance. The Germans were taken by surprise at first. When they did open up, lads were killed all around me and I was spattered with mud and blood."

Casualties worsened when progress of the 36th Division on the left was halted, and the 13th Yorkshires walked into a hail of machine-gun fire from their unprotected flank.

Despite these losses, which included three more dead officers, the Green Howards managed to cross the German trenches, in line with the 20th Middlesex, which had also cleared their objective in the wooded spur. Both battalions were pressed into a narrow front of advance under heavy fire from the west, but struggled on, the 20th Middlesex with their right foot in the edge of the wood. The 21st Middlesex formed up behind them in support to prevent any rear attack from pinching off the forward troops.

Despite being under fire from the front and both sides, a fighting patrol of the 13th Yorkshires reached the edge of the village at 1.00 p.m. Bourlon was crawling with Germans who had converted virtually every building into a pillbox and were heavily armed with many Schwarzlose machine-guns. The advance party was seen to enter the village, the company commander fell dead, and the other men scattered out of sight.

In the wood, the Welshmen had made so much progress that a company of South Wales Borderers had also reached the eastern edge of Bourlon village. They and reinforcements from the 17th Welch Regiment proceeded to winkle out enemy machine-gunners from cellars and barns. "There was no quarter given on either side," said Jones. "After our men were cut down like corn, it was no good anybody shouting 'Nix schiessen!'"

At 4 o'clock, two determined counter-attacks by the German 175th and Grenadier Regiments threw back the surviving Welshmen from the village and also dislodged the 19th Royal Welch Fusiliers from around Bourlon's western edge. The battalions were now exposed to fire from the village garrison and artillery in Fontaine, which still held out against repeated assaults by the 51st Division to the right.

The 119th Brigade seemed ready for another effort against the village when Lieutenant Colonel Kennedy rode up on his horse with two companies of the 18th Welch panting along in his wake. Rallying the men as he came, Kennedy flung himself from the saddle, rushed in front of the position and waving his cane charged the enemy. "The gallant commander of the 18th Welch had only gone a dozen yards when he was shot down by the Boche." Two more officers were shot down within minutes of taking command and the battalion was taken over by the Adjutant, Captain F. H. Matthias. Very few officers survived long, so that platoons and even companies were led by N.C.O.'s and resourceful private soldiers. Company Sergeant Major Davies of the 18th Welch led a counter-attack so aggressively that he knelt down in the open to allow his shoulder to be used as a mounting for a Lewis gun, until he fell with a head-wound.

Over in the 121st Brigade sector, the 20th/21st Middlesex were hard-pressed to hold the perimeter of Bourlon village, while fending off attacks from the east. Their battalion scouts had gone into the buildings to link up with other British skirmishers but had not been seen again. The Green Howards also were probing the rubbled streets, and managed to capture sixty prisoners. A few minutes later, the Germans sent a strong rescue party which freed the captives and killed over twenty of their escorting Yorkshiremen.

Reinforcements started to come up from the 120th Brigade to stiffen the attack and replenish the severe casualties. Clumps of small bodies in khaki lay along the line of advance, and stretcher-bearers braved sniper-fire and shells to evacuate the squirming forms of several hundred wounded men. Through this field of blood, two companies of the 12th Royal Suffolks picked their way, moving towards the trenches south of Bourlon village, which they reached in mid-afternoon.

One of their company commanders was Lieutenant (acting Captain) Harold Leeming, whose near-miraculous survival of six months as a front line infantry officer had been rewarded by two promotions that summer. Leeming's luck held when he dropped his revolver into deep mud, only to look up into the barrel of a Luger a moment later. The Germans had come across on a counter-raid and blundered into the Suffolks. Leeming braced himself for the bullet but his sergeant fired from the hip and killed the German. Lieutenant Leeming scooped up the 9 mm. Parabellum to help his men dispatch the raiders, and carried it as his preferred sidearm throughout the rest of the war.

When darkness began to fall, the situation along the divisional front was confused. The Welsh Brigade was in command of most of the wood, but was under constant attack by German infantry from Bourlon village and artillery in Fontaine. The 121st Brigade had units inside the village but had lost touch with them, and all battalions were by now scattered and intermingled. At 5.15 p.m., a gloomy message was received by General Campbell at his forward headquarters in the chalkpit near Cambrai road – "The Yorks and 21st Middlesex are practically obliterated. "In truth, remnants of these battalions were still fighting south of Bourlon, though they had been savagely mauled.

Edgar Robinson explained how the remaining Green Howards held on, though ammunition supplies were running low. "At dark, we went back to the starting point to carry up bombs to the front line. In my party, ten of us had to carry a heavy box of Mills bombs in each hand. On the way up, we passed the entrance to a German pillbox where two of our lads were making tea. We stacked our boxes of bombs outside, crowded round the entrance and begged a drink. I was the last in the trench.

"Suddenly, there appeared in my mind a photo we had hanging up at home of my father who had been dead fourteen years. His voice said, "Move son, move!" It seemed to sound so real and urgent that I instantly said, "Just a minute lads, let me pass." As I got to the other side of the group, a German shell burst just where I had been standing, and it exploded all the Mills bombs we had stacked. The lad who had been standing in my place, also named Robinson, was blown to bits; the others were killed and five badly wounded.

"I was blown about thirty feet on to the side of the trench at the corner. My gas mask was blown off, my tunic blown up around my neck and my trousers down around my ankles. Almost naked, I fell back into the trench. When I came round, it was dark and I heard groaning behind me. I picked myself up and ran for help at the first-aid dug-out. There I fell and somersaulted down the dug-out steps, calling for stretcher-bearers. Very much shaken, I landed at the feet of one. He gave me four tablets and a drink of warm tea, put me on a stretcher wrapped in a blanket, and I passed out until next morning."

When Robinson went back up the line next morning, he found that most of the surviving 121st Brigade had been pulled back to regroup. Their place was taken by dismounted cavalry troops of the 19th Hussars. As the reserve 120th Brigade had been split up during the night – the 14th Argyll and Sutherland Highlanders were now reinforcing the Welsh in the wood – the 14th Highland Light Infantry and the 12th Suffolks were assigned to renew the attack on Bourlon village.

The 14th H.L.I. Commander, Lt. Col. Battye, was put in charge of the operation and received verbal orders from General Campbell. The 120th Brigade was to capture Bourlon village that day, and help the Welch battalion take the rest of the wood. To do this, the 14th H.L.I. would attack on the right, while the 12th Suffolks went in from the left of the village. They would be supported by twelve tanks while attacking the village.

A heavy artillery bombardment pasted the village for twenty minutes, then the infantry moved forward at three o'clock in the afternoon. They were unaware that orders postponing the attack until more tanks were available had been issued by General Ponsonby. These orders could not get through in time, as shellfire had cut telephone wires and killed the runners sent forward with written countermands.

The Scots lost heavily even before reaching their jumping-off point. Just before zero-hour, a single shell dropped into the middle of No. 7 Platoon, killing or wounding all but two of them. There were more casualties when they were caught by machine-guns in an unexpected belt of wire. An observer wrote, "To tried troops, this would have been nothing, but to untried like ours it was very unnerving. The men never flinched, just plodded on."

Ahead of them, the twelve tanks lumbered into the village, lost touch with their supporting infantry, and were picked off one by one. Guns blazing, the vehicles supported each other like wounded buffalo, but only five of them managed to withdraw to their rallying point. When the infantry later fought their way in, they no longer had tanks to help them mop up. The Suffolks came under accurate artillery fire and had to pull back to trenches outside the village.

The H.L.I. pushed three companies right through the village, discovering on the way the dead bodies of many Green Howards who had disappeared the day before. When the H.L.I. reached the railway north-east of the village, they were pinned down by fire from all sides and cut off from the rest of their battalion. They set up headquarters in a ruined farmhouse, and herded their growing flock of German prisoners into the barn for safe-keeping. Behind them, the German garrison came up from its cellars and took over the streets of Bourlon again. The forward companies of the H.L.I. were completely cut off. They settled down to fight or die.

During this second day of the battle, the Welsh Brigade had been withstanding repeated counter-attacks as fresh German battalions tried to throw them out of the wood. Each time the enemy fell back, red flares would go up and a sleet of shells would descend. High-explosive, air-bursts, and poison gas deluged the Welsh, until only a few ragged clumps of splintered tree-trunks remained to hint that this had recently been a dense forest.

Incessant rain and snow added to the difficulties of the troops, and to the suffering wounded of both sides who lay everywhere. Out-numbered, shell-shocked, and almost asleep on their feet, the hardy little Welshmen settled in for another night in purgatory, not giving an inch of ground.

Viewed from the comfortable distance of Third Army Headquarters in Albert, the fight for Bourlon was regarded by Field Marshal Haig somewhat differently. He issued a special Order of the Day: — "The capture of the important Bourlon position crowns a most successful operation and opens the way to a further exploitation of the advantages already gained."

After three years of trench warfare, machine-guns, massed artillery, and tanks, the Commander-in-Chief of the British Armies still yearned for a cavalry charge. He ordered Lieutenant General Kavanaugh to stand by for an expected breakthrough, when he was to bring up the five cavalry divisions champing at the bit at Fins. Near the horses at Fins Depot, tank repairmen sweated to patch up collandered vehicles and send them back to Bourlon where no more tanks were available for the renewed attack on Monday morning.

The 13th East Surrey were brought up early on the morning of the 25th, the only complete battalion left in the entire division. They were sent through Bourlon village to try to link up with the three beleaguered companies of the 14th H.L.I. holding the north-east corner of Bourlon. The East Surreys reached the Scottish battalion headquarters just in time to help repel another attack. During it, a machine-gun bullet struck the heart of Lieutenant Colonel Battye. That indomitable man staggered back to find Lt. Col. Warden of the East Surreys and turned over his command before dying. The grieving Highlanders buried him in the garden of a house, reslung their shovels, and grimly went out to deal some retribution.

Their comrades marooned near the railway line were being slowly annihilated, though the survivors could be heard keeping up a steady fusilade against their attackers. They held out until nine-thirty on the morning of the third day, until they had run out of ammunition. Only eighty men survived to surrender. Few Scottish Bantams at all survived Bourlon; total casualties of the entire 14th Battalion, Highland Light Infantry, were seventeen officers and four hundred and twenty-six other ranks.

By the end of the second day, the casualties among the 119th Brigade were equally horrendous – particularly among the 17th Battalion, The Welch Regiment, every one of whose officers were dead or wounded. Reinforcements had been sent up the ridge by the 14th H.L.I. and the 11th King's Own, among them Harry Stansfield. "We helped hold the high ground on the north-east edge of the wood, blasting the Germans back four separate times. The Taffies (Welsh) were so dead beat, some actually fell asleep between attacks. I remember hearing one snoring loudly away in a shellhole, with mortar bombs banging all around him.

"Just behind our lines, German prisoners and our men tended to each other's wounded, regardless of the uniform. I could not help but contrast this with the way in which Jerries had shot every Welsh prisoner they caught and how the Welsh had given no quarter the first day. Both sides now were sick and tired of the whole stupid business."

Though Bourlon village was twice declared free of Germans, strong parties of them were soon back again in parts of it, methodically killing off scattered bands of Scots, Green Howards, and Middlesex men. The entire wood was in Welsh hands at midnight on the second day. They had triumphed where others had failed, but at such a terrible cost that the 40th Division could never again be a Bantam unit. The Welsh battalions were so weakened by casualties and battle-fatigue after over forty-eight hours of ceaseless combat that their position was now very precarious. Orders came through that the 62nd Division would come up next day to relieve the decimated 40th Division in the sector they had wrested from the enemy with so much bloodshed.

Gradually throughout November 26th, the 119th Brigade disengaged itself from the wood and came straggling back. The number of men who could walk to Anneux Chapel was shockingly few. The South Wales Borderers reached the road first. "We were marching in step," Jones noted firmly. Their casualties were ten officers and one hundred and twenty-three men killed and missing presumed dead, twelve officers and two hundred and forty-three men wounded. The battalion was awarded two D.S.O.'s, six M.C.'s, six D.C.M.'s and eleven M.M.'s.

The two Glamorgan Bantam battalions of the Welch Regiment had suffered even more hideous casualties. The 17th Welch lost eighteen officers and three hundred and one other ranks, and was awarded eight M.C.'s, four D.C.M.'s, and fifteen M.M.'s. The battalion was that day declared to have "ceased to exist." The few survivors numbered only enough to be later formed up into No. 9 Entrenching Company.

The 18th Welch sustained two hundred and seventy-three casualties, and was awarded one D.S.O., one M.C., two D.C.M.'s and fourteen M.M.'s. The 19th Royal Welch fusiliers paid a costly butcher's bill too; one hundred and twenty-five dead, and two hundred and forty-seven wounded.

When the 121st Brigade was relieved from Bourlon village, the Green Howards fought their way back past the German right flank and regrouped at the Sugar Factory. Twenty-five officers and four hundred and fifty men of the battalion went into Bourlon on the morning of November 23rd. Three days later, less than one hundred men and eight officers came back.

Edgar Robinson had survived once more, to recall, "Only sixty-five of us were left to march out with one senior officer, Col. Baker. We must have looked a shocking sight to the fresh troops we passed going in, tired, dirty, and blood-spattered, with our Colonel ahead of us shouting, 'Make way for my poor lads.' There were tears in his eyes."

So it went on — 12th Suffolks, one hundred and fifty casualties; 11th King's Own, ninety-four casualties. In just over two days of fighting, the 40th Division altogether lost one hundred and seventy-two officers and four thousand and seventeen N.C.O.'s and men. They had been awarded scores of awards for bravery, captured over seven hundred prisoners and taken the previously-impregnable heights of Bourlon. Field Marshal Haig sent a message that he "personally wished all ranks of the 40th Division to be congratulated on their success."

Within a week, the Germans regained control of the wood that had been bloodily won by the 40th Division, but their valour was not unrecognized. Though it ceased to be a Bantam Division after the battle, the divisional sign was changed in honour of their final achievement. To symbolize Bourlon Wood, two acorns were placed inside the white diamond, and behind it proudly strutted a golden Bantam rooster.

Like so many men who came back from serving in the Great War, returning Bantams did not enjoy an easy time in what politicians promised would be "a land fit for heroes." Some entered trades or the professions, dozens emigrated, a few became popular entertainers, and one businessman even gained a knighthood. However, judging by their life stories since, most found that employment opportunities were always somehow just a little scarcer for undersized men. Once more, they were in a society inclined to judge them by their stature only, and one less moved by their offering to work for a living than the army had been to let them volunteer to fight. In a few years, the Bantam battalions were forgotten, curiously unmentioned in unit histories; perhaps a too uncomfortable reminder of the lengths to which officialdom had once been willing to go to feed a war of attrition.

For all this, not one of the surviving Bantams voices

resentment of being forgotten or regret for having served. Ex-Lancashire Fusilier Frank Heath summed up the feeling of his still-jaunty old comrades, "I was very much afraid, wounded and ill several times, but I was lucky and survived, and I would not have missed it for all the gold in Fort Knox."

Their best epitaph of all was written by Robert Campbell Irvine. He served as an Highland Light Infantry Bantam for three years and one hundred and seventy-four days, and then was discharged after suffering two severe wounds. When he applied for a job with the Glasgow Tramways, he was turned down because he was "too small." Politically active for ex-servicemen's rights, he himself remained unemployed most of his life, while managing to raise five children. When the eighty-one-year-old Irvine died penniless in Erskine Hospital, he left a number of unpublished poems he had written. One goes like this:

> Two minutes silence for the dead.
> I thought of the fields when the fields were red.
> Red, not with poppies, but with blood,
> The blood of men, the image of God.
>
> Two minutes silence for the dead.
> Stood in the crowd and bowed my head,
> Not in reverence, but in shame,
> At the insult in memory of their name.
>
> Two minutes silence for the dead.
> Last Post is sounding, eyes are red.
> But Reveille is sounding for me instead
> Of Last Post in memory of the dead.

Those words have an appropriate echo today, and would have read well on a Bantams' war-memorial – if one had ever been built.

Toronto, Canada,
May 31st, 1980

– END –

Acknowledgements

The book could not have been written without the generous assistance of many individuals and of the dozens of publications which helped to put me in contact with them.

The surviving Bantams, and most of their relatives who shared their memories with me, are now very elderly. One may ask, how reliable are such recollections after so long a time when expressed in personal interviews or in letters? In fact, I found without exception that the many individual accounts which I managed to gather corroborated each other to a remarkable degree. They were further well authenticated by the official records, battalion war diaries, newspapers, and other contemporary accounts.

I was continually impressed by the natural facility which men of their generation have with language, and greatly enjoyed their irrepressible sense of humour. My only problem was with their modesty; an ingrained understatement which frequently made it difficult to obtain colourful details of their combat experiences.

A score of times during two years of researching this book, I received the sad news that yet another of them had reached the end of the trail. Nearly all the Bantams are gone now, we shall not see their like again.

Among the many people who helped to make this book possible, I would like to thank the following: –

Mrs. Millicent Ayrton, Hoylake, Cheshire, for permission to quote from Lt. Col. H. Johnston's diary; W. Adams, Panania, N.S.W.; J. J. Atkins, Tranmere, Birkenhead; Mrs. M. Asselbrough, Sunderland; John S. Archer, Leeds, Yorks; Mrs. Ivy Allinson-Bailey, Toronto; C. Allinson, Starbuck, Manitoba; Mrs. Rose Ash, Hartlepool; my brother, Mr. W. G. Allinson, Southport, Lancs; Tim Ashley, Maghull, Liverpool; Miss Vi Bretherton, Heswall, Wirral; J. Booth, Hyde, Cheshire; Hugh Brown, Philadelphia, Pa.; E. Butler, Birmingham; Mrs Ann Briggs, Kirkcaldy, Fife; Mr. J. Baptie, Scarborough, Ontario; George Batty, Royal Chelsea Hospital; Bill Bryant, Glossop, Derby; Mrs. Barbara Baker, Wirral; Mrs. B. Briggs, Thetford, Norfolk; Mrs. Catherine Barker, Whitley Bay; Sir William Butlin, St. John, Channel Islands; Mrs. Edith Bradbury, Dover, Kent; Rear-Admiral F.B.P. Brayne-Nichols; the late Alexander Batchelor, Toronto, Ontario; WO 2 Patrick Cracknell, Wessex Regiment; George Cunningham, Glasgow; Peter Campbell, Sidney, B.C.; Mrs. Frankela Corries, West Derby; Melton Campbell, Bath, Somerset; Miss Gladys Bree, Arlesly, Beds; Edmund Conroy, South Dartmouth, Mass.; Miss Lydia Crook, Woodchurch, Wirral; Horst Priess, Nordeney, Germany; Mrs. Bessie Cockburn, Birkenhead; Mrs. Sheila Carter, Stroud, Ontario; P. Cassidy, Glasgow; Tom Culshaw, Liverpool; Graham Carr, Vancouver, B.C.; Mrs Margaret Davidson, Greasby, Merseyside; Mrs. H. Dick, Belfast; Tommy Dickson, Hayes, Middx; G. K. Embley, Darlington, Durham; Mrs. J. Eldridge, Stockton-on-Tees; Joseph W. Ewing, Centre of Military History, Washington, D.C.; Mrs. Joan Foster, Victoria, B.C.; David Fox, New Hamburg, Ontario; Roland Fitzpatrick, Shipley, Yorks; R. F. Freeman-Wallace, Bristol; George Fisher, Preston, Lancs; Mrs. Gwynneth Foster, Chessington, Surrey; Gilbert Farrington, Manchester; Mrs. Ruby Goodall, Leven, Fife; Andrew Gilmour, Gifford, East Lothian; Miss Roseann Galloway, Leeds, Yorks; W. Griffiths, Criccieth, Wales; Mrs. Mary Garrity, Greenock; Donald Gray, Hemet, California;

Miss Catherine Grey, Berwick-on-Tweed; Mrs. Ivy Godden, Nedlands, Western Australia; Mrs. Annie Hudson, Sunderland; Jack House, Glasgow Evening Times; H. M. Hurst, Belfast; William Hurley, Lawrence, N.Y.; Frank Heath, Huddersfield; Mrs. Mary Hardacre, Preston, Lancs; J.J. Hutchinson, Rock Ferry; Miss Noele Heymann, Chichester; Edward Hillison, Portsmouth; Miss Elizabeth Humble, Sunderland; C.W. Hayes, Pugwash, Nova Scotia; F. Harris, Liverpool; Mrs. Shirley Hinns, Northrop Hall, Clwyd; A.J. Heaton, Richmond Hill, Ontario; Alex Hood, Bailey's Bay, Bermuda; David Hammond, New York City; Robert Irvine, Glasgow, for permission to quote his late father's poem, "Two Minute's Silence"; H.R. Ingham, Littleborough, Lancs; Mrs. Mary Jones, Shotton, Wales; Ken Jackson, Kitchener, Ontario; Miss Edna May, Sidney, B.C.; the late Morgan Jones, Bryn Asaph, Wales; David Jenkins, Cardiff; John Jones, Warrington; the late David Karstadt, London; David Preece, Llandudno, Wales; the late Mrs. Adelaide Kemmel, Toronto, Ontario; Edwin Lofthouse, York; James Lewis, Edinburgh; John A. Lawson, Ingatestone, Essex; George Lim, Hong Kong; Mrs. Dorothy Leeming, Woodstock, N.B.; the late Bill Leyland, Toronto, Ontario; Mrs. S. Laybourn, Hatfield, Herts; Victor Lill, Lyndhurst, Hants; Sidney Marven, Halstead, Essex; Arthur Morris, Gately, Hants; Lewis Morgan, Cardiff; George Marr, Wanganui, N.Z.; Joseph Mainwaring, New York City; Mrs Elizabeth Marchbank, Heswell; V. Merrick, Hartlepool, Cleveland; W.G. Mitchell, Newcastle-upon-Tyne; Mrs. Ethel Lavin, Ngongotha, N.Z.; G. Millington, Birmingham; Mrs. V. Moore, Harrogate, Yorks; Roderick Mitchell, Durham City; Ronald Marsden, Bournemouth; Len Marks, London; Brigadier H. D. McGregor, Lingfield, Surrey; George P. McLeod, Glasgow; Mrs. Frances McArthur, Winsford, Cheshire; A.W. McGill, Basildon, Essex; Mrs. E. McLarey, Birkenhead; Roland Mackie, Narrabun, N.S.W.; Mrs. I. McLaren, Dundee; Alan R. MacKenzie, Durban, South Africa; Albert Noble, Lowestoft, Suffolk; Klaus Dreiber, Salzburg, Austria;

Mrs. Lily Owens, Heswall, Cheshire; Richard Pierson, Westmount, Quebec; Bob Parker, West Islip, N.Y.; Mrs. P. Pressburger, Munich, Germany; Thomas Pemberton, Wirral; George Pearson, Houghton-le-Spring; George Palmer, King's Heath; Jack Paget, Amering, Sussex; Arthur Priestley, Toronto, Ontario; Mr. E. Pursell, St. Helens, Lancs; Jeffery Pritchard, Toronto, Ontario; Winnie Parker, Manchester; W.S. Pickford, Congleton, Cheshire; James Pringle, Bury-St.-Edmunds; E. Quickenden, Wanborough, Swindon; Mr. & Mrs. Allan E. Raw, Benoni, South Africa for permission to quote from Mr. A. Bigland's book, "The Call of Empire", 1926; William Ryan, Dublin; Reg Rimmer, Chester; D.F. Robinson, Bromsgrove; A.G. Robson, Hexam, Northumberland. Mrs. Iris Riches, Southend-on-Sea; James Robertson, St. Catherines, Ontario; Arthur Swift, Huddersfield, Yorks; Peter Sullivan, Barrie, Ontario; G.A.D. Smith, Tetbury, Glos; the late J. Nelson Spencer, Bebington, Wirral; John Smith, Tranmere; R.E. Swift, Bebington; the late Harry Stansfield, Ottawa, Ontario; H.R. Statham, Guildford, Surrey; Alfred Spindlow, Yiewsley, Middx; Edward Scales, Sunderland; Sidney Sears, Vancouver, B.C.; Colonel John Forbes, The Green Howards Museum, Richmond, Yorks; L. Owen and Mrs. J.L. Sears, Prince Consort's Library; Bryn Owen, Museum of The Welch Regiment, Cardiff; John J. Slonaker, U.S. Army Military History Institute; Captain D.N. Anderson, The Royal Highland Fusiliers; J. Pavey and R.H. Forey, Army Historical Branch, Ministry of Defence; J.S. Lucas, Ms Jane Carmichael, D.B. Nash, Imperial War Museum; Stephen D. Shannon, Durham Light Infantry Museum; K.M. White, Staff College, Camberley; Edward Grimshaw, Bristol Central Library; Major G.G. Egerton, South Wales Borderers; Major R.F. Tomlinson, The Prince of Wales Own Yorks Regiment; Hywel Rees, National Museum of Wales; W.A. Thorburn, Keeper, Scottish United Services Museum; The Director-General, Commonwealth War Graves Commission; Adjutant G.M. Rachaine, Division Logistique, Paris;

Brian Clark, Military History Society of Ireland; H. J. Woodend, Royal Small Arms Factory, Enfield Lock; Major P.A. Mauldon, The Queens Lancashire Regiment, Preston; Major G.E. Dodd, The Sherwood Foresters Museum; Michael J. Moore, Appalachian State University, N.C.; Lt. Col. A.A. Blacoe, The Cheshire Regiment; Brian Barnes, Director of Leisure Services, Wirral; G. Langley, Avon County Library, Bristol; South African National Museum of Military History, Johannesburg; Ron Chesterman, Cheshire Records Offices; Frances Gundry, Provincial Archives, Victoria, B.C.; William Doig, Glasgow Herald; Miss S. M. Challenor, Chester Library; Lt. Col. G.B. Eastwood, Royal Military Academy, Woolwich; Brigadier D.B. Riddell-Webster, The Cameronians; N. Thomas, City of Bristol Museum; Major R.H.S. Woodward, The Gloucester Regiment; Mrs Edith Tyson, Lancaster City Museum; M.G.H. Wright, Royal Military Academy, Sandhurst; David A. Smith, Public Archives Canada; Col. A.V. Tennuci, RAMC Historical Museum; Andrew Cook, British Records Association; Colonel T.D. Lloyd-Jones, Cadet Training Centre, Camberley; M.R. Barker, Lancashire Fusiliers Museum, Bury; Major T.P. Shaw, The Royal Regiment of Fusiliers; Major B.W.R. Baker, The King's Regiment; Col. B.A. Fargus, The Royal Scots; James Benzies, Rotary Club of Portobello, Edinburgh; Miss Judith Phillips, City of Bristol Archives; Major G.E. Dodd, The Sherwood Foresters Museum; Major E.L. Kirby, The Royal Welch Fusiliers Museum; Hal Gibbin, Orders & Medals Research Society; Mrs. Patricia Moore, Glamorgan Archivist; Royal British Legion; Royal Canadian Legion; American Legion; South African Legion; U.S. Veterans of Foreign Wars; Australian Returned Soldiers League; Veterans of World War I; J.F. Thomson, Dick Institute, Kilmarnock; M.A. Smith, Central Library, Manchester; B. Millan, Diplomatist Associates; L.F. Murray, Canadian War Museum; Peter Newark, Historical Picture Service; Ian Mackenzie, British Association of Retired Persons; K.I. Taylor, Australian Defence Force Journal;

Major D.I. Mack, The Royal Highland Fusiliers; Mr. David Pearson, Military History Department, Toronto Central Reference Library; John L. Summers, Holliston, Mass.; I. Sydenham, Aberdare, Glamorgan; Mrs. Kathleen Scroggie, Winnipeg, Manitoba; Lt. Col. H.W. Sporrell, Aberporth, Cardigan; the late Nobby Streeter, Beaumaris, Anglesey; E.E. Taylor, Stamford, Lincs; Peter Townsend, Knaresborough, Yorks; Edward Tottenham, Kirkcaldy, Fife; Parry Thomas, Llanfoist, Gwent; Mrs Alice Turner, Bradford, Yorks; the late John Taylor, Winnipeg, Man.; Algernon Villiers, Sunningdale, Berks; Ramon Villaporte, Buenos Aires; J.M. Whilde, Wellingborough, Northants; Jock Wilson, Perth, W.A.; George Wiggins, Edinburgh; Carlos Williams, Jujuiy, Argentina; Eric Willey, Greenock; Mrs. Frances Worrall, Sidney, B.C.; Johnny Wright, Liverpool; F.R. Waley, Sevenoaks, Kent; Neil Williams, Liverpool Echo; T. Ward, Cape Town, S.A.; Lt. Col. Sam Warwick, Durham; H. Willoughby, Grimsby, Yorks; Cyril Wright, New York City; Mrs. Grace Walker, Blackpool, Lancs; Robert Wild, Paignton, Devon; Col. Minter J. Wilson, Washington, D.C.; Noel Wainwright, Brixham, Devon; the late Billy Watson, Newcastle-on-Tyne; Lt. Col. Jamie W. Walton, Fort Leavenworth, Kansas.

A particular note of thanks must go to Mr. Edgar Robinson, Marske, Yorkshire, for generous permission to quote excerpts from his unpublished journal, "A Teenager In The Great War", and to the late Jack Enrique Jones, of Miami, Florida, for permission to quote his personal war reminiscences.

The manuscript itself could not have been finished without the patient typing skills of Pierina Minna, Leilah Pohl, and Elizabeth Rowan.

Most of all, I owe special gratitude to my dear wife, Beverley, and my sons for their affectionate understanding while I spent so many pre-occupied months away in the trenches.

Index